# SEEKING SHALOM

**About the cover art**

One of the most transformative texts of the Second Vatican Council was its 1965 declaration on the relationship of the Catholic Church to non-Christian religions, known by its opening Latin words as *Nostra Aetate* ("In Our Time"). It repudiated centuries of Christian claims that Jews were blind enemies of God whose spiritual life was obsolete. This contemptuous teaching had been depicted on many medieval churches by the female figures of Church *(Ecclesia)* and Synagogue *(Synagoga)*, the former crowned and victorious, the latter defeated and blindfolded, her crown fallen at her feet. *Nostra Aetate* repudiated such images. It declared that Jews are beloved by an ever-faithful God whose promises are irrevocable, and called for dialogue between Christians and Jews.

To celebrate the fiftieth anniversary of *Nostra Aetate*, Saint Joseph's University commissioned an original sculpture by Joshua Koffman entitled *Synagoga and Ecclesia in Our Time*. Today *Synagoga* and *Ecclesia* are able to learn about God from each other. As Pope Francis has written: "Dialogue and friendship with the children of Israel are part of the life of Jesus' disciples. There exists a rich complementarity between the Church and the Jewish people that allows us to help one another mine the riches of God's word" [*Evangelii Gaudium,* 2013]. The cover photo shows the full-size clay version of the sculpture, which will be cast in bronze.

# SEEKING SHALOM

*The Journey to Right Relationship*
*between Catholics and Jews*

Philip A. Cunningham

WILLIAM B. EERDMANS PUBLISHING COMPANY
GRAND RAPIDS, MICHIGAN / CAMBRIDGE, U.K.

Published 2015 by
Wm. B. Eerdmans Publishing Co.
2140 Oak Industrial Drive N.E., Grand Rapids, Michigan 49505 /
P.O. Box 163, Cambridge CB3 9PU U.K.

Printed in the United States of America

21  20  19  18  17  16  15       7  6  5  4  3  2  1


**Library of Congress Cataloging-in-Publication Data**

Cunningham, Philip A.
    Seeking shalom: the journey to right relationship between Catholics and Jews /
    Philip A. Cunningham.
        pages        cm
    ISBN 978-0-8028-7209-8 (pbk.: alk. paper)
    1. Judaism — Relations — Christianity.    2. Christianity and other religions —
    Judaism.    3. Judaism — Relations — Catholic Church.    4. Catholic Church —
    Relations — Judaism.    I. Title.

    BM535.C86    2015
    261.2′6 — dc23

                                                        2015020228


www.eerdmans.com

*This book is dedicated*
*to the many Christian and Jewish colleagues and friends*
*who have been companions in seeking shalom*
*between Jews and Christians.*

O chavruta o mituta!
*(BT Ta'anit 23a)*

# Contents

vii

# Charting an Unprecedented Journey

*Seeking Shalom* charts the story of a remarkable journey from antipathy and suspicion to a new, mutually enriching relationship between two ancient traditions, Judaism and Christianity. It especially focuses on the Catholic-Jewish relationship. This is because its author is Catholic, because the Catholic community has a centralized teaching magisterium that for several decades has been addressing relations with Jews with great seriousness, and because the fiftieth anniversary, or Jubilee, of the Catholic document that made a new relationship possible is now at hand.

On October 28, 1965, the Second Vatican Council, a conclave of the world's Catholic bishops in union with the Bishop of Rome, Pope Paul VI, issued a pioneering and highly authoritative statement: *Nostra Aetate,* The Declaration on the Church's Relationship to Non-Christian Religions. As this volume will examine in some detail, this event proved to be a momentous milestone.

Any celebration of this and similarly pioneering statements from other Christian traditions, however, must be tempered with the realization that they were composed in response to the unspeakable abomination of the Shoah. The massacre of two-thirds of the Jews of Europe on a continent with a predominantly Christian population challenged many churches and individual Christians to examine their own ideas and histories with respect to Jews and Judaism. Had Christian teaching contributed to the Nazi horror? In a way, this book shows how this process has unfolded in the teachings of the Catholic community.

The Catholic focus of this volume is not meant in any exclusivist way. Other Christians have also grappled with the issues raised by the mass murder of European Jews. But the process has unfolded and continues to unfold differently among the various Christian traditions because of divergences in polity, theological approaches, resources, history, and a host of other factors. Hopefully, this examination of the developments in Catholic teaching can be beneficial to other Christians, just as Catholic thought draws upon their specific theological creativity.

In some ways the different sections of this volume unfold in parallel to the development over the past five decades of the new relationship between Catholics and Jews. Just as the drafters of *Nostra Aetate* turned to the New Testament as they struggled to describe the church's relationship to Judaism, this book proceeds by beginning with questions of biblical interpretation before turning to theological exposition. Due to the rapid developments in studies of the Jewish and Christian relationship, some of the chapters significantly rework, expand, and update previously published articles, while others are entirely new.

Part One, then, considers biblical topics. It was through the reinterpretation of scripture that the churches began to reverse their previous hostility to Jews and their religious traditions. It begins with chapters on the adoption by the Catholic Church of historical- and literary-critical methods of biblical interpretation, moves to consider some of the scriptural topics that have figured most prominently concerning Jews, and ends by drawing upon the perspectives of one New Testament author to develop a biblically-grounded theological perspective for a post–*Nostra Aetate* church.

Part Two takes up the theological task more directly, turning to Christology, ecclesiology, soteriology, and other theological disciplines in the light of a renewed appreciation of Jewish covenantal life.

Another way to explain the two parts of this book is to observe that for the past seventy years or so the relevant Catholic ecclesial documents have advanced along two independent but complementary and eventually converging trajectories. The first track specifically concerned biblical interpretation. It began with a 1943 encyclical of Pope Pius XII and intensified with the Second Vatican Council's 1965 *Dei Verbum,* The Dogmatic Constitution on Divine Revelation. These were followed by several pertinent studies by the Pontifical Biblical Commission.

The other documentary tradition, which explicitly addressed relations with Jews, originated with the *Nostra Aetate.* That declaration sparked a continuing evolution in Catholic theological reflection and teaching as reflected in subsequent documents of the Pontifical Commission for Religious Relations with Jews and in numerous addresses given by Popes John Paul II, Benedict XVI, and, most recently, Pope Francis. Part One's focus on biblical interpretation and Part Two's on theologies of the church's relationship to the Jewish people echo the development of Catholic teaching along these two documentary paths.

Each of the two parts begins with chapters that examine the relevant Catholic ecclesiastical statements. This is a useful way to proceed for several reasons. First, such statements reflect the exegetical and theological labors that were undertaken over the past decades. Second, they are officially "Catholic" in that they emanate from popes, official curial offices, church-sanctioned advisory committees, etc. Third, because the Catholic tradition seeks both continuity with earlier precedents and new understandings in the light of changing times, they provide a convenient means to trace the steady developments that have transpired over the years. After considering the relevant ecclesiastical documents, each of the two parts of the volume then proceeds to demonstrate putting their principles into practice through specific scriptural and theological examples.

This is the fifth volume in which I have included the Hebrew word *shalom* in the title.[1] This is because I find the many connotations of this word to be particularly relevant to the relationship between Judaism and Christianity. Usually translated into English as peace, *shalom* in its fuller meanings actually denotes prosperity, well-being, and a sense of being whole and healthy. It involves being in right relationship within one's own community and with others. *Shalom* is also sometimes understood as the outcome of walking through life with God.

Clearly, Christianity has not been in "right relationship" with Judaism throughout most of the two millennia of its existence. As Cardinal Edward Cassidy has concisely summarized:

> There can be no denial of the fact that from the time of the Emperor Constantine on, Jews were isolated and discriminated against in the Christian world. There were expulsions and forced conversions. Literature propagated stereotypes, preaching accused the Jews of every age of deicide; the ghetto which came into being in 1555 with a papal bull became in

---

1. The others are: *A Story of Shalom: The Calling of Christians and Jews by a Covenanting God* (New York/Mahwah: Stimulus Foundation/Paulist Press, 2001); *Sharing Shalom: A Local Interfaith Dialogue Process,* edited with Rabbi Arthur Starr (Mahwah/New York: Paulist Press, 1998); *Proclaiming Shalom: Lectionary Introductions to Foster the Catholic and Jewish Relationship* (Collegeville, MN: Liturgical Press, 1995); and *Education for Shalom: Religion Textbooks and the Enhancement of the Catholic and Jewish Relationship* (Collegeville: Liturgical Press, 1995).

Nazi Germany the antechamber of the extermination. . . . The church can justly be accused of not showing to the Jewish people down through the centuries that love which its founder, Jesus Christ, made the fundamental principle of its teaching.[2]

Given this tragic assessment, one ponders to what extent the church's lack of *shalom* with Judaism has impeded its continuation of the mission of Jesus to prepare the world for the Reign of God. As Cardinal Walter Kasper has poignantly written, "[C]utting itself off from its Jewish roots for centuries weakened the church, a weakness that became evident in the altogether too feeble resistance against the [Nazi] persecution of Jews."[3] To put it another way, if over the centuries the Christian community has not been in right relationship with its Jewish roots, its Jewish neighbors, and indeed in some ways with its Jewish Lord, then how successful could it be in being an agent of *shalom* in the world?

The Catholic Church, together with most Christian denominations, has now renounced its past contempt for Judaism as replaced, obsolete, or outmoded. It seeks to cultivate *shalom* with those now recognized to also be covenantal partners with God. Such *shalom* brings both external "right relationship" with the Jewish people and internal "right relationship" between the church's own Jewish heritage and its Christian self-definition. This wholeness seems essential if either Jews or Christians are to fulfill their covenanting responsibilities before God toward the rest of humanity.

The final chapter in this book suggests that the fledgling new relationship between Christians and Jews has the potential to mature into an unprecedented period of profound friendship and mutual enrichment. Through close study and conversation together, both Jews and Christians recount occasionally discerning the presence of the Holy One in the other's religious heritage and practice. Such moments are powerfully transformative of one's religious self-understanding before God.

This has certainly been my own experience, which is why this book is dedicated to the dozens of Jewish and Christian colleagues and friends who have been my fellow travelers over the years in Seeking Shalom. In particular,

2. Edward Cardinal Idris Cassidy, "Reflections: The Vatican Statement on the Shoah," *Origins* 28/2 (May 28, 1998): 3.

3. Walter Cardinal Kasper, "Foreword," in Philip A. Cunningham, Joseph Sievers, Mary C. Boys, Hans Hermann Henrix, and Jesper Svartvik, eds., *Christ Jesus and the Jewish People Today: New Explorations of Theological Interrelationships* (Grand Rapids: William B. Eerdmans, 2011), xvi.

I want to thank those with whom I have had the privilege of team-teaching courses on the historical and theological relationships between Christians and Jews at Notre Dame College, Boston College, and Saint Joseph's University. I am especially indebted to Adam Gregerman, Jewish studies professor at Saint Joseph's University who directs its Institute for Jewish-Catholic Relations with me. He carefully examined the entire manuscript and offered many penetrating insights and invaluable criticisms that improved the book significantly. To slightly paraphrase Genesis Rabbah 69:2, "Just as a knife can be sharpened only on the side of another, so a student improves only through his *chaver* [friend/learning partner]."

As always my love and gratitude goes to my wife Julia Anne Walsh and our children Francis and Diana for their constant understanding and support.

*Trinity Sunday, 2015*

# PART ONE

# SCRIPTURE

# CHAPTER 1

# The Word of God in Human Language: The Catholic Biblical Renaissance

## Introduction

For the past seventy years or so, major developments in Catholic thinking on biblical hermeneutics — the methods of interpreting the scriptures — have made crucial contributions to positive relations between Catholics and Jews. These developments can be seen in relevant ecclesial documents, beginning with a 1943 encyclical of Pope Pius XII and intensified with the Second Vatican Council's 1965 *Dei Verbum,* The Dogmatic Constitution on Divine Revelation. These were followed by several pertinent studies by the Pontifical Biblical Commission.

In order to grasp how a virtual renaissance in the Catholic understanding of the Bible played a crucial role in the process of seeking *shalom,* one must understand the pertinent biblical documents. Ecclesial texts in regard to Catholic-Jewish relations are also helpful, because they utilized certain aspects of the emerging church teaching on the scriptures. This chapter explores the question: How does the Catholic tradition understand the nature of the Bible and its proper interpretation? It should be kept in mind that these are *developing* teaching traditions. Some of the earlier documents that

---

This chapter and the following one draw in part upon the Fifth Annual Driscoll Lecture in Jewish-Catholic Studies delivered at Iona College, New Rochelle, NY, on March 10, 2004, entitled "Catholic Biblical Perspectives on Judaism and the Jewish People" and also on a portion of my "Paul's Letters and the Relationship between the People of Israel and the Church Today," in Reimund Bieringer and Didier Pollefeyt, eds., *Paul and Judaism: Crosscurrents in Pauline Exegesis and the Study of Jewish-Christian Relations* (London/New York: T&T Clark, 2012), 141-162.

will be quoted below introduced concepts that later documents took up and elaborated upon.

## "What the Sacred Writers Really Had in Mind"

The year 1943 was very important for Catholic biblical scholarship. Previously, Catholic scripture scholars were discouraged from reading texts in their original languages, and from employing archaeological discoveries, or "scientific" methods of biblical textual analysis. They were officially prohibited from utilizing the analytical or critical tools that had developed in other academic disciplines, such as literature, which had been applied to biblical texts by other Christians, particularly Lutherans and other Protestants in Europe. Catholic scholars were also required to work from the Latin Vulgate translation of the Bible, which dates back to the late fourth century. They could not study scriptural texts in their original languages of Hebrew, Aramaic, or Greek.

These restrictions began to disappear in 1943 when Pope Pius XII issued his encyclical — an authoritative papal letter — entitled *Divino Afflante Spiritu* (Inspired by the Divine Spirit). This instruction required the use of the original languages and urged interpreters to "go back wholly in spirit to those remote centuries of the East with the aid of history, archaeology, ethnology and other sciences, and accurately determine what modes of writing, so to speak, the authors of that ancient time would be likely to use, and in fact did use."[1] This fundamental orientation of trying to go back into the original context of a biblical writing became a defining principle of the Catholic approach to the Bible. With this approach the reader or interpreter must appreciate the biblical writings in their historical contexts (e.g., what were the circumstances at the time of the text's composition? why was the author writing?) and in their literary contexts (e.g., what genre of writing is it? what types of argumentation, metaphors, figures of speech, and/or prevailing cultural conventions of the time are employed?). Both historical and literary investigations are needed to understand the original contexts of the scriptures.

In preparing his encyclical to mark the anniversary of a previous pope's statement on biblical topics, Pius XII realized that by 1943 there had been many important archaeological discoveries of both physical and textual artifacts that were crucial to understanding the ancient biblical world. No one

---

1. Pope Pius XII, *Divino Afflante Spiritu* (Sept. 30, 1943), §35.

could know, of course, that only four years later the single most important biblical archaeological find of the twentieth century would occur with the unearthing of the Dead Sea Scrolls. These texts brought to light the amazing creativity and diversity of late Second Temple period Judaism and totally revised the understanding of the world of the New Testament. Pius XII had already concluded in 1943 that the critical study of archaeology and history was essential to discerning the meanings of biblical texts, but this was made even more self-evident with the finding of these scrolls from Qumran by the Dead Sea.

Pius XII's acceptance of and even mandate to use critical scholarly tools to interpret the Bible was ratified and deepened by the Second Vatican Council, which issued in 1965 *Dei Verbum,* The Dogmatic Constitution on the Divine Revelation. The title is significant because a dogmatic constitution has the highest level of authority among the various types of documents issued by a council. And a council of all the Catholic bishops of the world in union with the bishop of Rome, the pope, has the highest teaching authority within the Catholic tradition. *Dei Verbum,* then, articulated Catholic dogma when it stated: "Those things revealed by God which are contained and presented in the text of sacred scripture have been written under the inspiration of the Holy Spirit."[2]

That the Bible was inspired by the Holy Spirit was not a new idea, of course, but the orientation set forth by Pius XII twenty-two years earlier quickly followed in the conciliar document: "Seeing that, in sacred scripture, God speaks through human beings in human fashion, it follows that the interpreters of sacred scripture, if they are to ascertain what God has wished to communicate to us, should carefully search out the meaning which the sacred writers really had in mind, that meaning which God had thought well to manifest through the medium of their words."[3]

In other words, a concern for the scriptures' historical contexts implies an effort to try to get into the perspectives of the sacred writers. Although according to Christian faith the Bible is the word of God inspired by the Holy Spirit, its actual writers were human beings, immersed in particular cultural and social situations, and so shaped by human modes of thinking and language. In Catholic understanding, the interpreter must reckon with this reality.

---

2. Second Vatican Council, *Dei Verbum* (Nov. 18, 1965), §11. http://www.vatican.va/archive/hist_councils/ii_vatican_council/documents/vat-ii_const_19651118_dei-verbum_en.html. Accessed Nov. 16, 2013.

3. *Dei Verbum,* §12.

Recalling that in these documents one can trace a development of thought, it is today more evident that *Dei Verbum*'s injunction to discover what "the sacred writers really had in mind" represented an overly optimistic view of our ability to get into the minds of people who lived thousands of years ago. There are limits as to how much today's readers can really know about the thinking of, say, Isaiah of Jerusalem in the eighth century B.C.E. Later ecclesial documents reflect an awareness of this limitation, and suggest that it is the modern interpreter's concern to be aware of the realities of the ancient world that is crucial. The guiding principle is that in the sacred writings divine inspiration is mediated through human authors. The Bible is the word of God expressed in human speech.

*Dei Verbum* went on to note that the interpreter of the Bible

> . . . must look to that meaning which the sacred writers, in given situations and granted the circumstances of their time and culture, intended to express and did in fact express through the medium of a contemporary literary form. Rightly to understand what the sacred authors wanted to affirm in their work, due attention must be paid to the customary and characteristic patterns of perception, speech and narrative which prevailed in their time, and to the conventions which people then observed in their dealings with one another.[4]

This is a pivotal move. For example, in the Genesis 1 creation account, the writers describe the placing of the stars in the underside of the inverted dome of the sky that rests upon a flat earth. By understanding that the scriptures reflect the cultural perspectives of their authors, it should not be disconcerting for readers today to recognize that the Genesis writers thought that the world was flat and so depicted God creating a flat earth. Twenty-first-century readers do not happen to share that cosmology, that view of the earth's shape, but they can appreciate that the significance of the text lies in the authors' religious claim that God is the creator of the universe. Genesis 1 is not important to Christian (or Jewish) faith for its pre-scientific understanding of the shape of the cosmos.

That the authors of this text were motivated by religious concerns in their imaginative description of the world's creation is evident in the otherwise puzzling conclusion that God rested on the seventh day after completing all these labors. This element is not about divine fatigue but about es-

---

4. *Dei Verbum*, §12.

tablishing the Sabbath as holy. The writers ended their creation narrative in this way to encourage their contemporaries to observe the Sabbath carefully.

## Biblical Interpretation as a Dialogue between Generations of Faith

In the decades after the Second Vatican Council, Catholic ecclesial teaching on biblical matters was developed in the instructions of the Pontifical Biblical Commission (PBC). Since 1971, this has been a group of about twenty biblical scholars from around the world, appointed by the pope. It operates under the aegis of the Congregation for the Doctrine of the Faith (CDF) whose head is also the Commission's *ex officio* president. The Commission advises the CDF on matters of biblical interpretation and their impact on Catholic doctrine. Sometimes the CDF will ask the Commission to investigate a certain topic or pursue a certain question. After study, the Commission reports back to the Congregation, which then often publishes the research under the authority of the cardinal president as an instruction for the universal Catholic Church. The documents published by the PBC under such auspices thus acquire a certain degree of ecclesiastical weight, although not having the same degree of authority as a papal or conciliar document.

The Commission issued a major document in 1993, called "The Interpretation of the Bible in the Church." Its presentation of the Catholic approach to the Bible expanded upon and furthered the trajectory of *Divino Afflante Spiritu* and *Dei Verbum:*

> Catholic exegesis [biblical scholarship] freely makes use of the scientific methods and approaches which allow a better grasp of the meaning of texts in their linguistic, literary, socio-cultural, religious and historical contexts, while explaining them as well through studying their sources and attending to the personality of each author. Catholic exegesis actively contributes to the development of new methods and to the progress of research.[5]

Note that the Catholic Church's pre-1943 aversion to using the tools from other disciplines has been totally replaced by the encouragement to use every interpretative tool available. This change alone exemplifies the renais-

5. Pontifical Biblical Commission, "The Interpretation of the Bible in the Church" (April 15, 1993), III. *Origins* 23/29 (Jan. 6, 1994): 497-524.

sance in Catholic biblical scholarship that occurred in the second half of the twentieth century.

In addition, the PBC went beyond the earlier documents by observing that there is a rich diversity of biblical perspectives:

> Granted that tensions can exist in the relationship between various texts of sacred Scripture, interpretation must necessarily show a certain pluralism. No single interpretation can exhaust the meaning of the whole, which is a symphony of many voices. Thus the interpreter of one particular text has to avoid seeking to dominate at the expense of others.[6]

In other words, once the interpreter attempts to situate biblical texts in their historical or literary contexts, there is a need to respect the diversity among those texts. That diversity is often complementary; it may enrich God's self-disclosure, as "a symphony of many voices," but if readers flatten that music to a monotone, they will have destroyed the multi-dimensionality of the scriptural tradition. This is just as true for all of the books of the Christian Old Testament as it is for the four individual Gospel portraits of the life of Jesus.

While all readers probably have their own preferred passages in the Bible that they elevate and privilege above others, the PBC urges caution. Often the Bible offers contrary voices or at least voices with a different nuance. To respect the Bible requires attention to those voices that seem dissonant to readers' preferred readings.

"The Interpretation of the Bible in the Church" also insisted that

> The historical-critical method is the indispensable method for the scientific study of the meaning of ancient texts. Holy Scripture, inasmuch as it is the "word of God in human language," has been composed by human authors in all its various parts and in all the sources that lie behind them. Because of this, its proper understanding not only admits the use of this method but actually requires it.[7]

This quotation prompts two theological comments. First, the idea that in the Bible God's word is expressed in human words touches on a quintessential aspect of Christianity. Christianity is an incarnational religion. Chris-

---

6. "Interpretation of the Bible in the Church," III, A, 3.
7. "Interpretation of the Bible in the Church," I, A.

tians not only believe that the word of God has taken tangible expression in inspired biblical literature, but distinctively that the Word of God became flesh in Jesus of Nazareth. It is precisely because Christians believe that God's Word has entered into the limitations of the mortal human condition that they also affirm that the biblical word is of God despite all the limitations of human language, culture, and history. To hold that the word of God in the Bible is unaffected by the messiness of human life is to make the Bible so divine as to remove it from human experience. From the Catholic perspective, a failure to appreciate the human origins of the Bible, albeit composed by humans graced with divine inspiration, runs the risk of turning a tangible written collection into an idol. It would violate the fundamental character of Christianity itself, which understands God to be intimately involved in all the ambiguities of human life.

Second, there are Christians who prefer not to look at the biblical texts in their literary and historical contexts. They would be stunned by the PBC's statement that the Bible "has been composed by human authors in all its various parts and all of its sources." This is a defining difference among Christians in the United States today. Catholic teaching and the approach of so-called "mainline" Protestants embrace the Bible as incarnational, while *some* Evangelical and Fundamentalist Christians so revere the divine character of the biblical inspiration that they resist the notion of any human limitations influencing the scriptures.

A final insight from "The Interpretation of the Bible in the Church" is very significant. Whereas *Dei Verbum* had perhaps an almost overly optimistic sense of our ability to identify the intentions of people who lived thousands of years ago, the 1993 PBC study nuances that effort substantially by adding an important further dimension: "Sacred scripture is in dialogue with communities of believers: It has come from their traditions of faith. . . ."[8] When Christians, and Jews as well, read the scriptures today, they are reading the faith testimony of the ancestors of their current communities of faith. They are, in a sense, engaging in a dialogue with the experiences of God in the lives of people of long ago and relating them to today's experiences of God in the present-day lives of their faith communities. There is a give-and-take process that unfolds.

Therefore, the effort to comprehend the scriptures in their historical and literary contexts is only one step in the process of biblical interpretation. Readers must also ask what the biblical authors' insights might mean for

---

8. "Interpretation of the Bible in the Church," III, A, 3.

today's world. The biblical authors had their own issues to contend with, but they did not include some that confront us in the twentieth-first century, such as global warming or genetic manipulation.

In Catholic teaching, then, biblical interpretation is a dialogical or dialectical process. Sometimes later readers might find the biblical witness inadequate or inconsistent. For instance, in the nineteenth century the United States was torn asunder by the question of slavery. The Bible lends itself to contradictory opinions about this subject, as seen by the fact that both slaveholders and abolitionists quoted it to support their diametrically opposed views. Some Christians cited the New Testament telling slaves to obey their masters (Col. 3:22; Eph. 6:5), while others argued that since all human beings were made in God's image (Gen. 1:26) everyone is deserving of freedom. So the interpretative dialogue between present readers and the biblical authors can critique the biblical witness because it echoes the avoidable messiness of human existence.

On the other hand, the biblical witness can, and should, also challenge modern readers. It can show us that we may not be living up to the vision or the ideals that the biblical writers value. Who can fail to contrast Isaiah's vision of a world in which God's peace prevails even among predatory animals and their prey (Isa. 11:6) with our own conflicted world of violence and injustice?

From a Catholic perspective, then, biblical interpretation resembles a kind of wrestling match between faith communities of today and those of long ago. (And this metaphor resonates with a Jewish self-understanding seen in the meaning of the word *Isra-el:* "to wrestle with God.") As the PBC put it in 1993:

> Dialogue with Scripture in its entirety, which means dialogue with the understanding of the faith prevailing in earlier times, must be matched by a dialogue with the generation of today (actualization). Such dialogue will mean establishing a relationship of continuity. It will also involve acknowledging differences. Hence the interpretation of Scripture involves a work of sifting and setting aside; it stands in continuity with earlier exegetical traditions, many elements of which it preserves and makes its own; but in other matters it will go its own way, seeking to make further progress. [9]

The earlier example of the debate over slavery illustrates this. Neither Jews nor Christians today hold those biblical texts that tolerate or condone slavery

---

9. "The Interpretation of the Bible in the Church," III, A, 3.

as having binding authority on their respective communities of faith. We have "gone our own way" in that regard. We can develop biblically-based arguments for doing so, but that is precisely the "work of sifting and setting aside" that the PBC mentioned. This requires "a dialogue with the generation of today" as well, meaning that twenty-first-century readers need to examine the presuppositions and expectations that they bring to their engagement with the biblical text and how today's circumstances shape their thinking during their reading.

Furthermore, because Christian faith "has had to renew itself continually in order to meet new situations . . . the interpretation of the Bible should likewise involve an aspect of creativity; it also ought to confront new questions so as to respond to them out of the Bible."[10] A fundamental "new question" confronted the church in the aftermath of the Nazi genocide of Jews in the heart of Christian Europe during the Second World War. For nearly two millennia the prevailing stance was that the Jewish people had been replaced by Christians as the People of God (or at best relegated to a very subordinate status) because God's wrath was upon them for their alleged rejection of Christ. This assertion, known as "replacement theology" or "supersessionism," was not seriously critiqued until the abomination of the Shoah.[11] Today, however, as Cardinal Kasper, president of the Pontifical Commission for Religious Relations with the Jews from 2001-2010, has remarked: "[T]he old theory of substitution is gone since the Second Vatican Council. For us Christians today the covenant with the Jewish people is a living heritage, a living reality."[12]

With *Nostra Aetate's* repudiation of the idea of a biblically-justified divine curse on Jews, and with its recognition that Jews remain in covenant with God, the Catholic Church has found itself in a theological context that is virtually unprecedented in history. It is a historic fact that the theological nature of the church's relationship to Jews and Judaism received little sustained analysis from New Testament times up until the twentieth century because an uncritiqued supersessionist stance became the norm. As this vital theological task is being pursued today, however, the Catholic community's recent approach to scriptural interpretation as a dialogical process plays an

10. "Interpretation of the Bible in the Church," III, A, 3.

11. This explains why *Nostra Aetate,* §4 could not cite any ecclesiastical councils or papal declarations to counteract supersessionism, but had to reach back to New Testament texts, especially its earliest books, Paul's epistles.

12. Walter Cardinal Kasper, *"Dominus Iesus,"* paper delivered at the 17th meeting of the International Catholic-Jewish Liaison Committee, May 1, 2001, 3.

important, indeed indispensable, role. This becomes clear by further examining the idea of a process of dialogue with the biblical text.

Sandra M. Schneiders has offered a comprehensive biblical hermeneutic or interpretive schema that complements and more comprehensively examines the principles outlined by the PBC in 1993. Drawing on the work of such scholars as Hans Georg Gadamer and Paul Ricoeur, Schneiders sees biblical interpretation as a dialectic between the *explanation* of what a text says and an *understanding* of the implications of the text for our own world of today.[13]

In Schneiders's system, the "ideal meaning" of a text is constructed by historical and literary analysis. Through analytic tools the reader seeks to explain "the World behind the Text" out of which it emerged and "the World of the Text" itself in terms of its literary features. This explanation, then, is put into dialogue with or actualized in our own world in order to understand what meanings the text has for *today*. By entering into "the World before the Text," the reality that the text imperfectly projects, modern faith engages biblical faith, constructs a cognitive "Meaning of the Work" for today, and, as a result, the transformative power of God may be unleashed. For example, a dialectical examination of what Paul's famous olive tree metaphor in Romans 11 should mean in our post-Shoah, post–*Nostra Aetate* world illustrates the process of actualization (see chapter 4 below).

In our conversation with the biblical text we may find ourselves disagreeing with part of what a biblical author says because of our scientific knowledge (e.g., Genesis 1's depiction of a flat earth), or because we don't share the urgent emotions of the writer (e.g., Psalm 137:9 ["Blessed is the one who takes *your* babies and dashes them on the rocks"]; or John 8:44 ["You [Jews] are from your father the devil"]).

Today's readers also have a different "effective history" than the biblical authors. They have been shaped by all the intervening events and developments that have occurred since the text was first written. Twenty-first-century Westerners, for instance, all live in a post-Freudian world, a post-Darwinian world, and a post-Einsteinian world — among other things! Unlike earlier generations, we tend to think in terms of the individual human psyche, of processes of development, and of the relativity of different perspectives. Therefore, even the way we conceive of the past, as represented by ancient texts, is different. "By 'effective history' is meant historical reality not only as initiating event but also as modified and amplified by all that the

---

13. Sandra M. Schneiders, *The Revelatory Text: Interpreting the New Testament as Sacred Scripture* (HarperSanFrancisco, 1991).

initiating event has produced. . . . The past . . . is constantly being reconstituted within its own effective history."[14]

For instance, modern readers will bring to the text questions that were not on the minds of the biblical authors. To cite a central concern of this book, Christians today cannot avoid reading New Testament passages about Jews without an awareness of what happened under the Nazis. That event is part of our "effective history." We will therefore "actualize" those passages differently than earlier generations of readers. Their significance will be different for us. Part of the process of biblical interpretation, then, involves some conscious self-critique on the part of today's readers. What are we bringing to our engagement with the text? What presuppositions, prejudices, or needs are at work? The import of such questions will become evident throughout this volume.

On the other hand, by getting to know the scriptural writers as human beings who encountered God amid all the ambiguities of human history and society, today's readers may find themselves transformed by being challenged by the biblical vision — even if that vision is only imperfectly realized in the Bible itself.

The flowchart on page 14, based on Schneiders's work, graphically summarizes the movements of this dialectical biblical hermeneutic, one which has proven crucial in the recent rapprochement between Jews and Christians. It is the interpretive method that will be utilized in the following chapters.

14. Schneiders, *The Revelatory Text,* 159-160.

# A Dialectical Biblical Hermeneutic

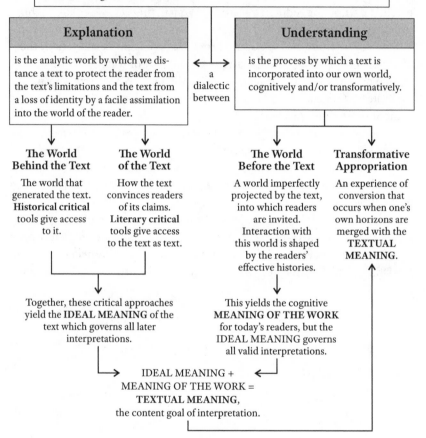

## INTERPRETATION

has two goals: (A) what the text means cognitively for today and (B) personal or social transformation. It begins with a pre-understanding, a first guess to the text's meaning, but then moves to:

### Explanation

is the analytic work by which we distance a text to protect the reader from the text's limitations and the text from a loss of identity by a facile assimilation into the world of the reader.

a dialectic between

### Understanding

is the process by which a text is incorporated into our own world, cognitively and/or transformatively.

**The World Behind the Text**

The world that generated the text. **Historical critical** tools give access to it.

**The World of the Text**

How the text convinces readers of its claims. **Literary critical** tools give access to the text as text.

**The World Before the Text**

A world imperfectly projected by the text, into which readers are invited. Interaction with this world is shaped by the readers' effective histories.

**Transformative Appropriation**

An experience of conversion that occurs when one's own horizons are merged with the **TEXTUAL MEANING.**

Together, these critical approaches yield the **IDEAL MEANING** of the text which governs all later interpretations.

This yields the cognitive **MEANING OF THE WORK** for today's readers, but the IDEAL MEANING governs all valid interpretations.

IDEAL MEANING +
MEANING OF THE WORK =
**TEXTUAL MEANING,**
the content goal of interpretation.

# CHAPTER 2

# Interpreting the Bible in a Post–*Nostra Aetate* Church

## The Catholic Approach to the Gospels

The key Catholic understanding that the Bible is the word of God expressed in human speech — as discussed in the previous chapter — applies in a special way to the four Gospels. In 1964, the year before the Second Vatican Council issued *Dei Verbum,* the Pontifical Biblical Commission was composed entirely of cardinals. It thus exercised a direct magisterial authority when in that year it issued a document called "An Instruction on the Historical Truth of the Gospels." In 1965, *Dei Verbum* took some of the ideas in this document and affirmed them with its higher conciliar authority.

In "The Historical Truth of the Gospels," the Commission, informed by a scholarly consensus that the Gospels were written decades after the life of Jesus, noted that in the four Gospel accounts one can find materials that date from three different periods of reflection on the significance of Jesus' life, death, and resurrection. The document used the expression of "Stages" One, Two, and Three:

*Stage One: The Ministry of Jesus* — traditions put in writing in the eventual Gospels that go back to Jesus' words and deeds during his ministry in the early 30s of the first century. Stage One materials include descriptions of Jesus as a healer, as a preacher in parables, and as proclaimer of the coming of the Reign of God. Stage One traditions recall Jesus' actual life and death.

*Stage Two: The Post-Resurrectional Preaching of the Apostles* — insights about Jesus that began to develop soon after his execution around the year 30. Gospel narratives about Jesus' words and deeds are embedded in texts written by people convinced that the one who was crucified had been raised to transcendent new life. All the Gospel narratives, including Stage One materials, are framed by this "post-resurrectional" perspective.

Naturally, there is a difference between "pre" and "post" resurrection attitudes and perspectives on Jesus. For instance, when the earliest apostles went out and preached about the Crucified and Raised One they begin to speak of him as sharing in the divine power of judgment by calling him "Lord." The word "Lord," in Greek, *kyrios,* is also the way that Israel's holy name for God, the Tetragrammaton ("I Am Who Am" — Exodus 3:14), was rendered into Greek. So calling the raised Jesus "Lord" was actually giving him God's own name, thereby claiming for him a divine status.

According to most scholars, the seven letters attributed to Paul in the New Testament were all written a decade or more before any of the canonical Gospels. They thus provide excellent illustrations of Stage Two perspectives, as in the famous passage from Philippians 2:9-11 which explains why the title "Lord" is fittingly ascribed to Jesus:

> Because of [Jesus' obedience even unto death], God greatly exalted him and bestowed on him the name that is above every name, that at the name of Jesus every knee should bend, of those in heaven and on earth and under the earth, and every tongue confess that Jesus Christ is Lord [*kyrios* = "I Am Who Am"], to the glory of God the Father.

Likewise, the phrase "Son of God" has different cadences in pre- and post-resurrectional (or Stage One and Two) perceptions, which might be indicated by using upper and lower case letters. The Bible refers to all Israel as "son of God" (e.g., Exod. 4:22) and to individuals, particularly David, as "son of God" (e.g., Ps. 2:7), as those whom God especially loves. But when Paul in Romans 1:3-4 proclaims Jesus as "descended from David according to the flesh, but established as Son of God in power according to the spirit of holiness through resurrection from the dead," one senses that the expression has assumed a far more exalted meaning among the post-resurrectional followers of Jesus.

With regard to the Gospels, the PBC in 1964 noted that such post-resurrectional convictions are often conveyed in accounts whose narrative setting is the pre-resurrectional context of the ministry of Jesus. Thus, when John 9 portrays a healed blind man saying to Jesus, " 'I do believe, Lord,' and he worshiped him" (v. 38), it is expressing a post-resurrectional faith in Jesus as having divine status even though the episode is set during Jesus' public ministry prior to his crucifixion. Similarly, when at Jesus' baptism, "a voice came from the heavens, saying, 'This is my beloved Son, with whom I am well pleased'" (Matt. 3:17), the Gospel reader is given a post-resurrectional knowledge of Jesus' identity that the characters in the narrative at the start of Jesus' ministry quite properly do not possess. This is shown by the fact that the spectators to the baptism scene in no way react or even seem to have heard the heavenly voice's startling announcement.

*Stage Three: The Writing of the Gospels by the Evangelists* — portrayals of Jesus shaped by the situations, concerns, and insights of the Gospel writers themselves. Stage Three is the time when the Gospels achieved the written form in which we have them today, decades after Jesus' ministry in the 70s, 80s, and 90s of the first century. Some of the four Gospels seem to have been written in a relatively short span of time, while others, particularly the Gospel of John, may have evolved over decades. In any case, the writing of the Gospels by the individual evangelists is yet another layer in the development of the written traditions about Jesus. The narratives about Jesus reflect the contexts, interests, unique gifts and perceptions, and — according to Christian faith — the inspired insights each evangelist has about the significance of Jesus.

One of the Stage Three concerns of the Gospel writers is when Jesus as Lord would return to mete out God's justice and establish God's Reign: next month, next year, in twenty years, in the unknown future? The different viewpoints among the four Gospels can be seen in how they tell the story of Jesus. In Mark 13:30, for instance, Jesus declares, "this generation will not pass away until all these things [including the coming of the Son of Man in glory] have taken place." By the time of the writing of the Gospel of John, however, such imminent expectations have waned. The Johannine Jesus says to Peter about the Beloved Disciple, "'What if I want him to remain until I come? What concern is it of yours? You follow me.' So the word spread among the brothers that that disciple would not die. But Jesus had not told him that he would not die" (John 21:22-23) before Jesus would come again.

Another question for the evangelists in Stage Three concerned the requirements for Gentiles to enter into the newly-forming assemblies of Jesus Christ. Need they observe the Torah as Jewish believers did? This debate is laced throughout the Gospels. For example, in the Gospel of Mark there is a discussion between Jesus and some other Jews about purity. Jesus says it is not the food that goes into somebody's mouth that makes them impure, but rather what words come out of their mouth (Mark 7:15). But Mark adds a little editorial comment, "Thus he declared all foods clean" (7:19). This indicates that in Mark's church, kosher food laws were not being observed since the Marcan Jesus is here portrayed as abolishing them. Matthew, however, has a very different position on this subject. In the Sermon on the Mount, the Matthean Jesus declares, "Do not think that I have come to abolish the law or the prophets. I have come not to abolish but to fulfill. . . . Therefore, whoever breaks one of the least of these commandments and teaches others to do so will be called least in the kingdom of heaven. But whoever obeys and teaches these commandments will be called greatest in the kingdom of heaven" (Matt. 5:17, 19). Since Matthew's presentation of the Marcan discussion about purity drops any suggestion that Jesus had "declared all foods clean," the logical conclusion is that all foods were not clean in Matthew's church. Torah commands were not being abolished. It would appear that Gentiles coming into Mark's church would not have to observe Jewish kosher food laws, whereas those entering Matthew's church community would likely be required to somehow respect them.

The realization that there is a disagreement about food laws among the evangelists leads to the unavoidable conclusion that Jesus himself never gave any authoritative instructions about Gentiles and Torah observance. Otherwise, there would not have been any debate. Without such a directive, the matter remained contentious into the 70s, 80s and 90s, and different Gospel writers approached the question according to the practices of their own churches. Attitudes toward Judaism and the "Law of Moses" would be affected by the way various church communities observed the Torah.

A further Stage Three question was how to live the Christian life in a particular situation. Of course, this is a question that all Christians ask themselves in all eras. But for the Gospel writers this question was posed in rather distinct circumstances that will be examined in chapter 5: what does it mean to live a Christian life in a church that has recently been persecuted (as seems to have been the case in Mark's community), or in a church that is struggling to have influence in the Jewish world after the Romans destroyed the Temple in the year 70 (as apparently the case of Matthew's community), or in a community that is trying to present itself to the (Gentile) Roman Empire as a peaceful, law-abiding movement (as evidently the case of Luke's community)?

One could provide many more examples of how the Stage Three concerns of the Gospel writers shaped their telling of the story of Jesus. But all these considerations lead to a number of important points about the Catholic approach to reading the Gospels, especially in the light of the recognition of the three stages of Gospel development:

First, the evangelists did not write the Gospels to give us "history" as we would understand the term today. They wrote, "so you may come to believe that Jesus is the Christ, the Son of God, and that through believing you may have life in his name" (John 20:31). The Gospels were written to promote Christian faith. For Christians, the truths that they express are inspired insights about the significance of Jesus written in the hope that readers will enter into a faith-relationship with him. They do not, of course, use twenty-first-century writing styles in attempting this task, but first-century ones.

For Christian faith the most important "stage" is Stage Three because it discloses the evangelists' inspired reflections on the significance of Jesus' life, death, and resurrection. It is what the writers want to tell their readers about Jesus that has been inspired and gives meaning to believers' hope in Christ. For this reason, today's readers ought to pay attention to the differences among the Gospels that show the evangelists' particular understanding of Jesus. It is very significant, for instance, that in the Gospels of Mark, Matthew, and Luke a distressed Jesus prays before his arrest that the Father "might remove this cup from me" (Mark 14:36; Matt. 26:39; Luke 22:42), whereas the Johannine Jesus, as always in full control of the scene, confidently asks, "Am I not to drink the cup that the Father has given me?" (John 18:11). Such differences make clear the distinctive christological perspectives of the Gospel writers, which, again, are of the utmost importance for Christian faith. As the Pontifical Biblical Commission has put it, "one must learn to look for the Christology of each evangelist. . . . The New Testament authors, precisely as pastors and teachers, bear witness indeed to the same Christ, but with voices that differ as in the harmony of one piece of music."[1]

Being aware that the New Testament Gospels contain materials from these three discrete "stages" is crucial because without this awareness the average reader simply assumes that everything they read is pretty much a verbatim eyewitness account of the events in the life of Jesus. With this perhaps unconscious presupposition, readers will tend to minimize or try to harmonize the differences found among the Gospel narratives and so will overlook each evangelist's distinctive (and what Christians know to be inspired) perceptions.

Most significantly for the modern Jewish and Christian rapprochement, such readers will construct an image of the life of Jesus and the interactions with his Jewish contemporaries that anachronistically incorporate elements and ideas from the decades after his crucifixion. Given the perennial "Christ

---

1. Pontifical Biblical Commission, "Instruction on the Bible and Christology" (January 6, 1984), §2.2.2.2(c).

killer" charge leveled by Christians down the centuries against Jews, the need to try to discern how their resurrection faith shaped the evangelists' portrayals of opposition to Jesus on the part of some Jews is of heightened importance. This is absolutely vital when considering such passages as the blasphemy accusation leveled against Jesus in the Sanhedrin hearing scene in Matthew 26:63-66. Did Caiaphas act against Jesus because he "blasphemously" claimed to be the divine Son (a post-resurrectional or Stage Two claim) or because Caiaphas feared that Jesus' "blasphemous" presumptuous arrogance imperiled the survival of the Temple (cf. John 11:48)?[2] Or to put it another way, was Jesus executed primarily for religious reasons because he violated the norms of the Jewish Torah, or primarily for what we might call political reasons because he proclaimed the imminent establishment of the rule of the God of Israel over the hegemony of the Roman Empire?

Thus, while Stage Three is most important for Christian faith, seeking to accurately reconstruct Stage One is crucial for understanding Jesus as an "authentic son of Israel"[3] in the late Second Temple period.

## The New Testament and Christian Attitudes toward Jews and Judaism

In an address given by Pope Saint John Paul II in 1997 he noted that "In the Christian world . . . erroneous and unjust interpretations of the New Testament regarding the Jewish people and their alleged culpability [for the crucifixion of Jesus] have circulated for too long, engendering feelings of hostility towards this people."[4] The pope was here referring to such passages as Matthew 27:25, "His blood be on us and on our children," or John 8:44, "You [Jews] belong to your father, the devil," which for centuries have been used by Christians to marginalize and oppress Jews. Such texts are *polemical*, written to argue against some opponent, to take a rhetorical punch at somebody. How does the Catholic approach to interpreting the Gospels understand these passages so as to conclude, as John Paul II did, that readings that promote hostility toward Jews are "erroneous and unjust"?

---

2. See the detailed discussion of the pre- and post-resurrectional connotations of blasphemy in Raymond E. Brown, *The Death of the Messiah: From Gethsemane to the Grave* (New York: Doubleday, 1994), I: 520-547.

3. John Paul II, "Address to the Pontifical Biblical Commission," April 11, 1997, §3.

4. John Paul II, "Address to Participants in the Vatican Symposium on 'The Roots of Anti-Judaism in the Christian Milieu,'" October 31, 1997, §1.

One simple answer is the Catholic teaching outlined above: interpreters should be aware that words attributed to Jesus in the Gospels (as if transcribed by Stage One eyewitnesses) are frequently expressions of perspectives being advanced by the Gospel writer (in Stage Three). Among the concerns of some of the evangelists was the desire to have the church seen as a legitimate religion within the Roman Empire. Christianity was not a legal movement in the first century and was subject to periodic persecution. If an evangelist is interested in presenting the church as an unthreatening, peaceful movement, he is not going to dwell on the fact that the founder of Christianity had been crucified by the orders of a Roman prefect for the seditious crime of being called "king of the Jews." This seems to be a very strong concern in the Gospel of Luke and the Acts of the Apostles in which there are many Roman characters who are almost always portrayed very positively (see chapter 5). When it comes to the particularly challenging task of narrating the Roman crucifixion of Jesus, the more imperial involvement is deemphasized, while the role played by Jewish characters becomes proportionally more prominent.

Contributing to the tendency to accentuate Jewish roles in Jesus' execution are the debates that occurred among different Jewish groups, including followers of Jesus as the Raised Lord, after the Roman destruction of the Jerusalem Temple in the year 70. As detailed in chapter 5, this dynamic is evident in the Gospel of Matthew, which argues that his church's way of being Jewish, of living out the covenant with God, is the way God wants Jews to live in a world without the Temple. Thus, Matthew portrays Jesus as the definitive interpreter of the Torah, as in the Sermon on the Mount scene, reminiscent of Moses' bringing down the Torah from Mt. Sinai. Matthew is competing for influence with other Jewish groups in the aftermath of the Temple's destruction, most notably the Pharisees.[5] It is for this reason that Matthew's Gospel has the harshest anti-Pharisaic rhetoric of all the Gospels (see Matthew 23). The intense opposition that Matthew portrays between Jesus and the Pharisees is more indebted to the rivalry at the time this Gospel was written (Stage Three) than to the actual relations between Jesus and the Pharisees during his ministry (Stage One), which were probably more varied. As the Pontifical Commission for Religious Relations with the Jews put it in a 1985 document:

---

5. So, e.g., Anthony J. Saldarini, *Matthew's Christian-Jewish Community* (Chicago/London: University of Chicago Press, 1994), and Daniel J. Harrington, *The Gospel of Matthew,* Sacra Pagina Series (Collegeville, MN: Liturgical Press, 1991).

An exclusively negative picture of the Pharisees is likely to be inaccurate and unjust. If in the Gospels . . . there are all sorts of unfavorable references to the Pharisees, they should be seen against the background of a complex and diversified movement. . . . The Gospels are the outcome of long and complicated editorial work. . . . Certain controversies reflect Christian-Jewish relations long after the time of Jesus.[6]

The upheaval in the Jewish world after the Roman destruction of the Jerusalem Temple in 70 C.E. is the backdrop for the inner-Jewish competition evident in Matthew. It is also seen in how Matthew narrates the execution of Jesus. Like many Jewish writers of the time, Matthew felt it necessary to explain why the Temple was destroyed. Most Jews interpreted the event as a divine punishment.[7] Some Jews such as Josephus argued that the Zealots had polluted the sacred space, which God therefore purified with fire.[8] Matthew's distinctive claim is that the corrupt leaders of Jerusalem misled its inhabitants into demanding Jesus' death. Therefore, that generation and their children's generation were destroyed. This is the background for the uniquely Matthean exclamation by the crowd: "His blood be on us and on our children" (27:25). Although writing in the latter third of the first century, Matthew explains the Temple's destruction in 70 C.E. by his presentation of the circumstances of Jesus' death around 30 C.E. He is presumably telling his readers not to follow the corrupt Pharisaic leadership of his own day (around 90 C.E.), and so be destroyed as were those Jerusalemites (in 70 C.E.) who followed the corrupt priests in Jesus' time (30 C.E.).

Tragically, when later read over the centuries in the context of an entirely Gentile Christianity, Matthew's work was understood to denote the imposition of a divine curse on the Jewish people in all times and places. Since the modern Catholic approach to the Bible requires that such passages be interpreted in their historical and literary contexts, it becomes clear that a

6. Pontifical Commission for Religious Relations with the Jews, "Notes on the Correct Way to Present Jews and Judaism in Preaching and Catechesis in the Roman Catholic Church" (1985), III, 8; IV, 1, A.

7. Adam Gregerman, " 'Have you despised Jerusalem and Zion after you had chosen them?': The Destruction of Jerusalem and the Temple in Jewish and Christian Writings from the Land of Israel in Late Antiquity," doctoral dissertation, Columbia University (2007), 205-213. UMI Number 3266586.

8. Josephus, *The Jewish War*, §§250, 323, 419, 539. Cited by Luke T. Johnson, "The New Testament's Anti-Jewish Slander and the Conventions of Ancient Polemic," *Journal of Biblical Literature* 108/3 (Fall 1989): 437.

timeless and universal curse upon all Jews is not being asserted by Matthew. This is why John Paul II could call such interpretations "erroneous." It is also why numerous magisterial or official Catholic documents have rejected such readings, beginning with *Nostra Aetate:* "Jews should not be spoken of as rejected or accursed as if this followed from Holy Scripture. Consequently, all must take care, lest in catechizing or in preaching the word of God, they teach anything which is not in accord with the truth of the Gospel message or the spirit of Christ" (§4).

An even more sweeping principle was articulated by the Pontifical Biblical Commission in 1993:

> Clearly to be rejected also is every attempt at actualization set in a direction contrary to evangelical justice and charity, such as, for example, the use of the Bible to justify racial segregation, anti-Semitism or sexism whether on the part of men or women. Particular attention is necessary, according to the spirit of the Second Vatican Council (*Nostra Aetate*, 4), to avoid absolutely any actualization of certain texts of the New Testament, which could provoke or reinforce unfavorable attitudes toward the Jewish people. The tragic events of the past must, on the contrary, impel all to keep unceasing in mind that, according to the New Testament, the Jews remain "beloved" of God, "since the gifts and calling of God are irrevocable" (Rom. 11:28-29).[9]

This is to be understood, I believe, as axiomatic for all Catholic interpretations of the New Testament. If someone reads New Testament passages in ways that promote hostility to the Jewish people, according to Catholic standards he or she has misinterpreted the text. I suspect that the most frequent explanation for such errors is a failure to appreciate the three stages of Gospel development.

## Reading the Christian "Old Testament"

When the followers of Jesus came to perceive him as raised from death, being Jews, they tried to make sense of their revelatory experience by turning to their sacred scriptures. However, they read them in ways that no Jews had ever read them before. They read them through the experience of the

---

9. PBC, "The Interpretation of the Bible in the Church," IV, A, 3.

Crucified One as raised. They read them through what we might call christological lenses.

Through this "rereading," texts such as the suffering servant songs in Isaiah or Psalm 22 took on meanings that would not have developed previously. The apostles brought their new readings of Israel's scriptures into their proclamation of the Good News of Jesus to fellow Jews and later to Gentiles. Their rereading enabled them to demonstrate that what God had done in Christ was in continuity with God's promises to Israel and with all of "salvation history."

With the exception of the contrary views of Marcion[10] in the second century, this basic orientation set the pattern for Christian approaches to what came to be called the "Old Testament." What was important about that "Old Testament" for Christians down through the centuries was what it revealed about Christ and the church. For them its significance in terms of the story of Israel and the Jewish people paled in comparison to the spiritual realities brought about with the coming of Jesus Christ.

Herein lies the difficulty. When combined with the polemical stance toward Judaism that grew in the church's early centuries (see chapter 3), an exclusively christological approach to the "Old Testament" contributed to the idea that Judaism was outmoded after Christ. Judaism, and therefore Jews, really had little religious reason to exist anymore. Even the term "Old Testament" could suggest obsolescence when contrasted with the "New" Testament. (To alert the reader to this potential, "Old Testament" appears in quotation marks throughout this section. The "Old Testament" is not "old" to Jews today, and ought not to be seen as obsolete by Christians either.)

Christians need to read the scriptures of ancient Israel in the light of Christ because that helps them understand Christ. However, problems arise if the text is understood as having a legitimate meaning *only* if read christologically.

The presence of a historical and literary consciousness about the Bible

---

10. Marcion was a mid-second-century Christian who, believing that many of the teachings of Christ could not be reconciled with the portrayal of the Old Testament's deity, argued that Jesus was actually the Son of the true, supreme and merciful God, not the Son of the wrathful creator deity whom Jews revered. Consequently, he insisted that Israel's scriptures were not normative for the church and should not be included in the Christian Bible. He was excommunicated by the church in Rome around the year 140. This was a decisive moment for Christianity because the inclusion of the "Old Testament" in the Christian Bible has defined the church's self-understanding ever since.

in Catholic teaching since 1943 (see chapter 1) is obviously important to this question. There has gradually developed an appreciation that biblical passages can have multiple valid meanings. In 1985, the Pontifical Commission for Religious Relations with the Jews had this to say:

> It is true then, and should be stressed, that the Church and Christians read the Old Testament in the light of the event of the dead and risen Christ and that on these grounds there is Christian reading of the Old Testament which does not necessarily coincide with the Jewish reading. Thus Christian identity and Jewish identity should be carefully distinguished in their respective reading of the Bible. But this detracts nothing from the value of the Old Testament in the Church and does nothing to hinder Christians from profiting discerningly from the traditions of Jewish reading.[11]

What is implied here (and would be made explicit in subsequent ecclesial documents) is that there is a spiritual value to Jewish interpretations of what they call the Tanakh (an acronym from the Hebrew words for Torah, Prophets, and Writings). Moreover, Christians can benefit from the traditions of Jewish interpretation. This is a reversal of hundreds of years of Christian preaching that urged the avoidance of Jewish biblical scholarship.

The same document goes on to talk about typological readings of the "Old Testament." A typological reading is searching an ancient text for parallels with later texts or later experiences. So, Christians, not inappropriately, have customarily read the "Old Testament" by drawing parallels to Christ and the church. A vivid example of this is the Binding or the Sacrifice of Isaac in Genesis 22. Isaac is a "type" of Christ, an anticipation. He carries the wood of his sacrifice up the hill; he is the only beloved son of the father, etc. This developed in Christian tradition as a way of scripturally understanding the significance of Jesus' death.

However, as *one* method of christologically reading the scriptures from ancient Israel, it not only runs the risk of reducing Judaism to being merely a preparation for Christianity but also deprives the scriptures of ancient Israel of their own integrity. With the rise of biblical criticism in Catholicism, however, there is today a greater appreciation for the multidimensional depth of the "Old Testament." Thus, the 1985 "Notes" conclude, "typological reading only manifests the unfathomable riches of the Old Testament, its inexhaustible content and the mystery of which it is full and should not lead

---

11. CRRJ, "Notes" (1985), II, 6.

us to forget that it retains its own value as revelation that the New Testament often does no more than resume (cf. Mk. 12:29-31)."[12]

This is a somewhat breathtaking analogy that compares the New Testament to a *Cliff Notes* summary of the "Old Testament." The first testament in the Christian Bible contains "unfathomable riches" that is not exhausted by christological readings of it. Christians ought to become more and more aware of this even while their lives of faith continue to be guided by the New Testament.

An earlier document from the Pontifical Commission for Religious Relations with the Jews concerning the implementation of *Nostra Aetate* also warned Catholics against simplistic contrasts between the "Old" and New Testaments: "The Old Testament and the Jewish tradition founded upon it must not be set against the New Testament in such a way that the former seems to constitute a religion of only justice, fear and legalism, with no appeal to the love of God and neighbor" (cf. Deut. 6:5; Lev. 19:18; Matt. 22:34-40).[13] This quotation rejects the invidious comparison of a supposed "Old Testament" God of justice and punishment with the God of love revealed by Jesus in the New Testament, a comparison which actually reprises the heresy of Marcion, who had so argued in the mid-second century. In reality, God's love for Israel is reiterated throughout the "Old Testament" (e.g., Exod. 34:6-7; Ps. 36; Ps. 136; Hos. 11) and judgment and punishment are themes also found in the New Testament (e.g., Matt. 25:31-46; Luke 6:24-26; John 3:17-21; Rev. 20:12-15). To dichotomize the two Testaments in this way disrespects them both.

## The Jewish People and Their Sacred Scriptures in the Christian Bible

In 2001, the Pontifical Biblical Commission published its most extensive study to date, which expanded upon many of the aspects of Catholic-Jewish relations introduced by earlier ecclesial documents. The study was accompanied by a glowing introduction by Cardinal Joseph Ratzinger, the future Pope Benedict XVI, who as president of the Congregation for the Doctrine of the Faith had to approve its publication. Because the document is over

---

12. CRRJ, "Notes," II, 7.

13. Pontifical Commission for Religious Relations with the Jews, "Guidelines and Suggestions for Implementing the Conciliar Declaration *Nostra Aetate,* 4" (1974), III.

two hundred pages in length, it is best to highlight its key points in three areas: Christian and Jewish retrospective rereadings of Israel's scriptures, the Hebrew prophets, and promise and fulfillment.

The term "rereadings" had appeared in earlier documents. It means to read old texts through new lenses, such as when the first Christians began to reread the scriptures of ancient Israel through resurrection lenses. Within the "Old Testament"/Tanakh itself such rereadings of earlier books by the authors of later books are evident. The Book of Chronicles is a rereading of the Book of Deuteronomy, for example. The 2001 PBC study took particular note of the Christian rereading of Israel's scriptures:

> In Judaism, re-readings were commonplace. . . . What is specific to the Christian re-reading is that it is done . . . in the light of Christ. This new interpretation does not negate the original meaning. . . . The Old Testament in itself has great value as the Word of God. To read the Old Testament as Christians then does not mean wishing to find everywhere direct reference to Jesus and to Christian realities. . . . Although the Christian reader is aware that the internal dynamism of the Old Testament finds its goal in Jesus, this is a retrospective perception whose point of departure is not in the text as such, but in the events of the New Testament proclaimed by the apostolic preaching.[14]

These words reiterate the insight of previous Catholic teaching documents which assert that the later christological readings of the "Old Testament" do not invalidate or supersede the text's "original meaning." In addition, though, the study characterizes this Christian reading as "retrospective." It understands the Christian rereading of the texts of Israel as having a "point of departure" that is not the words of the texts themselves, but the experience of Christ crucified and raised.

The 2001 study immediately proceeds to draw a conclusion of great importance for Christian-Jewish relations: "It cannot be said, therefore, that Jews do not see what has been proclaimed in the text, but that the Christian, in the light of Christ and in the Spirit, discovers in the text a surplus of meaning that was hidden there" (II, A, 6). For centuries, Christians had

---

14. Pontifical Biblical Commission, *The Jewish People and Their Sacred Scriptures in the Christian Bible* (May 24, 2001), II, A, 2, 6. http://www.vatican.va/roman_curia/congregations/cfaith/pcb_documents/rc_con_cfaith_doc_20020212_popolo-ebraico_en.html. Accessed Nov. 16, 2013.

accused Jews of blindness, of deliberate obstinacy, or even of being pawns of Satan for refusing to see that their own scriptures so self-evidently (to Christians) pointed to Jesus.[15] The Commission repudiates such ideas by explaining that to see christological meanings in the biblical texts of Israel demands resurrection faith as a prerequisite. That faith perspective enables the reader to derive a previously hidden "surplus of meaning" from the text.

In addition to these observations about Christian rereadings of the "Old Testament," the PBC study also comments on the distinctive *Jewish* rereadings of the Tanakh:

> Christians can and ought to admit that the Jewish reading of the Bible is a possible one, in continuity with the Jewish Sacred Scriptures from the Second Temple period, a reading analogous to the Christian reading which developed in parallel fashion. Each of these two readings is part of the vision of each respective faith of which it is a product and an expression. Consequently, they cannot be reduced one into the other. On the practical level of exegesis [scriptural interpretation], Christians can, nonetheless, learn much from Jewish exegesis practiced for more than two thousand years, and, in fact, they have learned much in the course of history. For their part, it is to be hoped that Jews themselves can derive profit from Christian exegetical research. (II, A, 7)

These words offer additional dramatic evidence of both the renaissance in Catholic biblical understanding and also in attitudes toward Judaism that have occurred in the past fifty years or so. Not only are christological readings of the "Old Testament" perceived to be retrospective, but the Jewish traditions of the rabbis, especially as contained in the Talmud, are themselves seen as retrospective interpretations. Most significantly, the Jewish rereadings are themselves deemed to be legitimate by being "analogous" to Christian retrospective interpretations. The difference lies in their respective and irreducible "points of departure": Christ in the case of Christians and the rabbinic writings in the case of Jews.

This perspective recalls the crucial assertion in the PBC's previous document, "The Interpretation of the Bible in the Church," that there are multiple legitimate meanings of a biblical text. Here it is seen that both Jewish and

---

15. See the helpful overview provided by David P. Efroymson, "The Patristic Connection," in Alan T. Davies, ed., *Antisemitism and the Foundations of Christianity* (New York/Ramsey/Toronto: Paulist, 1979), 98-117.

Christian traditions of interpretation have spiritual value. Pope Benedict reiterated this point quite powerfully when he wrote in 2011:

> After centuries of antagonism, we now see it as our task to bring these two ways of rereading the biblical texts — the Christian way and the Jewish way — into dialogue with one another, if we are to understand God's will and his word aright.[16]

Moreover, the Commission's hope that Jewish and Christian scripture study can be mutually beneficial is to some degree being realized in academia today. There are more and more Jewish experts in the New Testament and more and more Christian scholars of rabbinics. The former development is stunningly exemplified by the publication in 2011 of *The Jewish Annotated New Testament,* in which about sixty Jewish scholars comment on the books of the Christian New Testament and offer numerous thematic essays.[17]

Second, *The Jewish People and Their Sacred Scriptures in the Christian Bible* also discusses biblical prophecy and Israel's prophets in a very important way:

> It would be wrong to consider the prophecies of the Old Testament as some kind of photographic anticipations of future events. All the texts, including those which later were read as messianic prophecies, already had an immediate import and meaning for their contemporaries before attaining a fuller meaning for future hearers. (II, A, 5)

It is common for prophecy to be defined simply as predicting the future. Biblical prophecy is something much more. Most often it is speaking God's messages about current crises or decisions to the prophet's contemporaries. These decisions may indeed have consequences for the future, but the emphasis in the vast majority of biblical prophetic speech is on ethical behavior and choices. The prophets should be understood as the consciences of the covenant between God and the people of Israel, and not, as the PBC puts it, as providers of "photographic anticipations" — exact predictions of the future — either for their contemporaries or for generations of later readers.

---

16. Pope Benedict XVI, *Jesus of Nazareth,* Part Two, *Holy Week: From the Entrance into Jerusalem to the Resurrection* (San Francisco: Ignatius Press, 2011), 35.

17. Amy-Jill Levine and Marc Zvi Brettler, eds., *The Jewish Annotated New Testament* (Oxford University Press, 2011).

It might be helpful to give an example of the distinction the PBC is urging. As was mentioned earlier, the followers of Jesus consulted Israel's scriptures to try to make sense of the trauma of his crucifixion. Among other texts, they retrospectively reread the suffering servant songs in Isaiah (42:1-7; 49:1-7; 50:4-9a; and 52:13–53:12). These passages were also concerned with the suffering of God's "servant," perhaps the whole people of Israel in exile and/or the exiled Judean king. The prophet Isaiah suggests that God can bring unexpected blessing out of tragedy. The followers of Jesus saw this as particularly true in the case of Jesus, the suffering servant who gave his life in service to the Reign of God and who was therefore exalted by God (as in Philippians 2:5-11, e.g.).

If Isaiah's prophecy is wrongly approached as a "photographic anticipation," then the interactive nature of prophecy is flattened to one dimension: an ancient writer predicted something that later came to pass. Once the predicted event occurs, the prophecy has served its purpose. If some Christians say, "Look, Isaiah predicted that a righteous servant would suffer, and that's what happened to Jesus," then the suffering servant passages from Isaiah have little meaning for readers today except as proof-texts.

However, the PBC advocates that prophecy be seen more as the perception of a recurrent pattern of God's involvement with people, so that in the case of Isaiah's suffering servant, sometimes out of the suffering of the righteous, unexpected good can occur. Thus, Christians will certainly see that fulfilled superlatively in Jesus' resurrection, but they are also enabled to see Isaiah's prophecy about what happened in ancient Israel potentially recurring in their lives today whenever the innocent suffer unjustly. If prophecy is seen merely as prediction and accomplishment, it has been significantly emptied of its potential to be meaningful in people's lives today. Rather, prophecy seen as expressing an ongoing pattern of God's activities can help Christians (and Jews) cope with the horrible suffering in our world.

The Commission once again goes on to draw out an important implication for Catholic-Jewish relations, beginning with a description of biblical prophecy:

> The original task of the prophet was to help his contemporaries understand the events and the times they lived in from God's viewpoint. Accordingly, excessive insistence, characteristic of a certain apologetic, on the probative value attributable to the fulfillment of prophecy must be discarded. The insistence has contributed to harsh judgments by Christians of Jews and their reading of the Old Testament: the more reference

to Christ is found in Old Testament texts, the more the incredulity of the Jews is considered inexcusable and obstinate. (II, A, 5)

The Commission here explains that the practice of attempting to "prove" Christian claims by citing the biblical prophets has historically contributed to the Christian denigration of Jews. If Christians assert that direct, obvious predictions about Jesus are evident in Israel's scriptures, then why cannot Jews see that these "photographic anticipations" have been achieved?[18] The PBC rejects such conclusions, in this case identifying the problem as erroneous presuppositions about the nature of biblical prophecy.

Third, the 2001 PBC study offered some very significant comments on the topic of promise and fulfillment:

Beginning from a continuous re-reading of events and texts, the Old Testament itself progressively opens up a perspective of fulfillment that is final and definitive. The Exodus, the primordial experience of Israel's faith, becomes the symbol of final salvation. Liberation from the Babylonian Exile and the prospect of an eschatological salvation are described as a new Exodus. Christian interpretation is situated along these lines with this difference, that the fulfillment is already substantially realized in the mystery of Christ. (II, A, 5)

Christians believe that in Christ the establishment of the kingdom of God has emerged into human history, but they also believe that the kingdom of God has not yet arrived in all of its fullness. It is embryonically present. That is why the Lord's Prayer pleads "thy Kingdom come." Christians believe that it is inevitable that the Reign of God will come both because of God's promises to the children of Israel and because of what has happened in Jesus

---

18. One perennial Christian explanation, following a supersessionist reading of Paul, was that Jewish eyes were veiled so that they could not "see" Christ in the scriptures of Israel (see 2 Cor. 3:12-18). Another was that Jews were too physical or carnal in their way of reading scriptures. Origen, for instance, argued that the reason Jews "hold false opinions and make impious or ignorant suggestions about God appears to be nothing else than this, that scripture is not understood in its spiritual sense, but is interpreted according to the bare letter" (Cited in Robert L. Wilken, *Judaism and the Early Christian Mind: A Study of Cyril of Alexandria's Exegesis and Theology* [New Haven: Yale University Press, 1971], 16). The motif of Jews as blindfolded appears in dozens of medieval statuary depictions of Synagoga on churches and cathedrals. See Heinz Schreckenberg, *The Jews in Christian Art: An Illustrated History* (New York: Continuum, 1996), 31-65.

Christ. Here Christians and Jews have a commonality: they are both looking forward to something that they know is inevitable because God has indicated it to them in their respective traditions. Jews and Christians share some of these indications, such as the account of the Exodus from Egypt; others they do not. The PBC continues by discussing the eschaton, that time when all of the expectations of the Jewish and Christian traditions will be realized, when the Reign of God is fully established:

> What has already been accomplished in Christ must yet be accomplished in us and in the world. The definitive fulfillment will be at the end with the resurrection of the dead, a new heaven and a new earth. Jewish messianic expectation is not in vain. It can become for us Christians a powerful stimulant to keep alive the eschatological dimension of our faith. Like them, we too live in expectation. The difference is that for us the One who is to come will have the traits of the Jesus who has already come and is already present and active among us. (II, A, 5)

Two important points have been made here. First, Jewish expectations for the messianic Age to Come are "not in vain." They will be realized. This awareness helps Christians appreciate the unfinished aspects of their own expectations for the eschaton. Second, Christians will recognize the eschatological messiah on the basis of "the traits" of Jesus. These are traits consistent with the church's experience of Christ crucified and raised. But since Jewish messianic expectation is not in vain, then Jews will also recognize that eschatological figure as Messiah, obviously not on the basis of the traits of Jesus, but on the basis of traits conveyed in the Jewish tradition as to what the eschatological world will be like. This subject will be explored in more detail in chapter 10.

On the basis of its biblical studies, then, the Pontifical Biblical Commission implies a wonderful convergence in Jewish and Christian expectations. This is consistent with the perspective of the Pontifical Commission for Religious Relations with the Jews, whose 1985 "Notes" on the correct presentation of Jews and Judaism stated:

> [I]n underlining the eschatological dimension of Christianity we shall reach a greater awareness that the people of God of the Old and the New Testament are tending towards a like end in the future: the coming or return of the Messiah — even if they start from two different points of view. It is more clearly understood that the person of the Messiah is not only a

point of division for the people of God but also a point of convergence. Thus it can be said that Jews and Christians meet in a comparable hope, founded on the same promise made to Abraham. Attentive to the same God who has spoken, hanging on the same word, we have to witness to one same memory and one common hope in Him who is the master of history. We must also accept our responsibility to prepare the world for the coming of the Messiah by working together for social justice, respect for the rights of persons and nations and for social and international reconciliation. (II, 10, 11)

## Conclusion

It is clear that the adoption of biblical criticism in the Catholic community has opened up new possibilities for a fresh appreciation of the Jewish tradition. It has enabled the recognition of negative features of some Catholic traditions of biblical interpretation. Biblical studies have also greatly contributed to the new positive relationship between Catholics and Jews that has begun to grow since the Second Vatican Council.

As a result, the future holds great promise for extensive mutual enrichment and collaboration between Catholics and Jews, but this will require Catholics to continue to pursue the developments of the past several decades. This includes providing intensified education about biblical interpretation throughout the entire worldwide Catholic community.

# CHAPTER 3

# Christianity and Rabbinic Judaism:
# Branches from the Root of Second Temple Judaism

## A Complex Parting

The previous chapter surveyed the crucial contributions made by Catholic biblical scholarship to the recent rapprochement between Jews and Christians. The birth of this new relationship and the development of new research tools both in biblical and historical studies has led to an interest in the origins of Christianity as well as of post–Second Temple rabbinic Judaism. Already the earliest statements on Christian-Jewish relations after the Second World War had stressed the Jewishness of Jesus, his apostles, and the first churches,[1] but then the question of the so-called "parting of the ways" between the churches and Judaism came to the forefront. Study of this topic has effectively undermined a widely held assumption that Judaism and Christianity became separate and fundamentally opposed

---

1. For example, the "Ten Points of Seelisberg" (1947) urged Christians to remember that "Jesus was born of a Jewish mother of the seed of David and the people of Israel," and that "the first disciples, the apostles and the first martyrs were Jews." Likewise, *Nostra Aetate* (1965) stated: "The Church keeps ever in mind the words of the Apostle [Paul] about his kinsmen: 'theirs is the sonship and the glory and the covenants and the law and the worship and the promises; theirs are the fathers and from them is the Christ according to the flesh' (Rom. 9:4-5), the Son of the Virgin Mary. She also recalls that the Apostles, the Church's main-stay and pillars, as well as most of the early disciples who proclaimed Christ's Gospel to the world, sprang from the Jewish people."

---

This chapter is based on my "Jews and Christians from the Time of Christ to Constantine's Reign," in Albert S. Lindemann and Richard S. Levy, eds., *Antisemitism: A History* (Oxford: Oxford University Press, 2010), 47-62.

religious communities shortly after — or even during — the lifetime of Jesus. For centuries, some have traced hostility between Jews and Christians back to Jesus himself, depicting him as an opponent of an allegedly legalistic and heartless post-exilic Judaism. Others linked the "the parting of the ways" to a specific event: the crucifixion of Jesus (ca. 30 C.E.), to the activities of the Christian apostle Paul of Tarsus (35-65 C.E.), to the first Jewish-Roman War in which the Second Temple in Jerusalem was destroyed (66-70 C.E.) or to the second Jewish-Roman War, the Bar Kokhba revolt (132-135 C.E.).

Critical biblical scholarship and historical research over the past several decades[2] have caused a paradigm shift from such simplistic notions toward the model of a complex, irregular, and very gradual separation and delineation of Christianity from emerging rabbinic Judaism. Rather than being fundamentally antithetical, the boundaries between Jews and Christians are now seen as having been quite unclear for centuries. Their defining differences gradually deepened for diverse reasons in widely scattered places. Hindering an accurate reconstruction of the early relations between the two groups is a tendency to retroject later circumstances, teachings, and conflicts back to the time of their respective origins. This chapter sketches the origins and the gradual differentiation between rabbinic Judaism and Christianity, devoting special attention to the appearance of hostile attitudes between them.

## Late Second Temple Judaism

It has become almost axiomatic in recent studies to describe Judaism in the century or so before the destruction of the Second Temple in 70 C.E. as extremely diverse. There certainly was a common Jewish agreement that God had chosen the people of Israel to participate in a covenant centered on the Torah whose commands the people were to follow, on the Land where God permitted them to dwell, and on the Temple where God was to be worshipped. However, there were many competing interpretations about the

---

2. The topic of the "Parting(s) of the Ways" constitutes a significant sub-category of historical research in Christian-Jewish relations. Two of the most significant works are: Daniel Boyarin, *Border Lines: The Partition of Judaeo-Christianity* (Philadelphia: University of Pennsylvania Press, 2004); and Adam H. Becker and Annette Yoshiko Reed, eds., *The Ways that Never Parted: Jews and Christians in Late Antiquity and the Early Middle Ages* (Minneapolis: Fortress Press, 2007).

details of covenantal life beyond these basics. These diverse understandings gave rise to many different Jewish "groups" in this period, many of which we cannot clearly identify or distinguish two thousand years later.

One source of diversity within the Jewish world was geographic in nature. It appears that there were more Jews living outside the land of Israel than within it for centuries before the time of Jesus. Second Temple era Jews responded to the overwhelming influence of Greek culture and to their domination by a succession of imperial regimes in various ways. As is typical among subordinated peoples, some Jews assimilated into the wider culture, some rejected it utterly, and most fell somewhere between the two extremes. Although we lack much detailed information, Jews had been living in close contact with Greek culture since the days of Alexander the Great (356-323 B.C.E.). "Hellenistic Jews" who lived at a great distance from Jerusalem would speak Greek as their native language (hence the need for the Greek translation of Israel's scriptures called the Septuagint [ca. 200 B.C.E.]) and live out their religious traditions in different ways than their brethren in Israel.

In 63 B.C.E., the Roman general Pompey conquered Jerusalem and Jewish lands became subject to Roman tribute. A generation-long period of instability followed as rival Roman armies, competing Jerusalem aristocrats, and Parthian (Persian) forces devastated the region. In periodic campaigns, Roman armies burned entire towns, crucifying or enslaving the residents. In these circumstances, a certain outlook known as "apocalypticism" manifested itself in different ways among many Jewish groups. This perspective can be broadly defined as the conviction that the world had become so lawless that God would have to intervene to rout the forces of chaos and establish a divine reign of justice.

Jews speculated about how this divine intervention would occur. To sketch a wide range of apocalyptic concepts that arose in the first centuries B.C.E. and C.E.: some Jews wondered if God would use agents, human or angelic, to assert divine authority. Other Jews thought about the form of Jewish self-government in their own Land in the Age to Come, some picturing an ideal king like David of old, some a perfect teacher like Moses, and others a superlative priest who would lead the people in worshiping God in a renewed Temple, cleansed of corrupt clerical regimes. Some pondered the fate of the Gentile nations and peoples, some concluding that God would punish those guilty of idolatry but the righteous among the nations could be included in the kingdom of God. Some Jews expected or hoped for divine intervention in their lifetimes, while others were content that this would certainly occur at some point in the indefinite future. There were also some who anticipated that the righteous dead would be resurrected into the bliss of God's sovereign rule.

### Jesus, a Galilean Jew

A series of charismatic prophetic figures arose in this turbulent situation. Some of these individuals we know only by name, but the activity of Jesus from Nazareth in the Galilee was to have the greatest historical impact. Known as a popular teacher and healer, he traveled around Galilee and Judea. By means of illustrative parables, welcoming fellowship meals, healings, and symbolic deeds, he announced that the Reign of God was breaking into the world and that Israel was being restored.

Eventually, he brought this kingdom-centered message to Jerusalem during the always tense Passover season, a time when Jews from around the Mediterranean gathered to commemorate the festival of Jewish freedom from foreign domination. Roman authorities (and Jewish leaders concerned about a devastating Roman response to disorder) tried to avert the demonstrations against their rule that often erupted at Passover time. If unsuccessful in preventing unrest the Romans were poised to restore order forcefully. Some days before Passover, Jesus caused a disturbance in the Temple courts, apparently a prophetic protest against the widely-perceived corruption of the priestly leadership (whose chief priest, contrary to biblical norms, was effectively appointed by the Roman prefect). This incident sparked or reinforced alarm among the Romans and their priestly agents that Jesus might be intending to foment a Passover riot.

Preemptive action would seem to account for the Roman execution of Jesus just before Passover began. Crucifixions at prominent sites were used both to torture perceived insurgents and also to deter their followers. By taking the popular Jesus into custody under cover of darkness (Mark 14:2) and quickly dispatching him to a cross, a potential uprising would be blocked and a gruesome warning issued. The fact that Jesus was publicly crucified and not simply made to "disappear" supports this logic. Moreover, his mode of execution and the capital charge displayed on his cross of "king of the Jews" show that his activities on behalf of God's Reign or Kingdom were perceived by Roman overlords as seditious, though the failure to round up Jesus' followers also suggests a judgment that whatever threat he posed could be easily contained. The priestly elites — not unreasonably as later

37

events would prove — feared for the existence of the Temple if major turmoil erupted (John 11:8).[3]

This represents a mainstream consensus of current historical Jesus studies. In particular, it should be noted that such reconstructions depict Jesus as thoroughly immersed in the life of Second Temple Judaism. His activities and teaching were welcomed by some of his Jewish contemporaries and disliked or disputed by others, but there is no question that he operated well within the range of conventional Jewish diversity. Some might have challenged his statements, actions, or authority, but his "Jewishness" was not in question. As mentioned in the previous chapter and as will be further discussed below, this scholarly portrayal understands New Testament passages that suggest a rupture between Jesus' followers and other Jews as anachronistic, actually reflecting the controversies of several decades later.

## The Birth of the Church

Jesus of Nazareth was one individual among the thousands and thousands of Jews crucified by Roman forces. What sets him apart in terms of historical impact stems from the assertions that his followers, all of them Jewish, began to make about him shortly after his death. These Jews claimed to have experienced the crucified Jesus as raised by God to transcendent life. This divine exaltation of an executed prophet convinced them that the eschaton, the time for the in-breaking of God's Reign, was indeed commencing just as Jesus had declared. The idea of an eschatological general resurrection of the dead was adapted to the unexpected situation of a singular resurrection of a righteous individual, who would soon usher in the wider resurrection: "[Jesus] the first fruits, then at his coming all those who belong to [him]," as Paul of Tarsus put it about twenty years later (1 Cor. 15:23). Since Jesus had been executed as a pretender "king of the Jews," his followers saw his resurrection as divine confirmation that Jesus was indeed an anointed agent or messiah of God, recalling the anointed Davidic kings of old. Jesus was hailed as Messiah, in Greek "Christ," but in a particular sense: he was the one sent by God, faithful even to the point of death, raised to glory, and soon to return to complete the implementation of God's Rule.

The followers of Jesus began to read the scriptures of Israel with different eyes, searching its passages for texts that would explain their current

---

3. For further details on reconstructing the events of Jesus' passion, see chapter 6.

experiences to themselves and to other Jews. They continued to gather for the fellowship meals that had been a characteristic of Jesus' activity, but now transformed them into memorial meals, celebrating the one who had been crucified and raised. Hymns to God's Wisdom were adapted in praise of Jesus Christ, and they began praying to him as God's Son and as the Lord who would share in God's power of final judgment at the eschaton. Their eschatological enthusiasm — their excitement that God was evidently beginning to exercise divine sovereignty in the world — appears to have spread quickly to diaspora Jews visiting in Jerusalem and through them out into the wider eastern Mediterranean region. Local Jewish assemblies, called in Greek *ekklesiai* (churches, identical in meaning to *synagogai*), formed in many places and were centered on Jesus the Raised One.

All of these occurrences made the Jewish churches distinctive in comparison with other Jewish groups, presaging the eventual differentiation of Judaism and "Christianity" into separate religious communities. However, idiosyncratic practices, claims, or modes of interpreting the scriptures were not unusual in the diverse world of late Second Temple Judaism. In these early decades, the churches were still "Jewish," not just demographically, but also because they fell within the range of acceptable variety during this period (for a possibly idyllic view, see Acts 2:46-47).

A development with huge consequences transpired when early preachers (called apostles) sought to spread their good news of Christ crucified-and-raised in diaspora synagogues. Perhaps to their initial surprise, their proclamation greatly interested some Gentiles who had already admired Judaism and who were to some degree accepted in local Jewish communities. While a few of these so-called "God-fearing" Gentiles (see Acts 13:16, 26) had received circumcision and been fully incorporated into Jewish life as converts, most others, unwilling to take that step, seem to have informally adopted some Jewish dietary practices and participated marginally in the synagogue. Hearing the apostles of Christ, these God-fearers saw a way of becoming more closely involved in Jewish life and inquired about the possibility of joining the emerging churches. Although the Jewish apostles probably saw this Gentile interest as further confirmation that the eschaton was approaching, a defining controversy erupted within the churches. Given the inclusive nature of Jesus' own activities, there does not seem to have been much resistance to the idea that Gentiles might be admitted into the Jewish churches, but there was considerable disagreement about admissions requirements. Opinion ranged from the requirement that Gentile believers undergo circumcision and take on total observance of the Torah, to the radical eschatological perspective that the Torah's authority had expired now that God's Reign was approaching and need not be observed by anyone in the churches, Jew or Gentile.[4] Various intermediate positions required some minimal ethical standards (no adultery, murder, or idolatry) among Gentiles in the churches, or that the Jewish dietary laws be observed at community fellowship meals.

This dispute raged for many decades with different practices operative in different churches. Thus, as mentioned in chapter 1, in the Gospel of Mark, written around 70 C.E., Jesus is said to have eliminated kosher laws by declaring "all foods clean" (7:19), while in Matthew's Gospel, composed around 80-90 C.E., Jesus declares, "whoever breaks one of the least of these commandments [of the Torah], and teaches others to do the same, will be called least in the Kingdom" (5:19). While the churches observed various customs in regard to Gentile members, gradually more and more Gentiles joined, becoming the majority in some places. This phenomenon was another wedge that would contribute to the separation of an originally entirely Jewish eschatological movement from its origins among the people of Israel.

As the leaders of the original Jewish churches debated the issue, they mounted arguments about the authority of the Torah that would be read quite differently in later social contexts. Most influential in the long-term was Paul of Tarsus, whose letters to diverse early churches, written in the decade of the 50s in the first century C.E., are the earliest books in the New Testament. An advocate of admitting Gentiles without requiring circumcision or Torah-observance, Paul addressed in his letters specific issues or controversies in particular circumstances that we cannot fully discern. He often tried to convince his opponents with arguments that became difficult for later generations of readers, unfamiliar with Paul's immediate context, to understand. Recent Pauline scholarship stresses that he was writing mostly to newborn Gentile churches and so was more interested in the Torah's condemnations of Gentile idolatry, rather than in its observance by Jews or its inherent value. He seemed particularly disturbed by opponents, possibly Gentile converts to Judaism who treated circumcision as a magical ritual that automatically put one right with God, but who had little interest in the entirety of the Torah (for example, Gal. 5:3). When his arguments were af-

4. See the range of views presented in Raymond E. Brown and John P. Meier, *Antioch and Rome: New Testament Cradles of Catholic Christianity* (New York/Ramsey: Paulist Press, 1983), 2-9. Also see the discussion of whether circumcision might have been expected in the Matthean community in Anthony J. Saldarini, *Matthew's Christian-Jewish Community* (Chicago/London: University of Chicago Press, 1994), 156-160.

terward read in a thoroughly Gentile Christianity that had become alienated from Judaism, Paul's words were used to support a caricature of Judaism as a futile and legalistic effort to earn God's favor through the strict, heartless observance of impossible commandments. (See chapter 4 for further discussion of Paul.)

## Between Two Revolts: Growing Estrangement

The first of two Jewish revolts against the Roman Empire effectively ended with the destruction of the Second Temple in 70 C.E. This trauma had enormous repercussions for all contemporary Jewish groups, giving rise to potent forces that accelerated the differentiation of the followers of Jesus Christ from other Jews. The appearance of the term "Christian" to denote both Jewish and Gentile church members is likely a sign of this dynamic.

There is some evidence, for instance, that the Jewish believers in Jesus generally did not join in the Great Revolt of 66-70 C.E.[5] Their belief that the returning, glorified Christ would be the one to establish God's Reign would naturally deter their participation in an insurgency against the Empire led by other Jews. Moreover, the persecution of Christians in Rome by the Emperor Nero between 64 and 66 C.E., during which two prominent Jewish church leaders, Peter and Paul, were probably executed, demonstrated the new movement's vulnerability and weakness, arguing for its quiescence. The destruction of Jerusalem led to the demise of the "mother church," hastening a growing shift in authority from Jewish churches to Gentile ones. At the same time, the disappearance of the eyewitness generation likely encouraged the composition of narratives of the life of Jesus, called Gospels, which as part of the "New Testament" would in time supersede Israel's scriptures as the normative Christian textual authorities.

The destruction of the Second Temple also upset the equilibrium that had existed among the diverse Jewish groups. Although some expected the rapid rebuilding of the Temple (perhaps after seventy years, as had happened after the loss of the first Temple in the sixth century B.C.E.), the surviving Jewish leadership competed for influence in the decades after 70 C.E. Among the rivals were some churches, such as the community in which the Gospel of Matthew was composed. This narrative portrayed Jesus as the definitive interpreter of the Torah, whose teachings God now expected all Jews to

---

5. So Eusebius, *History of the Church*, 3.5.3

follow after the Temple's demise. As leadership in the post-Temple Jewish world began to coalesce because of the dramatically changed religious and political situation, there seems to have been a tendency to unify the diversity of movements and opinions that had characterized late Second Temple Judaism. In such an environment, the claims made about a crucified Jew in the churches tended to marginalize church members in the eyes of other Jews.

Gentile Christians, too, were subjected to conflicting forces in terms of the church's relationship to Judaism. God-fearing Gentiles already had some mixed feelings. Although attracted by the Jewish tradition's monotheism, ethics, and antiquity, the aversion many felt toward circumcision would have inclined them to be selective about which Torah commandments they would observe. This ambivalence was exacerbated after the unsuccessful revolt in 70 C.E., which made associations with a people under such close scrutiny potentially dangerous.

On the one hand, Jews in the Roman Empire were exempt from worshiping the emperor as a deity, a privilege that Gentiles in the churches also sought. On the other hand, after the Great Revolt the Romans levied a "Jewish tax" of two drachmas a year on Jews. At first it was ethnically based, but under Caesar Domitian (ruled 81-96) it was extended to Gentiles who claimed some allegiance to Jewish customs (God-fearers and Christians). This would have encouraged Gentile Christians to deny that they were in any way Jewish and so not liable to this tax, although in times of persecution they would be motivated to claim association with Jewish privileges in order to avoid being forced to worship the emperor.

It was in this environment of war, uncertainty, and shifting identities that the Christian Gospels were composed. Written in different church contexts and with different Christian audiences in mind, these narratives of the life and significance of Jesus shared a common purpose. Their writers, known today as the evangelists, all sought to promote faith in Christ as the divine Son who was appointed to bring about God's Rule. The story of his death and resurrection was, of course, key to their proclamation, but powerful social forces converged in shaping the ways in which they related this crucial episode.

In a church subject to occasional imperial persecution, the fact that Jesus had been found guilty of sedition by a Roman prefect could not be stressed. It was important to convey not only that Jesus historically was innocent of such charges, but also — despite all the evidence to the contrary — that Roman authorities at the time were not terribly concerned about the Kingdom-preacher from Galilee. In different ways, the Gospels depicted the Temple leadership, widely unpopular among Jews before the Great Revolt, as the prime movers behind Jesus' execution. At the time of the composition of the Gospels, the surviving Temple priests were bereft of the physical site of their authority, a vivid testimony in the eyes of many to divine anger with them. Additionally, portraying the crucifixion of Jesus as another instance of Israel's rejecting prophets sent by God enabled the evangelists to appeal to their fellow Jews to repent by believing in the one whom God had vindicated by raising him from the grave. Luke's Gospel repeatedly describes Jesus in such "rejected prophet" terms, while Matthew's Gospel offers the residents of Jerusalem, doomed to destruction by Roman legions in the Great Revolt, as negative models of those stained with blood for the death of God's chosen agent.

Thus, the foundational Christian scriptural narratives related the central story of the death and resurrection of Jesus in ways that minimized Roman culpability and accentuated the role played by Jewish figures. Motivated by the complex interplay of internal post-Temple Jewish rivalries and life under an overpowering imperial authority, the evangelists authored texts that were later used in very different social circumstances to justify hostility to Jews and Judaism. For instance, the decisive social situation would radically change three centuries later when the Roman Empire would cease to persecute Christianity and indeed actually embrace it.[6]

However at the time of the evangelists in the late first century, Roman authorities had difficulty distinguishing among Jews, God-fearers, Gentile converts who had been circumcised as Jews, Christian Jews, and Christian Gentiles. In some cases, they may have consulted with known synagogue leaders about the claim to Jewishness of other groups, and, depending on the local circumstances in the particular town, some synagogue leaders may have denounced Jewish or Gentile Christians as not authentic Jews. Such a scenario may lie behind the epithet "synagogue of Satan" found twice in the New Testament Book of Revelation (2:9; 3:9), a work widely thought to have been written during a Roman persecution of churches in Asia Minor in the 90s C.E. Similar circumstances may underlie scattered but hard to substantiate claims of Jewish violence against Christians here and there.

Why would Jewish leaders eventually come to view the churches as an increasingly marginal sect, and eventually as beyond the borders of ac-

---

6. See Adam Gregerman, " 'Have you despised Jerusalem and Zion after you had chosen them?': The Destruction of Jerusalem and the Temple in Jewish and Christian Writings from the Land of Israel in Late Antiquity," doctoral dissertation, Columbia University, 2007. UMI Publication Number 3266586.

ceptable Judaism? It should be stressed that Christianity really didn't merit much rabbinic attention for centuries. However, there were several factors at work, which over time took hold and played themselves out differently in different places.

First, despite the range of views in the internal church debate about Gentile admission, some Christians (first Jews then also Gentiles) argued against the continued validity of the Torah. Jews, for whom the Torah remained central regardless of the variety of interpretations of it, would have found this assertion unacceptable.

After the first Great Revolt, and especially after the second, Bar Kochba revolt (132-135 C.E.), Jewish leaders became increasingly wary of messianic fervor. Simon ben Kosba, who led the insurrection, was popularly hailed as God's anointed agent of restoration and given the messianic nickname of *bar Kochba,* "the son of the star." Christians, of course, rejected anyone other than Jesus Christ as messiah, but after the disastrous end of this second revolt Jewish leaders also became more cautious about such zealotry. Thus, they viewed with greater suspicion eschatologically enthusiastic movements such as the church.

In addition, as the first century ended, more churches were becoming entirely Gentile in composition. It would be difficult for local synagogue leaders to view such Christian communities — with their own emerging and independent leadership structures — as in any way "Jewish," despite their appeals to Jewish scriptures and traditions.

Finally, theological developments in emerging Christianity increasingly differentiated believers in Jesus Christ from other Jews. Certain churches, such as those that produced the Gospel and Letters of John, stressed the need for belief in Christ's divine status. Although by no means desiring to venture into polytheism, the originally Jewish Johannine community so emphasized the equality of the Father and the Son that to outside Jewish ears this amounted to a rejection of the central truth of Judaism, that God is One. Thus, in the Gospel of John, written near the end of the first century C.E., believers in Jesus are portrayed as being thrown out of the synagogue (9:22; 12:42; 16:2). This situation is impossible in the time of Jesus; instead it reflects the recent history of the Johannine community whose Jewish members had been shunned by the local synagogue.

Angered by this expulsion, the author persistently uses the term "the Jews" in the Gospel as unbelieving opponents of Jesus, even though almost every character is Jewish, including Jesus' followers. This literary device sarcastically conveys the alienation experienced by Johannine Jews who, from their perspective, have been cast from their Jewish heritage by so-called Jews. The factor which precipitated the expulsion is clearly what Johannine Jews had been saying about Jesus. In the Gospel, "the Jews" seek to kill Jesus. According to John, they say, "It is not for a good work that we are going to stone you, but for blasphemy, because you, though only a human being, are making yourself God" (10:33, also 5:18). Such a perceived breach of Jewish monotheism was intolerable to the synagogue and difficult for the evangelist to defend against prior to the development of Trinitarian theology.

It is hardly surprising in this rapidly changing and varied atmosphere at the turn of the first century, in which loyalties were in flux and in which wars and persecutions raged, that the separating Jewish and Christian communities would begin to define themselves oppositionally, one against the other.

## Supersessionism and the Institutionalization of Jewish and Christian Antipathy

Although these developments occurred without any uniformity in widely scattered locations, and that neither Jews nor Christians were governed by an authoritative central body that could enforce religious decisions, it is still possible to discern a growing confrontational trend in relations between the two groups in the second century C.E. Whereas earlier in the first century it was one group of Jews, those who held Jesus to be God's Christ, who were disputing with other Jews, in the new century it was more and more Gentile Christians and non-Christian Jews who contended. As the Christian "Letter of Barnabas" — a pseudepigraphal epistle written around the year 100 C.E. that is not part of the New Testament — shows, the logical possibility that both communities could affirm that both enjoyed covenantal relationship with the same God was rejected: ". . . do not be like certain persons [Jews] who pile up sin upon sin, saying that our covenant remains to them also" (4:6).

However, just because some Christian writers felt this way does not mean that their views were shared by the vast majority of Christians. For quite some time many Christians associated with their Jewish neighbors as if indeed the "covenant remains to them also." Even as the increasingly Gentile church was delineating its theological self-understanding, it did so in the presence of an influential Judaism that was reconstituting itself after the calamities of the two revolts.

In the years after the destruction of the Temple, the study of the written Torah, and the reinterpretation of its commandments for a world in which the sacrificial rituals could not be performed, gradually became the central activity of Jewish life. Scholars known as rabbis began to put into writing debates and traditions of interpretation that had been circulating for some time. A body of rabbinic literature developed that used the scriptures of Israel as the starting point for a reconstituted way of Jewish life.

The rabbis stressed the need for Jews to walk according to the commandments or *mitzvoth* of God as interpreted through their legal and narrative traditions of discourse. Jewish seasonal festivals of thanksgiving, recommitment, penitence and renewal became centered in the home and local community, and the observance of the *mitzvoth* was understood as replacing the sacrificial rites of the Temple. Though it took centuries, the rabbis' way of being Jewish would eventually become normative for all (non-Christian) Jews.

Thus, nascent Christianity and emerging rabbinic Judaism were simultaneously defining their distinct identities by drawing upon more-or-less the same scriptural traditions, but interpreted in radically different ways: the church through the lens of the coalescing New Testament and Judaism through the lens of the developing rabbinic literary corpus.

Although they shared the biblical texts, there were enormous social and political disparities between Jews and Christians in the Roman Empire in the second and third centuries. Jews were legally recognized as a legitimate religious association and continued to be exempt from worshiping Roman deities. Some diaspora Jewish communities undertook extensive synagogue building projects, sometimes prominently located on main city streets. Jews achieved positions of civic influence in many parts of Greece and Asia Minor, and were vital participants in the life of their towns and cities.

Although localized anti-Jewish violence flared from time to time, some Gentiles, including many Christians, continued to be strongly attracted by Jewish traditions. This fascination not only led these Gentiles to adopt some Jewish customs in an informal way, but also encouraged a significant number of Christians — both Jews and Gentiles — to continue or take on some degree of Jewish practice within church communities. Such "Judaizing" Christians, as they were sometimes polemically called by other Christians, could cite those New Testament texts written in first-century churches that had insisted on some measure of Torah observance for incoming Gentiles. Especially important for Jewish-oriented Christians were sayings of Jesus such as Matthew 5:17-18: "Do not think that I have come to abolish the law or the prophets; I have come not to abolish but to fulfill. For truly I tell you, until heaven and earth pass away, not one letter, not one stroke of a letter, will pass from the law until all is accomplished." It appears that for centuries some Christians would frequent synagogue functions as well as local church liturgies. The boundaries between the two groups, despite angry warnings against broaching those boundaries (especially from Christian leaders), remained quite porous for a considerable period.

On the other hand, Christians had a low social status in the Empire. The church had no imperial legal recognition and was subject to periodic persecution and popular disdain as a religion of slaves and women. Roman intelligentsia cast Christianity as a superstitious and heretical mutation of Judaism. The polemicist Celsus, for instance, writing toward the end of the second century, used a fictitious Jewish character to mock Christian claims that they understood the scriptures of ancient Israel better than did Jews:

> . . . Well, who is to be disbelieved — Moses or Jesus? Perhaps there is a simpler solution: perhaps when the Father sent Jesus he had forgotten the commandments he gave to Moses, and inadvertently condemned his own laws, or perhaps sent his messenger to give notice that he had suspended what he had previously endorsed. (Origen, *Contra Celsum*, IV, 18)

Church leaders had to respond to such charges and to combat Judaism's appeal to its own members. Taking polemical passages from the New Testament, which had mostly arisen as part of an inner Jewish debate, and reading the internal criticisms of the Hebrew prophets as evidence of constant Jewish failures, Christian teachers used the rhetorical customs of the time to attack Judaism's respectability.

The Roman destruction of the Second Temple and the Gospels' apologetic enlargement of the Temple priesthood's role in Jesus' crucifixion provided especially potent ammunition. Thus, Melito, bishop of Sardis in Asia Minor, would around the year 175 seek to counter the allure of Jewish Passover observances. His efforts turned vitriolic when he adduced the crucifixion:

> And where was [Jesus] murdered? In the very center of Jerusalem! Why? Because he had healed their lame, and had cleansed their lepers, and had guided their blind with light, and had raised up their dead. For this reason he suffered. . . .
>
> Therefore, the feast of unleavened bread [Passover] has become bitter to you [Jews] just as it was written: "You will eat unleavened bread with bitter herbs." Bitter to you are the nails which you made pointed. Bitter to you is the tongue which you sharpened. Bitter to you are the false wit-

nesses whom you brought forward. Bitter to you are the fetters which
you prepared. Bitter to you are the scourges which you wove. . . . Bitter
to you are your hands which you bloodied, when you killed your Lord in
the midst of Jerusalem. . . .

You [ Jews] forsook the Lord; you were not found by him. You dashed
the Lord to the ground; you, too, were dashed to the ground, and lie quite
dead. (*Peri Pascha,* 4; 72; 93; 99)

A slightly earlier but less polemical text similarly tapped into the New
Testament crucifixion narratives. In his *Dialogue with Trypho,* Justin Martyr
recounts a (probably fictitious) conversation with a Jew named Trypho in
which he scripturally argues for the legitimacy of Christianity:

For after that you had crucified Him, the only blameless and righteous
Man, . . . when you knew that He had risen from the dead and ascended
to heaven, as the prophets foretold He would, you not only did not repent
of the wickedness which you had committed, but at that time you selected
and sent out from Jerusalem chosen men through all the land to tell that
the godless heresy of the Christians had sprung up, and to publish those
things which all they who knew us not speak against us. So that you are
the cause not only of your own unrighteousness, but in fact of that of all
other men. (17)

Here Justin somewhat dispassionately uses the Septuagint (Greek version) of Israel's scriptures and selected Gospel passages to argue with a Jewish interlocutor over the correct interpretation of the sacred writings. Recent
historical studies are offering tantalizing glimpses of such early scriptural
debates between Christians and Jews, and are raising the possibility that
such exchanges further accelerated the growing separation of the church
and rabbinic Judaism in their formative decades. More research is needed,
especially on the question of how much normative Christian and Jewish
teaching was shaped by this oppositional dynamic.

On the Christian side, a helpful synthesis of the various elements of
its emerging anti-Jewish theology is provided by Origen, a scholar writing
around 248 C.E. against the contentions of Celsus:

For [the Jews] committed a crime of the most unhallowed kind, in conspiring against the Savior of the human race in that city [ Jerusalem] where
they offered up to God a worship containing the symbols of mighty mys-

teries. It accordingly behooved that city where Jesus underwent these sufferings to perish utterly, and the Jewish nation to be overthrown, and the invitation to happiness offered them by God to pass to others, — the Christians, I mean, to whom has come the doctrine of a pure and holy worship, and who have obtained new laws, in harmony with the established legal systems in all countries. . . . (*Contra Celsum*, IV, 22)

Here the contours of the widespread Christian response to invidious comparisons with Judaism are clear: God's covenant with the Jewish people always symbolized the promised coming of Christ and the church, Jerusalem was accursed and destroyed because of the Jewish rejection and crucifixion of Jesus, and as a result the divine covenant was transferred to Christians. Christians have been given new, universal laws and rituals that replace the temporary and preparatory Law of Moses. The reason that Jews do not recognize these truths, demonstrable from their own sacred writings, is because, again according to Origen, they do not read "Scripture according to its spiritual meaning, but interpret it only according to the bare letter" (*De Principiis,* 9). This theological delegitimization of Judaism has been called "supersessionism" because it is premised on the claim that the church has superseded the Jewish people as covenantal partners with God.

Supersessionism was born out of the vulnerable situation of Christians in the Roman Empire, especially in comparison with the more respectable Judaism. Its presuppositions circulated widely in the churches and are evident in the writings of virtually all the influential Christian writers of the early centuries. In addition, these developments occurred simultaneously with defining doctrinal debates about the nature of Christ's divinity and his relationship to the Father that reverberated throughout the Christian world. Thus, in the words of one scholar of the period, "Christian beliefs are so deeply rooted in attitudes toward Judaism that it is impossible to disentangle what Christians say about Christ and the Church from what they say about Judaism."[7] This theological stance became so embedded in Christian thought that it would not be seriously critiqued until after the Shoah in the twentieth century.

From its advantageous social position, rabbinic Judaism did not need, at least early on, to develop a similar opposing theological system. As long as Christianity was weak and marginal in imperial society, Jewish leaders

---

7. Robert L. Wilken, *Judaism and the Early Christian Mind: A Study of Cyril of Alexandria's Exegesis and Theology* (New Haven: Yale University Press, 1971), 229.

were content to warn their communities about the novel scriptural interpretations of Christians and to assert in various ways the Oneness of God
in the face of Christian claims about the divinity of Jesus. It is very unclear
if later medieval Jewish polemical writings against Christianity, such as the
*Toledot Yeshu,* have roots any earlier than the fourth century. This makes
sense given Judaism's high social status and the comparative impotence of
Christianity in the second and third centuries. There is some evidence of
mutual admonitions to avoid close contact with the members of the other
community, for example prohibitions of intermarriage, but based on extant
writing it appears that Judaism did not feel as threatened by Christianity as
Christians did by Judaism.

The dwindling numbers of Jewish members of the churches were in an
increasingly untenable position. Their degree of Torah practice and preference for less exalted claims about Christ made them suspect in the eyes of the
Gentile Christian majority. On the other hand, their association with Gentiles who appeared to non-Christian Jews as idolaters or polytheists would
tend to make Christian Jews unwelcome in Jewish communities. Such people were falling into the growing rift between the two groups.

Nonetheless, it must be stressed that despite the widening influence
of supersessionism, ordinary Jews and Christians in the Empire regularly
engaged in social interaction. Indeed, it was this day-to-day contact that
prompted efforts by their respective leaders to discourage too close an association, but this occurred differently in each local situation. Of interest
in this regard are two canons passed by the church council held in Elvira,
Spain, around 306 C.E., one threatening expulsion if landlords allowed Jews
to bless their crops (Canon 49) and another prohibiting clerics or laypeople
to eat with Jews (Canon 50).[8] Clearly Christians, at least in this part of Spain,
often asked Jewish friends to bless their crops and regularly dined with them,
or church leaders would not have felt the need to try to discourage these
interactions.

Crucially, during the fourth century C.E. the relative social positions of
Jews and Christians in the Empire changed dramatically. In 313, the Emperor
Constantine declared that Christianity would be tolerated in the Empire.
He followed this up during his long reign (until 337 and his death-bed ac-
ceptance of baptism) with imperial patronage of the church, which gave
Christian leaders unprecedented influence. Although some emperors after

---

8. Amnon Linder, *The Jews in Roman Imperial Legislation* (Detroit: Wayne State University Press, 1987), xxx.

Constantine were hostile to Christianity, or embraced deviant forms of it, in 380 Theodosius I made Christianity the preferred state religion, giving Christians considerable access to the power of the Roman legal system. Perhaps because they were now becoming free of the constant fear of possible state harassment, incidents of Christian attacks against Jewish synagogues increased during the fourth and fifth centuries, although imperial authorities at first sought to punish the miscreants. As time passed, Christian leaders promoted the passage of laws that curtailed the privileges of their Jewish rivals, leading ultimately to the marginalization of Jews in the medieval "Christendom" that arose after the collapse of the Roman Empire in the west. This too was a gradual process, most evident in hindsight, the full implications of which could not be foreseen. Nevertheless, a defining adversarial stance between Christianity and Judaism eventually came to prevail.

## Christianity, Anti-Judaism, and Antisemitism

In the aftermath of the Nazi genocide of Jews in the mid-twentieth century, a recurrent question that has confronted Christians was whether it was inherent in Christianity to be hostile to Jews and Judaism. Certainly, a quick survey of the preceding two millennia could readily lead one to think so. Another form of the question is whether the foundational Christian texts in the New Testament could be considered to be antisemitic. The newer historical understanding of the origins, gradual separation, and developing mutual opposition between Christianity and rabbinic Judaism is extremely relevant to this question.

The answer to the question will largely be determined by how "antisemitism" is defined, and in the case of the New Testament period by how "Judaism" is defined. If antisemitism is technically defined as a racialist hatred of Jews simply for being alive, then such antisemitism cannot be said to have existed during the first through fourth centuries c.e. In comparison to racial antisemitism, the delegitimization of Jewish traditions represented by Christian supersessionism is more properly termed "anti-Judaism" — opposition to Jewish religious tenets and practices. Even anti-Judaism is difficult to ascribe to those earliest Jewish church leaders who debated fiercely with Jewish contemporaries. They understood themselves to be part of an eschatologically-empowered Jewish community and contended with other Jews who disbelieved this. Their polemical assertions assumed a more anti-Jewish character when reiterated and assembled by later Gentile Christians.

The question is therefore very complicated because of shifting identity definitions and communal boundaries.[9]

If "antisemitism" is more broadly defined as animosity to Jews because of their different customs in comparison with other peoples, then such an antisemitism existed before the appearance of the church among those Gentiles who belittled diaspora Jews as clannish, elitist, and unreasonable and hostile to mankind for clinging to a single Deity while dismissing all others. Much of this rhetoric was taken up when later Christians competed with Jewish rivals for influence in the imperial world.

On the other hand, such an antisemitism directed against Jewish "difference" was accompanied, as we have seen, by a "philosemitism" held by other Gentiles who admired Jewish solidarity, venerability, monotheistic spirituality, and ethics. The appeal that Judaism held for a significant number of Gentile "God-fearers" partially accounts for the rapid inroads made in the Mediterranean world by the Jewish apostles of Jesus Christ. This philosemitism was also taken up as the church became more Gentile in its composition. The efforts of many Christians to observe Jewish customs to some degree, their frequenting of local synagogues, and their positive interactions with Jewish neighbors are all signs of this.

Nonetheless, social circumstances fostered the rapid dominance of a theologically-based antisemitism (in the broader sense of animosity to Jewish "difference," but here driven by theology) that became entwined with emergent Christian self-understanding: the church has supplanted Judaism, which has now become obsolete. It is important to appreciate the unique social and historical contexts that gave birth to a distinctively Christian religious antagonism toward Jews and Judaism. Although always latently present in medieval European Christendom, flaring into violence against Jews in times of economic and social turmoil especially after 1000 C.E., anti-Jewish perspectives are not religiously intrinsic to Christianity per se. The widespread post-Shoah Christian rejection of the allegation that Jews were divinely cursed for killing Jesus has shaken supersessionism at its roots, generating ongoing efforts to express Christian faith in ways that affirm ongoing Jewish covenantal life.

It is noteworthy that in recent decades a rereading of the epistles of the Apostle Paul has proven essential in rejecting supersessionism and in developing a positive Christian theological stance toward Jews and Juda-

9. See Luke Timothy Johnson, "The New Testament's Anti-Jewish Slander and the Conventions of Ancient Polemic," *Journal of Biblical Literature* 108/3 (Fall 1989): 419-441.

ism. Nothing more clearly shows how central our relationship to Judaism is for Christian self-understanding than the fact that it is the earliest New Testament books — the letters of Paul — that have proven transformational. (Notice, too, that in *Nostra Aetate* 4, the section that addresses Judaism, five of the seven footnoted biblical citations are to Paul's letters, while a sixth refers to a deutero-Pauline epistle.) It is therefore to the Apostle Paul that the next chapter turns.

# CHAPTER 4

# Paul's Letter to the Romans and Christian-Jewish Relations Today

## Rereading Paul

As is well known, *Nostra Aetate* relied heavily upon Paul's Letter to the Romans to state that the Jewish people remain "most dear" to God (Rom. 11:28), and that to them belong "the glory and the covenants and the law" (Rom. 9:4). As John Connelly's important study of the post–World War II revolution in Catholic theology about Jews and Judaism explains: "Without Romans and its confirmation of God's promises to the Jews as well as the eschatological hope for unity in an unspecified future, the church would not have had language to talk about the Jews after the Holocaust."[1] As a continuation of the themes found in the first three chapters, this chapter will first discuss the importance of the presuppositions that readers bring to their encounter with Paul's letters. After considering the historical

---

1. John Connelly, *From Enemy to Brother: The Revolution in Catholic Teaching on the Jews, 1933-1965* (Harvard University Press, 2011), 256. This important volume provides a vivid narrative of how Christians who sought to combat the appeal that Nazi antisemitism had for Christians turned to Romans, and over the 1940s-1960s gradually came to read it with new eyes. See also this comprehensive survey of the interpretation of a key verse in Romans: Joseph Sievers, "A History of the Interpretation of Romans 11:29," *Annali di storia dell'esegesi* 14 (1997): 381-442.

---

This chapter draws on my online essay on the website of the International Council of Christians and Jews, "Paul's Profound Identity as a Jew of His Day" and on "Paul and the Relationship between the People of Israel and the Church Today" in Reimund Bieringer and Didier Pollefeyt, eds., *Paul and Judaism: Crosscurrents in Pauline Exegesis and the Study of Jewish-Christian Relations* (London/New York: T&T Clark, 2012), 141-162. It has also been informed by the recent essay co-authored with Mark D. Nanos, "Implications of Paul's Hopes for the End of Days for Jews and Christians Today," *Studies in Christian-Jewish Relations* 9/1 (2014): 1-45.

context and literary purposes of the eleventh chapter of his Letter to the Romans, it will then pursue the meaning of Paul's words for a post–*Nostra Aetate* church.

There was more involved in the modern turn to Romans 11 than the simple rediscovery of ancient (if neglected) ideas from one of the earliest New Testament books. There was a need to *reread* Paul: the Nazi genocide of Jews demanded that Christians question their long-standing religious hostility to Jews. It was soon realized that certain traditions of interpreting Paul had played an important role in promoting negative sentiments toward the Jews and Judaism. For centuries, he was understood to have abandoned Judaism and converted to Christianity. He supposedly found the "Jewish" effort to earn "salvation" by obeying the commands of the Torah to be futile or unavailing, and therefore proclaimed the end of "the Law" for Jews and Gentiles alike. However, recent biblical scholarship has begun to see Paul in a very different light, though widespread consensus about every aspect of his thought has yet to emerge: Paul abandoned neither Judaism nor his Pharisaic background. Rather, he became a different kind of Jew, one who came to believe that God was intervening in human history, by raising Jesus Christ to new life, to initiate the Age to Come.

## Challenges in Reading the Pauline Epistles

Before discussing this paradigm shift in Pauline scholarship, it is important to note at the outset that even in ancient times, another New Testament writer described Paul's letters as "hard to understand" (2 Peter 3:16). Indeed, certain features of Paul's writings have always encouraged misinterpretation. There are several reasons for this.

### A. Textual Issues

It is widely agreed that not all the letters that the New Testament ascribes to Paul were actually written by him. Some were clearly composed decades after his death in his name. Although Christians deem the "deutero-Pauline" works of 2 Thessalonians, Ephesians, Colossians and the "pastoral letters" of 1 and 2 Timothy and Titus to be divinely inspired, readers should not automatically understand them as reflecting Paul's own thinking simply because they are attributed to him. For example, the author of 1 Timothy 2:12 stated that he did "not permit a woman to teach or to have authority over a man. She must be quiet." But in Romans 16:1-7, a letter that no one doubts comes from Paul himself, he greets a number of women, giving titles to them that surely suggest a considerable degree of authority: Phoebe is called a deacon of the church at Cenchreae (v. 1), Prisca or Priscilla is named a "co-worker" who with her husband hosts a house-church (vv. 3-5), and Junia is called "outstanding among the apostles" (v. 7).

In addition, some of the letters we have today may have originally been separate smaller ones. This is especially true of the letters to Corinth.

A further textual complication is that some of Paul's wording is occasionally ambiguous or hard to translate. For example, the Greek word *nomos* is usually rendered as "law," which is not the best English equivalent of the Hebrew Torah or teaching (of Moses). As noted below, similar uncertainties arise with the Pauline phrases *ergou nomou* (works/workings of the law) and *pistis iesou christou* (faith in/faithfulness of Jesus Christ). Much depends on the translator's presuppositions.[2]

### B. Paul's Writings Are Occasional Correspondence

Paul wrote to address specific situations in early local churches that cannot be reconstructed with certainty today. He often reacted to news or messages not in our possession, which makes it challenging to fully appreciate his replies.

Even though Paul was writing about particular local issues, many later interpreters felt they could construct a systematic "Pauline theology" on the basis of such "occasional" letters. This is a risky venture since Paul sometimes wrote impulsively without carefully weighing his words (see Gal. 5:12, for example!). The interpreters of later centuries also tended to discount the possibility that Paul may have developed his ideas from one letter to the next.

### C. Paul Argued in Jewish Categories

While Paul described himself as "circumcised on the eighth day, a member of the people of Israel, of the tribe of Benjamin, a Hebrew born of

---

2. See Pamela Eisenbaum, *Paul Was Not a Christian: The Original Message of a Misunderstood Apostle* (New York: HarperOne, 2009), 32-54.

Hebrews; as to the Law, a Pharisee; . . . as to righteousness under the Law, blameless" (Phil. 3:5, 6b), over time his letters were predominantly studied by Gentile Christians. They naturally read them through the lens of their own identities as non-Jews. In their mind's eye, Paul was a Christian, not a Jew. They assumed he lived as a Gentile and no longer followed the Jewish Torah. Their own experience of Christianity and Judaism as separate — even antithetical — communities was anachronistically projected back onto Paul himself. This habit was exacerbated by Paul's own pastoral practice of trying to speak to his primarily Gentile addressees on their own terms (see 1 Cor. 9:19-23).[3]

However, in Paul's time many of the churches were thoroughly Jewish demographically and so were part of the diverse world of late Second Temple Judaism. The fact that the words "Christian" or "Christianity" had not yet come into use and never appear in Paul's letters is an important signal to readers that Paul's religious world was quite different from today's.

Which brings us to the pivotal question: did Paul think of himself as a former Jew who became "Christian" (a Jewish apostate) or as a Jew who had come to believe he should announce that the messianic age was dawning (a Jewish apostle)?

The following very influential Pauline sentence is most relevant. It contains two uncertain terms. ". . . we know that a person is justified not by *the works of* the law but through *faith in* Jesus Christ" (Gal. 2:16). This sentence has been taken by most Christians over time to mean that unless people believe in Christ as Lord and Son of God, they are not in right-relationship with God, no matter what commandments ("works") they follow. However, the sentence could just as properly be rendered as: "we know that a person is justified not by *the workings of* the Torah but through *the faithfulness of* Jesus Christ." This construal is based on the idea that the Torah affects people's standing before God in different ways. For Jews, Torah-observance is a mark of being in covenant with a saving God. The Torah's "workings" for Jews is to keep them focused on conforming to God's will as an elect people. But the Torah's "workings" for pagan Gentiles is to expose their sinfulness as damnable idolatry.[4] Paul clearly was concerned about this because "the wrath of God is indeed being revealed from heaven against every impiety

3. See Mark D. Nanos, "Paul's Relationship to Torah in Light of His Strategy 'To Become Everything to Everyone' (1 Corinthians 9.19-23)," in Reimund Bieringer and Didier Pollefeyt, eds., *Paul and Judaism: Crosscurrents in Pauline Exegesis and the Study of Jewish-Christian Relations* (London and New York: T & T Clark, 2012), 106-140.

4. For a very cogent discussion of this, see Eisenbaum, *Paul Was Not a Christian*, 233-239.

and wickedness . . ." (Rom. 1:18ff.). Paul felt that Gentiles could not escape divine judgment as idolaters unless they began conducting themselves with the same faithfulness toward God that distinguished Jesus, "obedient to the point of death, even death on a cross!" (Phil. 2:8).

Surely these are two very different ways of understanding Galatians 2:16. The contrast shows that how a modern reader chooses to interpret the passage will be largely determined by whether they imagine that Paul has abandoned Judaism (the traditional option) or if he is seen as a Jew for whom Christ is central (the newer option).

The likelihood that Paul was not a Jewish apostate has led some modern scholars to observe that when Paul wrote about observance of the Torah, or even "the curse of the Law" (Gal. 3:10-13; referring to Deut. 27:26 — "Cursed be he who fails to fulfill any of the provisions of this law"), he seems to have been speaking more about the Torah's significance for Gentiles-in-Christ and not about its meaning for Jews, as later Christian readers assumed. Likewise, when he wrote Galatians 2:15, he may well have been citing a Jewish understanding about the Torah and the necessity of human faithfulness toward God with which most of his Jewish contemporaries would have been comfortable.

In other words, Paul's letters are construed in radically different ways depending on whether his readers think of him as a Jewish apostate who forsook Judaism or as always a Jew, though one who came to distinctive beliefs about Christ. If Paul in the first century wrote out of a certain messianically enthusiastic Jewish context to Gentiles on the fringes of Judaism, he would be easily misunderstood when his letters were eventually read in an entirely Gentile church that was unfamiliar with late Second Temple Judaism. This also includes the pharisaic, mystical, and apocalyptic features of Paul's thought.

### D. Paul's Letters Were Regularly Interpreted to Address Later Controversies

But the likelihood of misreading Paul was further increased by the understandable practice of reading Paul in order to support later theological arguments. The most vivid example of this is the use to which Paul was put during the debates between Roman Catholics and Protestants during the Reformation of the 16th century and beyond. Martin Luther likened Judaism to Roman Catholicism: both religions, he thought, were based on the futile effort to earn God's favor. His reformed Christianity based on his reading of Paul stressed the need to depend totally on God's mercy. Luther's Paul became the champion of "justification by faith" against all the rituals and practices of Roman Catholicism. Everything that Paul wrote was read as in opposition to Judaism and everything that Luther criticized about Roman Catholicism was projected onto Judaism: it was legalistic, loveless, filled with empty ritual, and corrupt.

Luther's introspection about his own sinfulness was also projected onto Paul, now seen as despairing of the Law as unable to bring him to right relationship with God. More recent biblical scholarship has questioned whether Paul was really filled with such existential angst and whether he would recognize himself in this portrayal.[5]

All of these factors have come under close examination in the past few decades. A key move was the recognition that Judaism has never been a religion of "works righteousness," an effort to earn God's favor. A more accurate description of the Jewish tradition understands that Jews seek to follow the divine will as expressed in the Torah *in gratitude* for having been elected as people in covenant with the One God.[6]

This has led to renewed study of Paul as remaining Jewish, and possibly Torah-observant, all his life.[7] In the new paradigm, his primary concern was the fate of Gentiles and their incorporation as non-Jews either as equal members into churches in which Jews were also members or into predominantly Gentile churches that would enjoy equal standing with churches with majority Jewish demographics. His difference with Jews disinterested in the Jesus-movement was his conviction that in Christ the end of history and the time of the redemption of all things were at hand. He was baffled why his Jewish kinfolk didn't perceive this end-time framework, but at no point did he stop thinking of himself as Jewish. Nor did he entertain the possibility that God's promises to redeem all Israel would be in vain.

---

5. The classic essay on this point is Krister Stendahl, "The Apostle Paul and the Introspective Conscience of the West," *Harvard Theological Review* 56 (1963): 199-215.

6. For a discussion of this perspective, which he calls "covenantal nomism," see E. P. Sanders, *Paul and Palestinian Judaism: A Comparison of Patterns of Religion* (Philadelphia: Fortress Press, 1977), 419-428.

7. This understanding has been cogently argued in many books and articles by Mark D. Nanos. For a concise summary of his perspective see his commentary on the "Letter of Paul to the Romans" and essay on "Paul and Judaism" in Levine and Brettler, eds., *The Jewish Annotated New Testament*, 253-286 and 551-554, respectively.

## Actualizing Paul Today

As explained in chapter 1, the 1993 study by the Pontifical Biblical Commission, "The Interpretation of the Bible in the Church," saw the need for a way of interpreting biblical texts that overcomes "the distance between the time of the authors and first addressees of the biblical texts, and our own contemporary age, and of doing so in a way that permits a correct actualization of the Scriptural message so that the Christian life of faith may find nourishment."[8] The PBC thus understood biblical interpretation as a kind of conversation:

> Sacred Scripture is in dialogue with communities of believers: It has come from their traditions of faith. . . . Dialogue with Scripture in its entirety, which means dialogue with the understanding of the faith prevailing in earlier times, must be matched by a dialogue with the generation of today. Such dialogue will mean establishing a relationship of continuity. It will also involve acknowledging differences. Hence the interpretation of Scripture involves a work of sifting and setting aside; it stands in continuity with earlier exegetical traditions, many elements of which it preserves and makes its own; but in other matters it will go its own way, seeking to make further progress.[9]

Historically, the nature of the church's relationship to Jews and Judaism did not really receive any sustained study from New Testament times up until the aftermath of the Shoah. As observed in chapter 3, for nearly two millennia the prevailing supersessionist model was not seriously critiqued.[10] With *Nostra Aetate*'s repudiation of the idea of a biblically-justified divine curse on Jews, and with its recognition that Jews remain in covenant with God, the Catholic Church has found itself in a theological context that is virtually unprecedented in history. Such a reform from a negative to a positive stance toward Judaism unavoidably has repercussions for Christian self-understanding. A dialogical approach to interpreting biblical writers such as Paul helps chart the dynamics of the interaction that occurs between the scriptural texts and readers of today who are grappling with the radically "new situation" after the Shoah and after *Nostra Aetate*.

8. PBC, "The Interpretation of the Bible in the Church," II, A, 2.
9. PBC, "The Interpretation of the Bible in the Church," III, A, 3.
10. This explains why *Nostra Aetate*, 4, could not cite any ecclesiastical councils or papal declarations to counteract supersessionism, but had to reach back to the earliest New Testament books, Paul's epistles.

Today's readers thus have a different "effective history" than both Paul and all the previous generations of Christian interpreters. Readers in a post–*Nostra Aetate* church are becoming aware that debates over the requirements for Gentile admission among the first Jewish members of the earliest churches, including Paul, contributed to a later caricature of Torah-observance as mindless legalism. They will thus likely react quite differently to Paul's words about "the curse of the Law" (Gal. 3:13) than prior readers.

The following pages will use the dialectical process set forth in chapter 1 to discuss the pertinence of Paul's letters for twenty-first-century relations between Christians and Jews. It will focus on the Letter to the Romans because it is the only one of Paul's epistles, and perhaps the only New Testament book, that grapples in a sustained fashion with the subject of Jews outside of the church. It will also read Paul as being *within* late Second Temple Judaism rather than one who saw himself as having gone beyond Judaism.

As the Jewish apostle to the Gentiles, Paul struggles in the Letter to the Romans with questions that have been bothering him: Why are his Jewish kinfolk proving to be less receptive than God-fearing Gentiles to the Good News (Gospel) that God, by raising Christ, was inaugurating the Age to Come? Why are they not joining with Paul in reaching out to the nations at this crucial time? Does this growing number of Gentiles-in-Christ suggest that God has not been faithful to the people of Israel? Are unbaptized Jews doomed to condemnation at the approaching time of God's judgment on the world? In thinking over these matters, Paul develops various ideas that I will seek to actualize for post-Shoah Christians today. We begin first with the task of "explanation" by considering the context of Paul's Letter to the Romans.

## The Situation behind Paul's Letter to the Church[11] in Rome

The Letter to the Romans is also unique because it is the only letter Paul sent to a church community that he did not personally establish. Moreover, the church in Rome had Jewish members, unlike the Gentile communities in Corinth, Galatia, or Thessalonica to which Paul wrote.

House churches among Jews in Rome probably came into being in the

---

11. For the sake of convenience, I refer to the Roman church in the singular, even though it is likely that there were a number of small "house churches" in the city. This scenario is vigorously pursued in Mark D. Nanos, *The Mystery of Romans: The Jewish Context of Paul's Letter* (Minneapolis: Fortress Press, 1996).

mid-40s, possibly as a result of the efforts of Jewish apostles from Judea. The Roman church would therefore have had a strongly Jewish orientation, even after Gentiles began to seek participation.

In 49 C.E., the emperor Claudius banished some Jews from Rome because of a commotion over someone name "Chrestus," probably a reference to Christ.[12] Some of those expelled were Jewish apostles such as Prisca and Aquila whom Paul is said to have met in Corinth (Acts 18), but it seems unlikely that the church in Rome was bereft of all its Jewish members. After Claudius's death (54 C.E.), prominent figures likes Prisca and Aquila could return to Rome, enabling Paul to greet them in his letter (Rom. 16:3-5a).[13]

By the end of the 50s, Paul was planning on ending his apostolic work in the eastern Roman Empire. He intended eventually to travel to Spain to begin a mission in the west, and planned to stop in Rome in order to organize this expedition (15:23-24, 28-29). His activity in the eastern Mediterranean had been controversial. His advocacy of Torah-free admittance of Gentiles into the church led to a public clash with Peter in Antioch (Gal. 2:11-14), caused a rift with his partner Barnabas (2:13), prompted him to look upon the leaders of the Jerusalem church with sarcasm (2:6), and provoked hostility toward other apostles who desired Gentiles to observe at least some of the Torah's commandments in order to be welcomed into the church (2:4). His claims that Gentiles must not take on Torah observance gave rise to the claim that Paul was encouraging baptized Jews to abandon Torah observance (Acts 21:21), a view not to be found in Paul's own letters.

Partially in an effort to dispel this cloud over his ministry, Paul encour-

---

12. According to the Roman writer Suetonius, Claudius "expelled Jews from Rome because of their constant disturbances impelled by Chrestus." Some commentators, following Acts 18:2, take this to mean that Claudius had ordered all Jews to leave Rome. Since this would banish perhaps 50,000 people, an eviction attested to nowhere else in contemporary literature, this seems highly improbable. It could mean that only Jews in the church were exiled, but, again, this seems unlikely owing to Roman difficulties in distinguishing among different types of Jews. Most likely, the edict expelled those who were the most outspoken in their debates over "Chrestus" — people like Prisca and Aquila. See Raymond E. Brown, "The Roman Church Near the End of the First Christian Generation," in Raymond E. Brown and John P. Meier, *Antioch and Rome: New Testament Cradles of Catholic Christianity* (New York/Ramsey: Paulist Press, 1983), 100-102, 107-109. Brown's insights greatly inform this section of the chapter.

13. It is debated whether Romans 16 is part of the original letter. The observation by Brown and others ("The Roman Church," 108-109) that Paul ends his letter with an exercise in name-dropping in order to introduce himself to the Roman church and also to acquire its support for his collection for the Jerusalem church is a convincing argument that Romans 16 is integral to the original.

aged each of the Gentile churches he founded to appoint delegates to represent them in carrying a donation for the well-being of the "mother church" in Jerusalem (1 Cor. 16:1-4; 2 Cor. 8:1-24). If this embassy was accepted by the leaders in Jerusalem, it would be a sign of solidarity between Jewish and Gentile churches and powerful evidence of the Spirit's presence in Paul's apostleship.

Before journeying westward to Rome, Paul planned to travel to Jerusalem to accompany the delegates with their contribution (Rom. 15:25-32). He wrote to the church in Rome before setting out both to introduce himself and Phoebe, a church official from the eastern seaport of Corinth, who may have carried the letter to Rome (16:1-2). Paul may have hoped that Phoebe, presumably a skilled businesswoman, would receive aid from the Roman church in mounting the expedition to Spain. Paul was also counting on Rome's prayers and support for the success of his mission to Jerusalem (15:30-32).

This provides a significant clue to the situation of the church community in Rome. Although by this time the Roman church was already predominantly Gentile (e.g., Rom. 1:13), and although it might have been composed of a number of smaller house-churches (e.g., 16:5), in general it must have resembled somewhat the more Torah-observant Jerusalem church to be able to offer Paul some credible support with its leaders. In other words, "the dominant Christianity at Rome had been shaped by the Jerusalem Christianity associated with James and Peter, and hence was a Christianity appreciative of Judaism and loyal to its customs."[14] By writing to the church in Rome, Paul was trying to disabuse its believers of any distorted versions of his preaching that they might have heard, but also to show them that his ministry was compatible with the outlook of the Jerusalem assembly upon which the Roman church had been founded, even if more recent Gentile members may have started to mock Jewish customs.[15]

Scholars who seek to reconstruct the setting of the Roman church find especially important Paul's written comments concerning the eating of meat which had been sacrificed to idols, and about the attitudes of the "strong" and "weak" toward such meat (14:1–15:13). Some scholars simply identify the "strong" and "weak" as Gentile and Jewish believers, respectively. They

14. Brown, "The Roman Church," 110. Note that the use of "Christianity" in this quote is anachronistic since the word does not appear in any of Paul's letters.

15. Brown, "The Roman Church," 111. Jacob Jervell, "The Letter to Jerusalem," in Karl P. Donfried, ed., *The Romans Debate* (rev. exp. ed.; Peabody, MA: Hendrickson Press, 1991), 53-64.

detect an internal debate within the Roman church between dominant Gentiles and the returning expelled Jews.[16] Others contest this identification, arguing that there are not neatly defined "groups" in the Roman church, but simply varieties of faith practice.[17]

It is best not to simply equate the "weak" and "strong" with Jews and Gentiles respectively. There were Jews and Gentiles in Christ who no longer felt bound by kosher laws (and hence could eat meat offered to idols without hesitation), and there were Jews and Gentiles in Christ who felt obligated not to consume idol-meat. More important is Paul's lack of enthusiasm for either position; instead he insists on unity. He seems more interested in distinguishing his opinions from extreme ideas that might have been erroneously associated with him.[18]

To summarize, Paul's aim in Romans is to offer an accurate and balanced summary of his preaching in order to win Rome's support for him personally, for his delicate diplomatic gesture to the Jerusalem church, and for his planned mission to Spain. He also seeks to promote oneness between Jews and Gentiles in the church, including the church in Rome. While Paul may have heard of some squabbles among Roman house churches over questions of practice, such wrangles cannot be neatly characterized as Jew-in-Christ versus Gentile-in-Christ. Paul avoids becoming immersed in such local exchanges, and instead tactfully focuses on the main theme of his preaching: the greater issues of unity and fellowship.

In furthering his purposes, Paul often seems concerned about the issue of boasting. He wants no boasting of strong over weak (Rom. 14:1; 15:1), of weak over strong (14:3b-4), of Jew over Gentile (2:17ff.), or of Gentile over Jew (11:18ff.). Boasting seems to function for Paul as a sign of failure to realize one's dependence on God's mercy (3:9, 27; 5:1-5). It also shows a lack of concern for the unity of the Body of Christ (12:1-21). For Paul, boasting demonstrates inadequate faithfulness.

In his reflections on boasting, he focuses on the boasting of Gentiles in the church over Jews outside the church (11:13-14, 25-26). This leads him for the first time to write about the status of unbaptized Jews and of the apostles' overall failure to successfully preach the Gospel to them.

16. E.g., Harrington, *Paul on the Mystery of Israel,* 41-42; Francis Watson, "The Two Roman Congregations: Romans 14:1–15:13," in Donfried, *The Romans Debate,* 203-215.

17. E.g., Robert J. Karris, "Romans 14:1–15:13 and the Occasion of Romans," in Donfried, *The Romans Debate,* 65-84.

18. Brown, "The Roman Church," 119-120.

## Paul's Argumentation in Romans 11

The problem of boasting is one which Paul had encountered before, especially in Corinth (e.g., 1 Cor. 1:26-31; 3:21; 4:7; 5:2, 6; etc.). In Rome the subject takes on a new twist because of the Jewish legacy and presence there. Thus a side of Paul not visible in his other letters is revealed; he not only desires Gentiles to be admitted into the church on an equal basis with Jews; in Romans it becomes clear that he also wants Jews respected by baptized Gentiles — whether or not those Jews have accepted that Christ has been raised. He gives many reasons why Gentiles in Christ have no grounds for boasting:

### A. All people depend on God's generous mercy.
Because everyone sins, Jew and Gentile alike, they are dependent on God's compassion (Rom 3:9; 11:6, 30-32). No one can merit or earn a right relationship with God. It can only be humbly accepted as an undeserved gift, as grace. This reality precludes anyone from boasting about a status which they didn't merit in the first place.

### B. Gentile believers in the Crucified and Raised One are indebted to Jews.
Gentiles have been admitted into Christ only because of the faithfulness of Jews to God's actions in Christ. Paul expresses this through a series of metaphors. Gentiles have been sanctified by a holy dough. They are grounded in a root which brings them to holiness (11:16). It is the Jews in Christ, graced by God with the faith of Christ (11:5-6), who have made it possible for the wild Gentile olive branches to be grafted among the Jewish branches of the domesticated olive tree of the People of God (11:17).[19] Since "wild" Gentile believers can only help produce oil by being grafted onto the domesticated

---

19. It should be noted that there is scholarly debate over who Paul means by "the root" (11:16). Some have seen it as referring to Christ, while others to the "remnant," Jews-in-Christ such as Paul himself. Other commentators understand "the root" to mean the patriarchs or biblical Israel. See Joseph A. Fitzmyer, *Romans,* Anchor Yale Bible Commentary (New Haven: Yale University Press, 1992), 609-610. See also his article "Romans" in Raymond E. Brown, Joseph A. Fitzmyer, and Roland E. Murphy, *The New Jerome Biblical Commentary* (Englewood Cliffs, NJ: Prentice Hall, 1990), 861. When the passage is understood in the context of a Torah-observant Paul functioning within Judaism, it is most likely that the "root" is his metaphoric way of speaking of the People of God: Jews who recognize that the New Age is dawning, Jews who are stumbling by being unconvinced of this, and non-Jews who have become part of God's People by putting on the life of the Raised Christ.

olive plant, they must recognize their ongoing debt to Jews. Gentiles in Christ have no justification to boast over Jews in Christ, because they owe their inclusion among God's People to the Jews in their midst.

## C. God has caused most Jews to be unconvinced about the Good News in order to provoke the apostles' mission to the nations.

Paul had become convinced that God, in Christ, was bringing to fulfillment all the Torah promises that Gentiles would come to share in the blessings of Abraham. He hoped that his fellow Jews would readily perceive this wondrous culmination and longed for them to join him and others in proclaiming God's mercy to the Gentiles (Rom. 9:3).

Paul theorized that Jewish hesitancy or skepticism toward the announcement of the in-breaking of God's Reign must, in fact, be God's doing! The purpose of God's action was to catalyze the apostolic mission to the Gentiles in the short time left before the dawning of the Age to Come (11:25).[20]

Therefore, baptized Gentiles had still less reason to look contemptuously on Jews outside the church. Their rapid admission to God's people had been made possible only by God's intervening to make most Jews blind to the importance of Christ. As a result, Gentiles should only marvel at God's gracious activity on their behalf.[21]

20. Paradoxically, the failure to perceive God's actions in Christ is Paul's principal criticism of his Jewish kinfolk throughout Romans, even though he can simultaneously attribute such blindness to God. This is evidence of the painfulness this subject had for Paul, a pain intensified by Paul's imminent eschatological expectations. His struggle with this matter also lies behind his metaphor of the veil over Jewish eyes in 2 Cor. 3. (His comments there on Jewish biblical interpretation would need to be actualized today along the lines of PBC 2001's statements that both rabbinic and Christian "re-readings" of the scriptures of ancient Israel are "retrospective" readings, which are analogous and parallel processes [see II, A, 6-7]).

In Rom. 3:27-31, he asserts that since God is the God of Gentiles as well as Jews, God can enter into relationship with Gentiles on the basis of Gentile faith. This for Paul does not up-turn the Torah (3:31) because, he argues, the Law itself anticipated this divine outreach to the nations independent of itself (3:21). In this way, Christ is the *telos,* the end or goal or climax of the Torah (10:4). Israel, in Paul's judgment, has failed to perceive this because they have come to identify only Torah observance, not faith, as the mark of relationship with God (9:30-32a).

21. This was not Paul's first effort to grapple with the apparent failure of God's promises to an Israel skeptical of the preaching of the apostles. First, he explored what makes a true Jew, hypothesizing that there were Jews who seemed so only superficially but really were not (Rom. 9:6ff.). Then he invoked the biblical image of the faithful remnant of Israel, applying it to Jews in Christ. God's promises were being realized in the fidelity to Christ of baptized Jews (9:27; 11:1-6). One gets the sense that Paul was groping for a way to maintain both the election of Israel and the need for faith in Christ. He came to consider the role of God's will and grace

**D. Jews remain the People of God because of their covenant.**

Jews who are not accepting of the Good News, to whom Paul refers as "stumbling" (11:1), "branches bent aside" (11:17-21) and (at one point) "broken off" (11:22-24), will have a much easier time being re-awakened to their responsibilities as God's People than did the Gentile believers in Christ who were unnaturally grafted onto an alien tradition. Again, Gentiles have little ground for feelings of superiority.

**E. Gentiles in Christ must demonstrate holiness with their lives.**

Jews and Gentiles in the church have a responsibility to make Israel "jealous" (11:11). By this, Paul means that the ethical life of the baptized must clearly manifest the presence of God. Paul expects that by seeing God at work among former pagans, his Jewish kinfolk would come to perceive the inauguration of the Age to Come by the raising of Christ. Gentile believers, then, cannot boast because by doing so they diminish their witness to God's activity among them. They become less holy.

**F. It is inevitable that all Israel will be part of God's Reign.**

Jews not in Christ are, for Paul, apparently in some sort of "theological limbo," to use Daniel Harrington's phrase.[22] Although currently unconvinced about God's covenantal actions in Christ, they are irrevocably destined for inclusion in the Age to Come because of God's faithfulness to divine promises (11:28-29). *All* Israel will be restored (11:26). Jews not in Christ have "stumbled" in order to make way for the Gentiles, but they have not "fallen" into perdition (11:11). Paul himself hopes to "rescue some of them" from their skepticism (11:14), but the inevitable participation of all Israel in the inbreaking New Age will result in nothing less than life from the dead (11:15).

Once more, baptized Gentiles can only respond with humble awe to the supreme graciousness of God. Despite Israel's (divinely-initiated) lack of sympathy to the Gospel, unbaptized Jews maintain their honorable standing as the Chosen People (9:4-5; 11:28-29), and are predestined to be included in the Age to Come. Gentiles, the beneficiaries of a similar divine generosity, can have no legitimate behavior other than to praise God (11:30-36).

Paul's arguments against Gentile boasting must be understood in the context of Paul's expectations for the future. Paul believed that the New Cre-

---

(9:14-18; 11:6) and this led him to his most developed conception: God's (temporary) veiling of Jewish perceptions had catalyzed the mission to Gentiles.

22. Harrington, *Paul on Mystery of Israel*, 55, 81.

ation, or the Age to Come, was in the final throes of erupting into human history (e.g., Rom. 8:18-25). The definitive establishment of the New Age would occur with the triumphant return of Christ enthroned in glory (e.g., 1 Cor. 15:23-28). Paul fully expected that Christ's return, his *parousia,* would occur within his own lifetime (1 Thess. 4:15) or, at least, shortly thereafter (Phil. 1:21-26; 3:20; 4:5). Indeed, Paul's perception that time was so short (e.g., 1 Cor. 7:26, 29) was probably the primary reason for the urgency with which he sought to save as many Gentiles as possible. Unless rescued from their idolatrous habits by the faith of and in Christ, they would fall victim to God's judgment and wrath as the present age came to its end (Rom. 1:18–2:11).[23]

With this imminent eschatological, or end-times, horizon, it is understandable why Paul could be comfortable imagining his unbaptized Jewish kinfolk in a sort of theological stasis. During the present transitory "ripple in time"[24] between the Present Age and the Age to Come (or between Christ's raising and return) God had frozen Jewish hearts in order to redirect the efforts of the apostles toward the saving of the Gentiles.

This is why Paul speaks about "life from the dead" (Rom. 11:15) in connection with the acceptance by unbaptized Jews of God's deeds in Christ. Although the sequence of events is probably not fixed in Paul's mind, the return of Christ in glory, the inauguration of the New Creation, and the unity of Jews and Gentiles were all anticipated to be roughly contemporaneous events.

By thinking this way Paul was able to reconcile several incongruous concepts: (1) the irrevocable election of all the People of Israel and the inevitable fulfillment of God's promises to them, (2) Israel's current failure to perceive these promises as being fulfilled in Christ, (3) the significance of Christ for all humanity, and (4) Christ's imminent *parousia* and the dawning of the New Creation.

## Actualizing Paul in a Post-Shoah, Post–*Nostra Aetate* Church

With this hasty "explanation" of Romans 11 in terms of the worlds behind and of the text, we turn to the "understanding" side of Schneiders's dialectical model (see chapter 1) and consider the actualization of Paul's ideas in our

23. That urgency may also explain the noxious rhetoric used by Paul in 1 Thess. 2:14-16, if those verses are not a later interpolation. Frustrated by assaults on the faith of the Thessalonian believers and on his own mission to Gentiles, he lashes out angrily.

24. I am indebted to Paula Fredriksen for this phrase.

different world of today. We are asking how the world before the text, the world projected by the text, sheds light on a post-Shoah, post–*Nostra Aetate* church two thousand years after Paul. To begin, some differences between Paul's vision and our own must be considered.

First, it should be observed that most twenty-first-century Christians do not share Paul's end-times expectations. The vast majority of Christians do not expect the return of Jesus and the ultimate establishment of God's Reign to occur within their own lifetimes.[25] Given the lapse of two millennia since Paul's day, most Christians today have consciously or unconsciously postponed the Eschaton into the indefinite future. Similarly, few modern Jews anticipate the dawn of the messianic age very soon. Rather, God's People are thought to have a duty to work with God in bringing the world to its eventual completion.

Since we do not share in Paul's sense that "all our futures are so foreshortened . . . for the present scheme of things is rapidly passing away,"[26] his efforts to hold together discordant theological convictions about Israel and Christ can seem to us to be strained.

In addition to living in a world with a different eschatological outlook, twenty-first-century Jews and Christians are heirs to a shared two millennia history that Paul did not dream would continue to unfold. We have a radically different "effective history" which shapes our consciousness, perceptions, and dreams.

For Catholics, this means that Paul's words are read today in a church community that has authoritatively renounced its history of anti-Jewish preaching, that is struggling to come to grips with the dreadful reality of the Shoah, that seeks to reform earlier anti-Jewish theologies, and that recognizes the ongoing spiritual vitality of the Jewish people and tradition.

This last point is a major divergence of the thinking of modern Catholics from that of Paul. Post–*Nostra Aetate* Catholic ecclesial instructions have stressed that "the history of Judaism did not end with the destruction of Jerusalem, but rather went on to develop a religious tradition . . . rich in religious values."[27] Jewish history is seen to continue especially in the Dias-

---

25. Though their eschatological expectations differ from his, it ought to be observed that, paradoxically, modern Catholics more closely resemble Paul's views about the dynamism of Jewish covenanting with God than almost all of their Christian forebears.

26. J. B. Phillips's dramatic rendering of 1 Cor. 7:29b, 31b. See his *The New Testament in Modern English* (rev. ed.; New York: Macmillan, 1972).

27. Commission for Religious Relations with the Jews, "Guidelines and Suggestions for Implementing the Conciliar Declaration *Nostra Aetate*, 4" (1974), III.

pora, "which allowed Israel to carry on to the whole world a witness — often heroic — of its fidelity to the one God and to 'exalt God in the presence of all the living' (Tobit 13:4)."[28] The recognition of such spiritual faithfulness has enabled John Paul II to declare that a "better understanding of certain aspects of the Church's life can be gained by . . . taking into account the faith and religious life of the Jewish people as professed and lived now as well." Likewise, Catholic preachers have been advised to "draw on Jewish sources (rabbinic, medieval, and modern) in expounding the meaning of the Hebrew Scriptures and the apostolic writings,"[29] and the Pontifical Biblical Commission has observed that Catholics can "learn much from Jewish exegesis practiced for more than two thousand years."[30]

These and numerous other possible examples demonstrate current Catholic appreciation of the theological richness of the post–New Testament Jewish tradition. Since Paul pre-dated the writing of the Mishnah and Talmuds, he did not know that post-Jesus Jewish creative vitality would renew Jewish life in a world without the Jerusalem Temple. With our different historical perspective, modern Catholics cannot relate to Paul's ideas about unbaptized Jews being in a temporary "not (yet) with the program" state. Paul could imagine this momentary state of affairs in his eschatological enthusiasm, but we, who two thousand years later have personally experienced the spiritual dynamism of Jewish friends, cannot agree that Judaism is in any sense languishing.

Another difference between Paul's day and our own can be seen in the nature and composition of the church. When Paul wrote his letters, the church was a movement within the diverse world of late Second Temple Judaism. The fact that Paul never uses the word "Christian" or "Christianity" probably reflects the reality that followers of Jesus Christ did not yet see themselves as a religion clearly distinct from Judaism. Moreover, in many places Jews were probably still in the majority among those baptized into Christ. Gentiles were becoming members, too, but their numbers were initially small. The ratio of Jews to Gentiles in Christ varied widely from place to place (compare the Jerusalem church to the Corinthian church, for example).

28. Commission for Religious Relations with the Jews, "Notes on the Correct Way to Present Jews and Judaism in Preaching and Catechesis in the Roman Catholic Church" (1985), VI, 1.

29. Bishops' Committee on the Liturgy, National Conference of Catholic Bishops, "God's Mercy Endures Forever: Guidelines on the Presentation of Jews and Judaism in Catholic Preaching" (Washington, D.C.: USCC, 1988), 31i.

30. Pontifical Biblical Commission, *The Jewish People and Their Sacred Scriptures in the Christian Bible* (2001), II, A, 7.

Today, however, the Christian religion can be called the Gentile church. The tiny fraction of Christians who are of Jewish heritage are not encouraged by most Christians to maintain Jewish practices and they are not considered Jews by their former co-religionists. This difference in self-understanding between Paul and us also influences the actualization of Paul's ideas today.

Despite such discrepancies, Romans 11 can readily be actualized for modern Catholic-Jewish relations (Schneiders's cognitive "Meaning of the Work" — see the chart at the end of chapter 1) because the post–*Nostra Aetate* church echoes Paul's respect for "the unrevoked covenant," as Saint John Paul II repeatedly described it. This can be done in several ways:

## A. Gentile Christians still have no ground for boasting.

A main Pauline theme in Romans (and other letters) is that boasting is contradictory to gratitude for God's graciousness. Among other things, he was concerned about baptized Gentiles bragging or feeling superior to Jews whether baptized or unbaptized.

One can only imagine Paul's reactions if somehow he were to learn the subsequent history of relations between Jews and the eventually totally Gentile church. His hope that his Gentile converts would live such ethical lives that his Jewish kinfolk would become "jealous" of God's obvious holiness among them failed miserably as history unfolded; indeed Christian conduct often had the opposite effect on Jews. If, over the centuries, Jews have at times been able "to serve God without fear in holiness" (Luke 1:74-75):

> . . . then it is certainly only in exceptional cases that this has been due to the behavior of Christians. The Jewish no to Jesus Christ, and even more to the Church, has therefore been legitimated countless times by the obedient behavior of Jews and the disobedient behavior of Christians. The Christian churches will only be what they are called to be for the People of God, as far as is humanly possible, when they have testified convincingly through their life and behavior for just as long a period as they filled the Jews with apprehension, that for Israel they are a reason not for fear but for fearlessness and perhaps even for confidence.[31]

This leads to the conclusion that Paul's explanation for the widespread Jewish skepticism toward apostolic preaching (God had temporarily made most

---

31. Peter von der Osten-Sacken, *Christian-Jewish Dialogue: Theological Foundations* (Philadelphia: Fortress Press, 1986), 81.

Jews unreceptive to save Gentiles) is certainly inapplicable today given all
the intervening history.

## B. The relationship between Jews and Christians is a Mystery.

Paul's uses the term "mystery" in his grappling with the difficult question of
the relationship between the people of Israel and the people of the church
(Rom. 11:25). He then concludes his ruminations by citing Isaiah 40:13 and
Job 35:7; 41:11 in a doxological exclamation, apparently expressing dissatis-
faction with his ability to fully grasp God's plans and activities:

> O the depth of the riches and wisdom and knowledge of God! How un-
> searchable are his judgments and inscrutable his ways! 'For who has known
> the mind of the Lord? Or who has been his counselor?' 'Or who has given a
> gift to him, to receive a gift in return?' For from him and through him and
> to him are all things. To him be the glory forever. Amen (11:33-36).

"Mystery" is a word rich with theological meaning and potential. It refers to the presence of the divine in human life that can be perceived but not
fully compassed by limited human understanding. There is always more to
be discovered. The "mystery" of the Jewish and Christian relationship, for
instance, was a theme in the 1974 Vatican Guidelines: ". . . it is when [the
Church is] 'pondering her own mystery' that she encounters the mystery
of Israel."[32]

Underlying Paul's use of the word "mystery" is his conviction that God is
at work in the relationship between Israel and the church. After the passage
of twenty centuries, this possibility suggests that God intends for the two
communities to have complementary, if different, roles in the world. The
same intuition is probably at work in Pope Saint John Paul II's now famous
words: "As Christians and Jews, following the example of the faith of Abraham, we are called to be a blessing for the world [cf. Gen. 12:2ff.]. This is the
common task awaiting us. It is therefore necessary for us, Christians and
Jews, to be first a blessing to one another."[33]

## C. Both Jews and Christians dwell in covenant with God.

As earlier observed, *Nostra Aetate* reaffirmed the covenantal bonding between God and the Jewish people, citing Romans 9:4-5 and 11:26, 28. Paul

---

32. Vatican, "Guidelines" (1974), V.
33. "Address on the Fiftieth Anniversary of the Warsaw Ghetto Uprising," April 6, 1993.

sought to maintain this fundamental conviction even in the light of his incomparable, transcending experience of Christ (Phil. 3:8). His perhaps personally unsatisfying solution was to relegate unbaptized Jews to a temporary condition of "stumbling" and being "bent aside" until they inevitably came to perceive that the Age to Come was breaking in — hopefully by seeing God's holiness reflected in the lives of non-Jews in Christ. As already noted, Christians today do not expect the *parousia* in their lifetimes and after two millennia cannot imagine Jewish religious life to be moribund. However, Paul's eschatological understanding of salvation has important implications today.

Paul spoke of salvation mostly in terms of being deemed righteous, in right-relationship with God, at the Eschaton. So, for example, he prayed for one of his Gentile churches that God would "so strengthen your hearts in holiness that you may be blameless before our God and Father at the coming of the Lord Jesus with all his saints" (1 Thess. 3:13; cf. 5:23; Phil. 1:9-11; 2:16-17; Rom. 8:18-25). Although over the centuries Christians have naturally developed many different definitions of salvation,[34] its intrinsically eschatological aspect has been preserved in traditions such as invocation in the Lord's Prayer, "Thy kingdom come." The Reign of God that Jesus proclaimed still has not transformed the world. The ultimate salvation of creation lies in the future.

If twenty-first-century Christians accept Paul's declaration that "all Israel will be saved" (Rom. 11:26) and understand salvation as culminating at the End of Days, then:

> . . . in underlining the eschatological dimension of Christianity we shall reach a greater awareness that the people of God of the Old and the New Testament are tending towards a like end in the future: the coming or return of the Messiah — even if they start from two different points of view. It is more clearly understood that the person of the Messiah is not only a point of division for the people of God but also a point of convergence. Thus it can be said that Jews and Christians meet in a comparable hope, founded on the same promise made to Abraham (cf. Gen 12:1-3; Heb 6:13-18).[35]

---

34. See, for example, Clark Williamson, "What Does It Mean to Be Saved?" in Philip A. Cunningham, ed., *Pondering the Passion: What's at Stake for Christians and Jews?* (Franklin, WI, and Chicago: Sheed & Ward, 2004), 119-128.

35. Vatican, "Notes" (1985), II, 10. Note also PBC, *Jewish People* (2001): "Jewish messianic expectation is not in vain. It can become for us Christians a powerful stimulant to keep alive the eschatological dimension of our faith. Like them, we too live in expectation" (II, A, 5).

In terms of Jewish salvation, such considerations lead to the conclusion that Christians should not seek to baptize Jews in pre-eschatological historical time. Rather, the church has a mission alongside Jews, not to Jews. Pope Benedict XVI put it this way (approvingly quoting Hildegard Brem): "In the light of Romans 11:25, the church must not concern herself with the conversion of the Jews, since she must wait for the time fixed for this by God, 'until the full number of the Gentiles come in' (Rom 11:25)."[36] Similarly, Cardinal Kasper has expressed things in very Pauline terms:

> Such petitions for the coming of the Kingdom of God and for the realization of the mystery of salvation are not by nature a call to the Church to undertake missionary action to the Jews. Rather, they respect the whole depth of the *Deus absconditus,* of his election through grace, of the hardening and of his infinite mercy. So in this prayer the Church does not take it upon herself to orchestrate the realization of the unfathomable mystery. She cannot do so. Instead, she lays the *when* and the *how* entirely in God's hands. God alone can bring about the Kingdom of God in which the whole of Israel is saved and eschatological peace is bestowed on the world.[37]

This means that for twenty-first-century Catholics there are two faith communities who experience covenantal bonding with God. While there has been much theological discussion about whether there is one overarching covenant, two separate covenants (through Torah and through Jesus), or multiple covenantal moments (see chapter 10), it must now be understood as a basic tenet of Christian faith, witnessed to by Paul, that God has entered into a saving relationship with Jews and Christians alike.

In some ways, for today's Christians this reopens the paradox with which Paul was trying to wrestle. The permanency of God's relationship with Israel must be related to the Christian conviction of the universal significance of Christ. If Jews are in a saving, covenantal bonding with God, independently of Christ, then how is Christ universally significant?[38]

36. Benedict XVI, *Jesus of Nazareth,* Part Two, *Holy Week: From the Entrance into Jerusalem to the Resurrection* (San Francisco: Ignatius Press, 2011), 47. However, see Cunningham and Nanos, "Implications of Paul's Hopes for the End of Days," for a critique of the "eschatological postponement" aspects of this sort of formulation.

37. "Striving for Mutual Respect in Modes of Prayer," *L'Osservatore Romano* (April 16, 2008), 8-9.

38. See Cunningham et al., *Christ Jesus and the Jewish People Today* (Grand Rapids: Eerdmans, 2011), and chapter 11 in this volume.

**D. The Relationship between Jews and Christians is an organic one.**
Additionally, it can be suggested that Paul's olive tree metaphor was based
on a sound intuition; whatever the covenantal configuration, the relationship between the two faith communities is an organic one. It is one which
touches on the very essences of the two traditions. Without advocating any
kind of syncretism, the relationship might even be described as symbiotic.

This understanding has frequently been voiced in Catholic documents
since *Nostra Aetate,* which have taken note of "the spiritual ties which link
the people of the New Covenant to the stock of Abraham."[39] John Paul II has
spoken eloquently of the bonds between Judaism and Christianity, stating
that "our two religious communities are connected and closely related at
the very level of their respective identities,"[40] and that "the Jewish religion
is not 'extrinsic' to us, but in a certain way is 'intrinsic' to our own religion.
With Judaism we have a relationship which we do not have with any other
religion. You [ Jews] are our dearly beloved brothers and, in a certain way, it
could be said that you are our elder brothers."[41] The pope's use of such familial language is indicative of the intimacy which post–*Nostra Aetate* Catholics
are able to feel for the Jewish community. This would seem to be a modern
actualization of Paul's organic imagery.

How this spiritual closeness is to manifest itself in Catholic practice
remains to be seen. The recognition of our rapport with the Jewish spiritual heritage must be reflected in Catholic liturgy, music, education, self-
definition, and Christology. Much has been accomplished in this regard, but
there is much that remains to be done.

It ought to be mentioned that while this attitude is new for Christians,
it is also a novel experience for Jews to hear themselves referred to in such
positive and familial ways. Given past history, it is only natural for Jews to
wonder if this unprecedented tone is only some temporary aberration from
the Christian norm, or if it is one more, even if unintentional, effort to as-
similate Jews into Christianity. Some Jews are opposed to entering into interreligious dialogue for these and other reasons:

> We feel that, emotionally, we are not as yet ready to enter into a fraternal
> dialogue with a church, a religion, that has been responsible for so much
> suffering, and which is ultimately responsible for the murder of our fathers

---

39. *Nostra Aetate,* 4.
40. John Paul II, "Address to Representatives of Jewish Organizations," March 12, 1979.
41. John Paul II, "Address at the Great Synagogue of Rome," April 13, 1986.

and mothers, brothers and sisters in the present generation. . . . All we want of Christians is that they keep their hands off us and our children![42]

Christians certainly have little basis to be offended by such sentiments. Our mutual history has been too painful and prolonged to anticipate the immediate establishment of *shalom* between the two communities. All that we Christians can do is undertake to reform our tradition's failure to heed Paul's warnings against arrogance and to commit ourselves to behaving as a covenanted people should. However, if God graces us with any measure of success, and we Christians succeed in reconfiguring our self-definitions accordingly, then, sooner or later, Jews will also be confronted with re-evaluating their views of Christianity. If such Jewish reflection sees validity in some sort of organic spiritual relationship between the two faiths, then Jewish communal self-definition will be affected as well.[43]

Assimilation need not be the inevitable result of a Jewish recognition of an organic link with Christianity. The Pauline metaphor of the olive tree can serve as the inspiration for a model which sees modern rabbinic Judaism and contemporary Christianity as both being branches of the biblical Hebrew root.[44] Both traditions are thereby related, although remaining distinctive.

### E. The Gentile church is nourished by its holy, Jewish roots.

Another Pauline theme that can readily be actualized among Christians today was explicitly applied in *Nostra Aetate:* "nor can [the Church] forget that she draws nourishment from that good olive tree onto which the wild olive branches of the Gentiles have been grafted (cf. Rom. 11:17-24)." Significantly, whereas Paul could have been thinking of Jews in Christ, such as himself, as the ones who mediated holiness to Gentile believers, such a construct is impossible in the virtually entirely Gentile church of the present day. It is noteworthy, therefore, that the Vatican Council used Paul's image in relation to the Jewish tradition as whole. The church is continuously enriched by the Jewish tradition, and, as several Catholic statements indicate, that enrich-

---

42. Eliezer Berkovits, "Judaism in the Post-Christian Era," in F. E. Talmage, ed., *Disputation and Dialogue: Readings in the Jewish-Christian Encounter* (New York: KTAV, 1975), 290, 293. A contrary viewpoint is found in David Novak, *Jewish-Christian Dialogue: A Jewish Justification* (New York/Oxford: Oxford University Press, 1989).

43. For more on this subject, see chapter 13.

44. E.g., Leon Klenicki and Eugene J. Fisher, eds., *Root and Branches: Biblical Judaism, Rabbinic Judaism, and Early Christianity* (Winona, MN: Saint Mary's Press, 1987). See also chapter 3 in this volume.

ment is not limited to biblical Jews, but includes the Jewish contemporaries of the church today.[45]

Indeed, it could be said that the reverse is also true: the church suffers and risks betraying the Gospel when it forgets its Jewish roots.[46] In the words of the bishops of the United States:

> By the third century . . . a de-Judaizing process had set in which tended to undervalue the Jewish origins of the Church. . . . [But] most essential concepts in the Christian creed grew at first in Judaic soil. Uprooted from that soil, these basic concepts cannot be perfectly understood. It is for this reason that *Nostra Aetate* recommends joint "theological and biblical studies" with Jews.[47]

Such collaborative ventures have occurred in the past several decades, and have produced much new insight. New lines of discussion are emerging especially in the areas of scripture, Christology, liturgy, and ethics. Future efforts in this regard should continue, but, following the principle that Catholics need nourishment from the Jewish tradition, they should also increasingly move beyond academic and clerical circles and into the lives of average believers. Some ways to do this are to encourage Jews and Catholics to visit

45. E.g., Vatican, "Guidelines" (1974), Preamble; Vatican, "Notes" (1985), VI, 1; and John Paul II, "Address to Episcopal Conference Delegates and Consultors of the Pontifical Commission for Religious Relations with the Jews" (March 6, 1982).

46. Cardinal Kurt Koch has made this point very forcefully: "Even though the primitive racist anti-Semitism of the Nazi ideology, which had of course developed already in the 19th century, has nothing in common with Christianity, we Christians nevertheless have every cause to remember our complicity in the horrific developments, and above all to confess that Christian resistance to the boundless inhuman brutality of ideologically-based National Socialist racism did not display that vigor and clarity which one should by rights have expected. Resistance by Christians may well have also been so inadequate because a Christian theological anti-Judaism had been in effect for centuries, fostering a widespread anti-Semitic apathy against the Jews. Thus an ancient anti-Jewish legacy was embedded in the furrows of the souls of not a few Christians. With shame we Christians must also acknowledge that Hitler, with his joint rejection of both Judaism and Christianity, had grasped the true essence of Christianity and its intrinsic relationship with Judaism better than not a few Christians themselves. This shared National Socialist hostility should have aroused among us Christians much more empathetic compassion than in fact did come into effect" ("Theological Questions and Perspectives in Jewish-Catholic Dialogue," address delivered at the annual meeting of the Council of Centers on Jewish-Christian Relations, October 30, 2011.)

47. National Conference of Catholic Bishops, "Statement on Catholic-Jewish Relations" (1975).

each other's houses of worship, to experience dialogue with one another on the local level, to pray together to the Creator of all, and to collaborate together in addressing social needs.[48]

The prayers and songs raised in Catholic worship must also reflect the church's new awareness of its connectedness to Judaism. References to Jews as dwelling in continuing covenant with God must replace supersessionist allusions or comments about Jews only in the past tense.

Additionally, "the Jews and Judaism should not occupy an occasional or marginal place in [Christian] catechesis: their presence there is essential and should be organically integrated."[49] Sustained and thorough education on Judaism is an important priority for Catholics today.[50]

This is probably the best place to observe that similar questions arise regarding typical Jewish knowledge of Christianity. Although Jews are obviously not nourished by any Christian roots, stereotypical views of "the other" are probably as common among them as they are among Christians.[51] As one Jewish commentator has put it, "Jews have thought little about the spiritual dignity of other faiths."[52]

### F. Jews and Christians must witness to the Age to Come together.

Finally, Paul's eschatological concerns have an additional implication in the present day, albeit with some adaptations. Like Jesus before him, everything that Paul did was ultimately directed toward the arrival of the Reign of God, the New Creation, when God "will be all in all" (1 Cor. 15:28). Although we do not share Paul's urgent timetable in this regard, Jews and Christians both believe that they must work on behalf of the Age to Come. It is a vocation that they can fulfill together.[53]

In an era beset with interreligious conflict, Christians and Jews can offer a badly needed model of collaboration and a vision of God's desires for the world. This is perhaps the strongest instruction that Paul would have for

---

48. Bishops' Committee on Ecumenical and Interreligious Affairs, National Conference of Catholic Bishops (USA), "Guidelines for Catholic-Jewish Relations" (1985 revision), Recommended Programs.

49. Vatican, "Notes" (1985), I, 2.

50. Vatican, "Notes" (1985), Conclusion.

51. See John T. Pawlikowski, "Rethinking Christianity: A Challenge to Jewish Attitudes," *Moment* 15/4 (Aug. 1990): 36-39.

52. Irving Greenberg, "Response to John T. Pawlikowski," *Moment* 15/4 (Aug. 1990): 39.

53. Vatican, "Guidelines" (1974), IV; Vatican, "Notes" (1985), II, 10-11; BCEIA, "Guidelines" (1985), Recommended Programs, 7.

Gentile Christians today. We have been grafted, through Christ, into God's plans for the world through no merit of our own. In humble thanks for that gift, we should join with the elder People of God in witnessing to and working toward God's New Creation.

# CHAPTER 5

# The Gospels and Their Presentations of Judaism

## Reading the Gospels Responsibly

*Nostra Aetate* taught that "Jews should not be spoken of as rejected or accursed as if this followed from holy Scripture," and suggested that such
preaching or teaching would not be "in accord with the truth of the Gospel
message or the spirit of Christ."[1] This directive repudiated the ancient and
fairly standard Christian practice of using the Gospels to portray Jews as a
people cursed by God because of the crucifixion of Jesus.[2]

Such a custom had persisted in the church until this century. Consider,
for example, a pre-Vatican II American religion textbook which explained
the parables in Matthew 21:33-43 and 22:1-14 by proposing that "[Jesus']
prophecy was partially fulfilled in the destruction of Jerusalem and more
fully in the rejection by God of the chosen people." Another textbook when

---

1. *Nostra Aetate*, 4.
2. See Edward H. Flannery, *The Anguish of the Jews: Twenty-Three Centuries of Anti-
Semitism* (rev. and exp. ed.; New York/Mahwah: Paulist Press/Stimulus Books, 2004). Although presenting what has been called a "lachrymose" overview of the history of the Jewish-
Christian relationship, it still remains a useful introduction to the subject. On the corrosive
influence of the so-called "deicide charge," see the more recent work by Mary C. Boys, *Redeeming Our Sacred Story: The Death of Jesus and Relations between Jews and Christians* (New
York/Mahwah: Paulist Press/Stimulus Books, 2013).

---

This chapter draws on my "The Synoptic Gospels and Their Presentation of Judaism" in David P. Efroymson, Eugene Fisher, and Leon Klenicki, eds., *Within Context: Essays on Jews &
Judaism in the New Testament* (Liturgical Press, 1993), 41-66, with additional new material on
the Gospel of John.

referring to Matthew 27:25 stated that "the chief priests took up a cry that put a curse on themselves and on the Jews for all time: 'His blood be upon us and our children.'" A third text opined that "since Pilate could not find anything wrong with Christ, he decided to disfigure his pure and beautiful body, so that even the bloodthirsty Jews would back down and say that Christ had had enough."[3]

The Gospels clearly contain passages that have been used in the past to promote animosity toward Jews and Judaism. That potential still exists.

However, there is another reason why Gospel references to Judaism must be read carefully. Any distortion of the Jewish faith and tradition will inevitably result in a distorted picture of Christianity as well because, as Pope Saint John Paul II observed, "our two religious communities are connected and closely related at the very level of their respective religious identities."[4] The Vatican's 1985 "Notes" insist that this wholly unique bond which joins us as a church to the Jews and Judaism requires that a true knowledge of Judaism must be "organically integrated" into catechetical curricula and not be denigrated to an "occasional and marginal" status.[5] Thus, accurate portrayals of Judaism are required not only because of legitimate concerns for justice and fairness, but also because this accuracy regarding Judaism is necessary for a proper understanding of Christianity.[6]

This chapter will discuss how preachers and religious educators, or just ordinary readers, might pursue these goals when considering the Gospels of Mark, Matthew, Luke, and John. Obviously, in a limited space each Gospel cannot be examined fully. Therefore, we will focus on specific passages that are particularly distinctive or especially disclose each Gospel writer's point of view. We begin by summarizing material presented more fully in chapter 2 about an important biblical principle that should be kept in mind when working with the Gospel texts.

---

3. These three quotes come from a 1961 textbook study by Rose Thering, O.P., as presented in John T. Pawlikowski, *Catechetics and Prejudice: How Catholic Teaching Materials View Jews, Protestants, and Racial Minorities* (New York: Paulist, 1973), 81-83.

4. "Audience for Representatives of Jewish Organizations," March 12, 1979.

5. Vatican, "Notes," I, 2.

6. One indication of this is that a textbook study in 1992 showed that nearly half of all lessons in American Catholic religion textbooks on the primary level contained references to Jews and Judaism as did 44% of all secondary-level textbooks. If Christian educational curricula inaccurately portray Judaism, then clearly distortions will enter into Christian self-understanding even during the process of Christian formation. See Philip A. Cunningham, *Education for Shalom* (Collegeville, MN: Liturgical Press, 1995), 100-120.

## The Origins of the Gospel Tradition

In 1964 the Pontifical Biblical Commission issued an "Instruction on the Historical Truth of the Gospels" which outlined the findings of biblical scholarship concerning the origins of the Gospels. It told modern readers to be aware that the Gospels contain materials that come from three different stages in the growth of the Christian movement.

*The first stage* or time period includes information dating from the actual ministry of Jesus in the early 30s of the first century of the Common Era.[7] *The second stage* comprises traditions that arose in the decades after his followers experienced Jesus as raised to transcendent new life. This period can thus be called the post-resurrectional preaching of the early apostles. It is characterized by the struggle to comprehend the significance for humanity of the life, death, and raising of Jesus and by the veneration of him as Christ, Lord, and Son of God. *The third stage* of Gospel formation encompasses the events contemporaneous with the actual composition of the written Gospel texts in the 70s, 80s, and 90s of the first century.[8] The issues and problems on the minds of the Gospel writers colored not only their presentations and conceptions of Jesus, but also affected their attitudes and depictions of Jews and Judaism.

As a further result of the three-layered nature of the Gospels' textual tradition, the evangelists' portraits of Jesus can sometimes be seen to be operating on more than one level. As shall be seen, a Gospel writer's concerns may occasionally prompt him to portray the "Stage One" Jesus as dealing with what is really a "Stage Three" issue.[9] Thus, for example, reading chapters 5 and 9 of the Gospel of John with an awareness of these different stages of development has led most scholars to conclude that the near-final form of that Gospel reflects a heated dispute between Jews in the Johannine group

---

7. The terms B.C.E. and C.E., respectively meaning Before the Common Era and the Common Era, are an alternative way of denoting the time before Christ and after Christ that is inoffensive to non-Christians.

8. This dating of the synoptics is based on the all but unanimous scholarly understanding that Mark is the earliest Gospel and served as a source for Matthew and Luke. Those interested in the details of the debate about the relationships of the Gospels should see Frans Neirynck, "Synoptic Problem," in Raymond E. Brown, Joseph A. Fitzmyer, and Roland E. Murphy, eds., *The New Jerome Biblical Commentary* (Englewood Cliffs: Prentice-Hall, 1990), 587-595. N.B. also 596, 631, 675-676.

9. This principle has been recognized as pertinent for the Gospels' treatment of Judaism by the 1985 CRRJ "Notes" (IV, 1, A), which explained that since "the Gospels are the outcome of long and complicated editorial work ... some references hostile or less than favorable to the Jews have their historical context in conflicts between the nascent Church and the Jewish community."

who have been expelled from the local synagogue community (9:22, 34; cf. 12:42; 16:2) because their exalted claims about Jesus were understood to be a violation of monotheism (5:18; cf. 10:30-33).[10] Such a social shunning as a result of a christological conflict is impossible during the life of Jesus around the year 30 and is clearly set much later in the first century.

## The Early Church

This all means that some awareness of the history of the first-century church is needed for a thorough reading of the Gospels. This section will highlight some important features of that history.[11] See also chapter 3 above.

### A. The Jewishness of the Early Church

The church as a distinct entity was born after the death and raising of Jesus, but it was only one Jewish group amid many others. It is significant that some of the church's earliest preaching, occurring in Stage Two, evolved in this context of debate with other Jewish groups. This intra-Jewish exchange operated according to contemporary cultural mores and customarily included fiery and abrasive language.[12]

Echoes of this debate, which eventually were incorporated into the written Gospels, transposed an originally "in-house" exchange into the very

---

10. The literature on this point is vast. Prescinding from numerous commentaries, the following are examples of key or specialized studies: Raymond E. Brown, *The Community of the Beloved Disciple: The Life, Loves, and Hates of an Individual Church in New Testament Times* (New York/Ramsey/Toronto: Paulist Press, 1979); Jerome H. Neyrey, *An Ideology of Revolt: John's Christology in Social Science Perspective* (Philadelphia: Fortress Press, 1988); and J. Louis Martyn, *History & Theology in the Fourth Gospel* (rev. & enlarged ed.; Nashville: Abingdon, 1979). Although many scholars today would question Martyn's assumptions about the relevance of the rabbinic "benediction against heretics" *(Birkhat HaMinim)* to the Johannine community, his study is an excellent example of redaction criticism, i.e., a focus on the evangelist's context. For the definitive study of that prayer see Ruth Langer, *Cursing the Christians?: A History of the Birkat HaMinim* (New York/Oxford: Oxford University Press, 2011).

11. For an excellent overview of the history of the New Testament church see Paula Fredriksen, *From Jesus to Christ: The Origins of the New Testament Images of Jesus* (2nd ed.; New Haven: Yale University Press, 2000).

12. See Luke Timothy Johnson, "The New Testament's Anti-Jewish Slander and the Conventions of Ancient Polemic," *Journal of Biblical Literature* 108/3 (Fall 1989): 419-441.

different social context of later readers. The early disputes between Jews in the church and other Jews took on a more dissonant tonality when later read by non-Jewish Gentiles.

## B. The Admission of Gentiles into the Church

One of the most crucial developments in the first-century churches was the admission of uncircumcised Gentiles into the Christ-assemblies. This question was the source of major controversy in the church's earliest decades, as the letters of Paul and the Acts of the Apostles make clear. The dispute indicates that Jesus had not given any instructions on the topic, probably because his ministry was addressed to his fellow Jews.[13] The subject of the admission of Gentiles is yet another instance of the transformative effects of the resurrection experience as the church passed from Stage One into Stage Two.

There was a wide range of views about the admission of Gentiles among the Jews who formed the early church. This diversity can be conveniently outlined by describing four basic opinions on the issue:[14]

*Type One:* Jews in Christ[15] and their Gentile converts who practiced full observance of the Mosaic Law, including circumcision, as necessary for receiving the fullness of salvation.

*Type Two:* Jews in Christ and their Gentile converts who did not deem circumcision to be salvific for baptized Gentiles, but did require them to keep some Jewish commandments such as the dietary laws.

*Type Three:* Jews in Christ and their Gentile converts who did not deem circumcision to be salvific for baptized Gentiles and did not require them to observe Jewish dietary laws. This type did not entail a break

13. See the 1985 CRRJ, "Notes," III, 1: "Jesus was and always remained a Jew, his ministry was deliberately limited 'to the lost sheep of the house of Israel' (Matt. 15:24). Jesus is fully a man of his time and of his environment — the Jewish Palestinian one of the first century, the anxieties and hopes of which he shared."

14. This schema has been suggested by Raymond E. Brown in his joint work with John P. Meier, *Antioch and Rome: New Testament Cradles of Catholic Christianity* (New York/Ramsey: Paulist Press, 1983), 2-8.

15. The Pauline term "Jews in Christ" is employed herein instead of the more conventional "Jewish Christians" in order to emphasize that these earliest church members did not consider themselves to have departed from their Jewish heritage. With the possible exception of late "Type Four" Christians, they were Jews "with a difference," not former Jews.

with the cultic practices of Judaism (feasts or Temple practices), nor did it impel Jews in Christ to abandon circumcision and the Torah.
*Type Four:* Jews in Christ and their Gentile converts who did not insist on circumcision and Jewish food laws and saw no abiding significance in Jewish feasts or the cult of the Jerusalem Temple, indeed eventually seeing these things as belonging to an abrogated and outmoded old covenant.[16]

The debates going back and forth among these various types of Jews and Gentiles in the first-century church are evident in the synoptic Gospels, as will be seen below. Obviously, a person's attitudes toward Jews outside the church would be greatly affected by their place in this typology. Whether Jew or Gentile, a "Type One" Christian would be the most favorably disposed toward Judaism, whereas a "Type Four" Christian, again whether Jew or Gentile, would be the most hostile toward Judaism.

## C. The Jewish-Roman War of 66-72 C.E.

The outbreak of a Jewish revolt against the Roman Empire, culminating in the Roman destruction of Jerusalem and the Temple in the year 70 C.E., was a major turning point in the histories of the Jewish people and of the early church. It had different effects on each group.

Briefly, the military disaster triggered a process of consolidation in a Judaism now bereft of the focal Temple cult. Over the following decades and centuries, the surviving Jewish religious leadership set the foundations for what would become the spiritual richness of rabbinic Judaism. As part of this redefinition process, boundaries between the slowly coalescing "mainstream" Judaism and various Jewish subgroups were clarified. Among the groups now being distanced from nascent rabbinic Judaism was the church, whose growing number of Gentile members alone called its Jewishness into question.[17]

The church, on the other hand, was seeking to establish itself in the Roman Empire and to distinguish itself from those Jews who had rebelled against Rome. It was imperative for the church to present itself as a peaceful,

16. Outline adapted from Raymond E. Brown, *Biblical Exegesis and Church Doctrine* (New York/Mahwah: Paulist, 1985), 133-134.

17. For more details, see chapter 3 in this volume. For more on the origins of rabbinic Judaism and its relations with the young church see Daniel Boyarin, *Border Lines: The Partition of Judaeo-Christianity* (Philadelphia: University of Pennsylvania Press, 2004).

non-threatening assembly worthy of imperial recognition as a legal religion. Such legal status was especially important for the growing number of Gentile Christians who sought the exemption from having to worship Roman deities which Jews (including Jews in Christ) had enjoyed for decades.[18]

Thus, the post–70 C.E. context — in which the Gospels of Matthew, Luke, and John were composed — encouraged an increasing separation between Judaism and the developing church.

### D. Jews in Christ in the Last Third of the First Century

The exact moment in which baptized Jews became the minority in the church is impossible to determine, and, of course, the ratio of Jews to Gentiles in local churches varied from place to place. Whether or not these Jews were a minority by the time the Gospels were written in the 70s, 80s, and 90s, they still played a major role in the church in the latter third of the century. The Gospels of Matthew and John were likely written by such Jews, and if the author of the Gospel of Luke was not Jewish, he was certainly a "God-fearing" Gentile who held the Jews in great reverence.

Yet baptized Jews were in a very awkward position. The growing likelihood that the church was becoming a completely Gentile assembly left them vulnerable to the charge that Christianity was just a heretical deviation from Judaism. As a result, the dwindling number of Jews in Christ (and their Gentile associates) had two urgent priorities: (1) to insist that the Hebrew Bible be interpreted in light of the life, death, and raising of Jesus Christ; and (2) to defend the church's mission to the Gentiles.[19]

## The Gospel of Mark

### A. General Background

Having thus sketched some of the historical factors which form the backdrop for the writing of the Gospels, we now examine the presentation of Jews and

18. Evidence of this can be seen in references to the "synagogue of Satan" in Revelation 2:9; 3:9. See, e.g., the discussion in Wilfrid J. Harrington, *Revelation*, Sacra Pagina Series (Collegeville: Liturgical Press, 1993), 59-60.

19. See "The Mighty Minority" in Jacob Jervell, *The Unknown Paul: Essays on Luke-Acts and Early Christian History* (Minneapolis: Augsburg, 1984), 26-51.

Judaism in each of them. This discussion will focus mostly on Stage Three of the Gospel tradition, the time of the evangelists or Gospel writers. In other words, this chapter doesn't directly examine Jesus' ministry around 30 C.E. but how and why the later evangelists shaped their accounts of it in ways that reflected their individual understandings of the movement's relationship to Judaism.

At the outset it should be stated that the Gospel of Mark is both the earliest and the shortest of the Gospels. It appears to have originated in a church community that had faced violence and chaos. Some suggest that it was written in Rome shortly after the persecutions under the emperor Nero (64-66 C.E.), others that it was composed in the eastern Mediterranean in the midst of the Jewish-Roman War (66-72 C.E.). It is always possible that the narrative was composed in stages in different locations or iterations as well. Whatever its exact provenance, the Gospel seems very concerned with suffering and forcefully asserts that true insight into the person of Jesus is possible only by reckoning with his suffering and death.

The Gospel can be neatly divided into two halves at the end of chapter 8, the scene that has come to be known as "Peter's Confession." Prior to this point the Gospel has been dominated by Jesus' performance of miraculous feats, but both his words and actions produce only amazement and bewilderment (e.g, Mark 1:22, 27; 2:12; 4:41; 5:20, 42; 6:2; 6:51; 7:18, 37; 8:21). Demons repeatedly demonstrate a supernatural knowledge of Jesus' identity, but no other character in the narrative benefits from their exclamations (Mark 1:23-25, 34; 3:11-12; 5:7). While it might be thought that the early mention of Pharisees and Herodians planning to destroy Jesus could reflect an anti-Jewish sentiment by the evangelist (Mark 3:6), it should also be noted that the Gospel portrays a universal inability to comprehend Jesus. Scribes charge him with conspiring with Satan (3:22-30), his family arrives to take charge of Jesus because they've heard that he's "out of his mind" (3:20-22, 31-34), the pig-herding Gerasenes request that he leave their region (5:17), his Nazarean townsfolk become angry with him (6:3), and his disciples are as befuddled as anyone else despite the private tutoring which they have received (e.g., 4:10-13, 33-34, 40-41; 6:35-52; 7:18; 8:4, 17-18, 21).

In the second half of the Gospel the tone is decidedly different. Following Peter's pivotal statement that Jesus is the Christ (8:29), Jesus begins a series of instructions that the Son of Man must suffer (8:31; 9:31; 10:33-34) and that those who would follow him must be prepared to suffer also (e.g., 8:34–9:1; 9:43-47; 10:29-31, 38-39; 13:9-13).

The Gospel reaches its climactic moment as the crucified Jesus expires.

"Now when the centurion, who stood facing him, saw that in this way he breathed his last, he said, 'Truly this man was God's Son!'" (15:39). This outcry marks the first time that a human character has been able to confess faith in Jesus as Son of God. The evangelist thereby asserts that such faith is possible only by standing at the foot of Jesus' cross and experiencing his suffering. Miraculous wonders, authoritative sermons, and private instruction all fail to provide true insight. For Mark, only the cross leads to authentic faith. This perspective is especially important for a church community that has known pain and misery.

Lastly, Mark understands his church's present troubles to be the final acts in the drama of salvation. He feels that his "generation will not pass away" before "they will see the Son of Man coming in clouds with great power and glory . . . [to] gather his elect from the four winds" (Mark 13:30, 26-27). Mark is not writing his Gospel for the sake of posterity because for him history is foreshortened. His aim is to narrate a "life of Christ" which will directly address the current needs of his community.

### B. Mark and Judaism

Even though relating the suffering of his community to Christ's passion and death is Mark's prime concern, there are portions of the Gospel that disclose the evangelist's stance toward Judaism. Of special note are three passages that discuss sabbath observance (Mark 2:23-28), purity (7:1-8), and kosher foods (7:18-19). In all three, Jewish norms are downgraded or eliminated. The Son of Man is said to be master of the sabbath (2:28), purity practices are characterized as mere "human precepts" (7:7), and all foods are declared to be clean — though notably the latter is an explanation provided in the evangelist's editorial "voice," not on the lips of Jesus himself (7:19).

There are a number of reasons for thinking that the topics addressed in these verses owe more to the evangelist's concerns around the year 70 C.E. than to problems arising during the ministry of Jesus in the early 30s. For instance, there is no evidence that either Jesus, his disciples, or any of their Jewish contemporaries seriously questioned the requirement to observe the sabbath or to eat only kosher foods. Jews — including Jesus — certainly debated what proper sabbath and dietary observances entailed, but there was no question of abandoning what was explicitly commanded in the Torah (e.g. Exod. 20:8-11; Deut. 14; Lev. 11). The finality with which the Marcan Jesus devalues key Torah concepts seems incongruous with the Jewish setting of Jesus of Nazareth. On the other hand, along with circumcision, the issues of kosher foods and of conformity to the sabbath were definitely controversial topics in the early church (e.g., Gal. 2:11-14; 4:10; Rom. 14:1-6; Acts 10:9-16; 15:19-29; 21:17-26). The very existence of such debates indicates that Jesus himself spoke no definitive word on these matters despite what these Marcan passages might suggest. If Jesus had indeed "declared all foods clean," why was there any doubt about it later?

The ongoing question of the legitimacy of these customary Jewish practices seems to have arisen only after non-Jews were being admitted into the church. It was the church's new context which provoked debate as to whether Jewish norms had any meaning in an increasingly Gentile assembly. The fact that in these passages it is the disciples of Jesus and not Jesus himself who receive criticism suggests that it is followers of Jesus in Mark's day that are being disparaged for their un-Jewish behavior, in other words, a "Stage Three" dynamic.

This does not mean that the evangelist created these scenes of Jesus disputing proper Torah observance out of thin air. Instead, it appears that Mark has taken the traditions that Jesus engaged in typical first-century Jewish debates about the interpretation of the Torah, and has rendered them according to the practice in his church community not to observe sabbath or kosher norms at all.

Further evidence of the evangelist's situation is seen in Mark's distant-sounding and not fully accurate editorial explanation of Jewish purity customs (7:3-4). The need of any explanation at all shows that Mark's intended readership is significantly Gentile. But as a matter of fact, not all Jews observed these Pharisaic purity practices, nor does it appear that Pharisees demanded that their fellow Jews do so or thought of them as sinners if they did not. In addition, the presentation of the Pharisees is somewhat stylized, reflecting a Stage Two or Three context. Pharisees did not regularly patrol grain fields on the sabbath hoping to catch people plucking grain, nor did they inspect the cleanliness of the hands of non-Pharisees.[20]

All of these items, especially Mark's editorial assertion that "thus he declared all foods clean" (7:19), betray the perspectives of a largely Gentile church which sees itself as not bound by kosher or sabbath laws, or Pharisaic purity customs. In this, Mark differs from both Matthew and Luke. For

---

20. For the preceding paragraphs I am indebted to the analyses of E. P. Sanders in *Jesus and Judaism* (Philadelphia: Fortress, 1985), 264-267; and his *Jewish Law from Jesus to the Mishnah* (Philadelphia: Trinity, 1990), 6-41.

example, Matthew omits the Marcan contention that Jesus declared all foods clean (Matt. 15:10-20), while Luke has deleted the entire scene. Furthermore, Luke depicts the Apostolic Council in Jerusalem as requiring Gentile converts to observe some dietary restrictions (Acts 15:19-29), and Matthew may have something similar in mind in his addition to the Parable of the Guests Invited to a Feast (Matt. 22:11-14).

Mark's attitude toward the Temple in Jerusalem is consistent with his stance toward other Jewish practices. Jesus' cursing of a fruitless fig tree and its subsequent withering (Mark 11:12-14, 20-25) brackets the scene in which Jesus overturns tables in the Temple (11:15-19). The next two chapters show Jesus in mounting contention with Temple authorities, including a pointed parable about the caretakers of a vineyard whose murderous failure to produce fruit will result in the vineyard being given to others (12:1-12). Finally, at the instant of Jesus' death, the curtain of the Temple is torn asunder (15:38). This suggests both the eventual fate of the sacrificial cult (cf. 13:2) and the opening of access to the Divine Presence to the Gentile nations. Notice that it is a Gentile centurion who expresses profound insight in the very next verse. (Again, Jesus' actual words and deeds concerning the Temple are not the issue here, but, rather, Mark's arrangement and interpretation of the traditions about Jesus which he has received.)

From all of these indications, it seems that Mark must be ranked as a "Type Four" Christian according to the schema given above. He rejects Jewish food laws and he sees no abiding significance in Jewish feasts or the cult of the Temple. For Mark, all of these things seem irrelevant in the community of Jesus. Perhaps his position is epitomized in the saying that "no one puts new wine into old wine skins" (2:22).

Although the Gospel of Mark is concerned with a crisis of faith that has arisen in a church experiencing suffering, upheaval, and possibly persecution, the writer's stance toward Judaism is perceptible. The Marcan Jesus' comments about food, purity, and the sabbath all convey the evangelist's belief that such customs are all but meaningless in the final days before the return of the Son of Man and, therefore, are not binding on either Jews or Gentiles in the church.

## The Gospel of Matthew

### A. General Background

It is commonly believed that Matthew's Gospel was composed about fifteen years after Mark's (circa 85 C.E.) and that the author actually used some form of Mark as one of his sources. The writer displays an impressive knowledge of Israel's scriptures (in the Greek Septuagint translation), which he uses extensively to illuminate his understanding of the significance of Jesus. Indeed, the uniquely Matthean reference to the "scribe who has been trained for the kingdom of heaven . . . who brings out of his treasure what is new and what is old" (Matt. 13:52) may reflect the author's estimation of his own work. He is a scribe who discloses the treasures of the Torah and the prophets in the light of Jesus' new conclusive interpretation of them.

While Jesus' passion is very important to him, Matthew's depiction of Jesus does not emphasize his suffering with the intensity that Mark's Gospel does. Instead, the Matthean Jesus is presented as the definitive expression of the Torah who authoritatively teaches what God expects his people to do. The evangelist artfully conveys this conception of Jesus in several ways. For example, events in the life of the Matthean Jesus are often reminiscent of the original law-giver, Moses. It is only in Matthew's Gospel that the newborn Jesus must be rescued from the homicidal designs of an evil king, recalling the events surrounding Moses' birth (Matt. 2:13-18; cf. Exod. 1:15–2:10). Similarly, the scene of Moses on Mount Sinai is echoed when the Matthean Jesus delivers his great sermon about Torah life while sitting on a mountain (Matt. 5:1-2ff.), an event that in Luke's Gospel occurs on a level place (Luke 6:17-19ff.).

It could also be said that the Matthean Jesus embodies the entire history of Israel. The implication of the genealogy at the opening of the Gospel (Matt. 1:1-17) is that the whole story of the Jewish people coalesces in the birth of Jesus. This idea is verified by: (1) allusions to God's occasional *modus operandi* of acting through women with unusual sexual histories (Matt. 1:3, 5, 6, 16, 18-20; cf. Gen. 38; Josh. 2; Ruth 3-4; 2 Sam. 11); (2) the portrayal of Joseph as the recipient of knowledge through dreams (Matt. 1:20; 2:13, 19, 22; cf. Gen. 37:5, 9, 20; 40:8-19; 41:14-36); (3) allusions to the whole People Israel coming up out of Egypt and being tempted in the desert (Matt. 2:14-15; 4:1-10; cf. Deut. 8:2; Exod. 16:1-3; 17:1-2, 7; 32:1-4); and (4) explicit assertions that in the life of Jesus the scriptures of Israel have been fulfilled (Matt. 1:22; 2:15, 17, 23; 4:14; 5:17; 8:17; 12:17; 13:14, 35; 21:4; 26:54, 56; 27:9).

On this last point, readers should be aware of how these Matthean "fulfillment" passages function. At first glance it might appear that Matthew has simply observed that predictions made in the prophets about the Messiah have come to fruition in Jesus. Actually, Matthew has done something far more subtle. This could perhaps be most vividly illustrated by examining Matthew 2:15 in which the evangelist suggests that Joseph's flight to Egypt with the child and his mother "was to fulfill what had been spoken by the Lord through the prophet, 'Out of Egypt I have called my son.'" The evangelist is alluding here to Hosea 11:

> When Israel was a child, I loved him, and *out of Egypt I called my son.*
> The more I called them, the more they went from me;
> They kept sacrificing to the Baals,
> and offering incense to idols. (Hos. 11:1-2)

When we look at the passage in its own context, it becomes clear that the prophet, speaking for God, is commenting upon the past history of God's relationship with Israel. The son of God, Israel, was brought up out of Egypt in the Exodus, and even though it thus owes its very existence to God, Israel still consorts with pagan idols. Far from being a prediction about the eventual arrival of someone out of Egypt in the *future,* the passage is a wistful recollection of the *past.*

Matthew, however, has detected a resonance between the stories of Israel, son of God, and Jesus, Son of God. Both have been called out of Egypt by God, both pass through waters (Matt. 3:13-17; Exod. 14), and both experience temptations in the desert (Matt. 2:1-10; Exod. 16ff.). Looking backwards into the Hebrew scriptures through the lens of his post-resurrectional experience of Jesus, the evangelist perceives implications not apparent in the text itself. The Matthean Jesus has not simply carried out predictions made about him, for in reality the scriptures of ancient Israel do not contain "predictions" about Jesus. Rather, by reading the Hebrew scriptures in the light of the Raised Jesus, the evangelist has come to believe that the story of Jesus recapitulates the story of Israel.[21]

---

21. As noted in chapter 2, this retrospective understanding of biblical prophecy and fulfillment was concisely stated in the Pontifical Biblical Commission's 2001 study: "It would be wrong to consider the prophecies of the Old Testament as some kind of photographic anticipations of future events. All the texts, including those which later were read as messianic prophecies, already had an immediate import and meaning for their contemporaries before attaining a fuller meaning for future hearers. . . . The original task of the prophet was to help his contemporaries understand the events and the times they lived in from God's viewpoint. Accordingly, exces-

Matthew can conceive of Jesus in this way because he also understands Jesus as the personification of the Wisdom of God. In several passages, the Matthean Jesus is described in terms reminiscent of God's Wisdom (Matt. 11:16-19, 28-30; cf. Sir. 6:18-37; 24:19-24; 51:23-27) with the result that those near Jesus are in the presence of something greater than the Temple, than Jonah, and than Solomon (Matt. 12:6, 41-42). Pre-Jesus Jewish writers understood God's Wisdom as residing in the Temple in Jerusalem (Sir. 24:8, 10) and as expressed in the Torah (Sir. 24:24). Therefore, the Matthean Jesus — as the supreme expression of that Wisdom — transcends the importance of the Temple and is able to authoritatively interpret the Torah (see the "but I say to you" verses from the Sermon on the Mount in Matt. 5:21-45).

Because Jesus thus brings the ultimate interpretation of the Torah, Matthew's Jesus is the teacher par excellence and Matthew's Gospel is the most consciously catechetical of the Gospels. In addition, Matthew emphasizes that the teaching of Jesus is something that must be put into actual practice and not merely spoken about (e.g., Matt. 5:17-19; 7:21, 24-26; 12:12; 21:28-31; 25:14-30; 25:31-46; 28:19-20).

One last feature of Matthew's Gospel will impact our assessment of the evangelist's position on Judaism. This is his attitude toward Gentiles. While there is no doubt that Matthew, like the other Gospel writers, supports the church's Gentile mission (e.g., Matt. 28:19), it is also true that his Gospel betrays a certain ambivalence toward Gentiles. For instance, there are several passages where Matthew urges his readers not to be like Gentiles, and where, occasionally, "Gentiles" is an epithet on a par with being a "tax collector." (See Matt. 5:46-47; 6:7, 32; 18:1. Note that in the Lucan parallels [Luke 6:32-33; 11:1-2; 12:30; 17:1-4] this anti-Gentile rhetoric is absent.) Similarly, it seems that it is Gentiles who are referred to as "dogs" (Matt. 7:6; 15:24-27; references again absent in Luke). Furthermore, it is made very explicit in Matthew that Jesus' mission is only to the "lost sheep of the house of Israel" (Matt. 15:24) and that likewise his disciples are to "go nowhere among the Gentiles" but are to "go rather to the lost sheep of the house of Israel" (10:5-6).

This orientation, combined with the other items mentioned above, leads to the conclusion that the evangelist is Jewish. He thinks of Jesus in very Jewish categories, exhibits an extensive knowledge of Israel's scriptures, may

---

sive insistence, characteristic of a certain apologetic, on the probative value attributable to the fulfillment of prophecy must be discarded. This insistence has contributed to harsh judgments by Christians of Jews and their reading of the Old Testament: the more reference to Christ is found in Old Testament texts, the more the incredulity of the Jews is considered inexcusable and obstinate" (II, A, 5).

picture himself as a "scribe" of the teachings of Jesus, and displays mixed feelings toward Gentiles.

Unlike the Marcan Jesus who "declared all foods clean" (Mark 7:19) and simply nullified Torah instructions, the Matthean Jesus states emphatically that he has not "come to abolish the law [Torah] and the prophets" and "whoever breaks [or annuls] one of the least of these commandments, and teaches others to do the same, will be called least in the kingdom of heaven" (Matt. 5:17a, 19a). It would seem that while Matthew agrees with admitting Gentiles to the church, he believes that they must observe at least some Torah behavioral norms. This would appear to be the point of Matthew's addition to the Parable of the Guests Invited to a Feast (Matt. 22:11-14). Though an uninvited guest is admitted to the banquet, he must be properly attired or face expulsion.[22]

Matthew, then, should be classified as at least a "Type Two" Christian according to the typology described above, and possibly a "Type One" disciple of Christ. He upholds the ongoing legitimacy of the Torah, albeit as authoritatively interpreted by Jesus, and sees it as binding, to an extent that we really cannot determine, on Gentile Christians as well.[23]

## B. Matthew and Judaism

The inherent Jewishness of Matthew's Gospel needs to be kept in mind when considering the Matthean attitude toward Judaism. This is particularly true when one comes upon the extremely polemical passages in chapters 21–23. Once again, the modern reader must be cognizant of the Stage Three context of the evangelist.

22. The ancient tradition that Matthew's Gospel was composed in the vicinity of Antioch in Syria bears on this passage. Galatians 2:11-14 relates that Peter and Paul argued publicly in Antioch about whether Gentiles should be required to observe certain dietary regulations (see also Acts 14:25–15:2; 15:19-21, 28-29). Since Peter seems to have prevailed, it is possible that in Antioch it became the established norm for Gentiles to eat kosher foods, a tradition which Matthew's Gospel reflects.

23. Anthony J. Saldarini has observed that while Matthew carefully articulates his community's modifications of such Jewish customs as alms-giving, sabbath observance, Temple worship, purity rules, tithing, and conformity to Torah, no mention whatsoever is made of circumcision. Since Matthew is uninhibited about expressing his other, numerous differences with other Jewish opinions, the absence of contention about circumcision strongly suggests that the Matthean church simply takes circumcision for granted. This would certainly put him in the "Type One" category. See Anthony J. Saldarini, *Matthew's Christian-Jewish Community* (Chicago/London: University of Chicago Press, 1994), 156-160.

Matthew's church is evidently a predominantly Jewish community in the mid-80s that understands itself as being authentically Jewish because it lives according to Jesus' authoritative presentation of the Torah. It is a community that feels itself called to incorporate Gentiles into its ranks, although with certain prerequisites. As such, the Matthean community is a minority sub-group among the various competing Jewish movements that are seeking to fill the vacuum created by the destruction of the Temple in 70 C.E. Consequently, the scribes and Pharisees are especially criticized in Matthew's Gospel because they are emblematic of those with whom the evangelist is vying for the post-Temple leadership of the Jewish community.

Matthew's polemic against contemporary opponents is evident in his version of the Parable of the Vineyard. This parable is found in one of Matthew's sources, the Gospel of Mark (Mark 12:1-12), but Matthew has added as an explanatory verse: "Therefore, I tell you the kingdom of God will be taken away from you and given to a people *(ethnē)* that produces the fruits of the kingdom" (Matt. 21:43). Additionally, the Matthean parable is addressed to the "chief priests and Pharisees . . . [who] realized that he was speaking about them" (Matt. 21:45), but the Pharisees are absent in the Marcan account (Mark 11:27).

Matthew often pairs the Pharisees either with the chief priests or with the members of the priestly governing class, the Sadducees (Matt. 3:7; 16:1, 6, 11, 12; 22:34; 27:62). Since the two groups are affiliated in this way, they become associated in his readers' minds.

In Matthew's estimation, the ethical poverty of the chief priests' leadership had been the cause of the Temple's destruction in 70 C.E. Their corruption is apparent in Matthew's passion narrative. It is the "chief priests and elders" (Matt. 27:20) who had orchestrated Jesus' death and who incited the people of Jerusalem to utter the uniquely Matthean exclamation: "His blood be on us and on our children!" (27:25).[24] Under such leadership, Jerusalem "kills the prophets" and is "desolate" (23:37, 38). Matthew's ideas about the fate of such leaders is plainly visible in his insertion into the Parable of the Guests Invited to a Feast. The king "sent his troops, destroyed those murderers, and burned their city" (Matt. 22:7; an idea notably absent in the Luke 14:21 parallel).

---

24. There has been debate about whether Matthew intends in this verse to issue a blanket condemnation of "the people as a whole" (27:25) or to impute guilt more precisely to "the chief priests and elders" (27:20). Such verses as 21:45-46 in which the "chief priests and Pharisees" fear the crowds who regard Jesus as a prophet favor the latter option.

By associating the Pharisees with the Temple leadership, Matthew implies that just as the leadership of the chief priests had been corrupt and had proven to be fruitless (Matt. 21:19, 33-44), so too the emerging leaders of Matthew's day are inauthentic blind guides who are also failing to produce true Torah living. In seven "woes" against the "scribes and Pharisees, hypocrites!" (Matt. 23:13, 15, 16, 23, 25, 27, 29), the evangelist goes on to castigate his competitors for the hearts and minds of both Jews and Gentiles (woes 1-2), to reject their understanding of oaths, tithes, and purity (woes 3-5), and to portray them as lawless killers (woes 6-7). Matthew seeks to undermine the developing power of this contemporary Jewish leadership because for him only a Jesus-centered understanding of Torah is legitimate. The evangelist insists that true guidance is to be found in the Jesus-centered Matthean community, a "people that produces the fruits of the kingdom" (21:43). Rival claimants to authority in the Jewish world are hypocritical blind guides who seem to be learned Jews but really are not. The fact that his Gospel is thus shaped against the background of what might be called an internal family feud only adds to the volatility of Matthew's rhetoric.

In later church tradition, as witnessed by the textbook quotations at the beginning of this chapter, it was common to understand these Matthean passages as meaning that the divine election of Israel as the Chosen People had been transferred to Gentiles and that non-Christian Jews were dispossessed and accursed. Within his own context, however, it is more likely that Matthew takes the ongoing election of Israel for granted. The conflict is about who accurately interprets Torah and, therefore, who should lead in the post-Temple epoch: the ascendant Pharisees or the Matthean assembly of Jews and Gentiles living according to the Torah taught by Jesus.[25]

## The Gospel of Luke and the Acts of the Apostles

### A. General Background

The third synoptic Gospel is the first part of a two-volume work that not only tells the story of Jesus' ministry but also recounts the growth of the early

---

25. On the importance of a Jewish or a Gentile context for the reading of Matthew, see Benno Przybylski, "The Setting of Matthean Anti-Judaism," in Peter Richardson, ed., *Anti-Judaism in Early Christianity*, vol. 1, *Paul and the Gospels* (Waterloo, Ont.: Wilfrid Laurier University Press, 1986), 181-200.

church. Therefore, our discussion of the Gospel of Luke needs to reckon with the second volume, the Acts of the Apostles, as well. The twin works seem to date from approximately the same time as the Gospel of Matthew (circa 85 C.E.), but the author appears not to have been aware of his fellow evangelist's activity. Like Matthew, Luke is also speculated to have had access to some form of the Gospel of Mark.[26]

One of Luke's central convictions is that the time has come for salvation from violence, division, and poverty to be extended to all people. Besides explicit statements to this effect (e.g., Luke 2:32; 3:6; Acts 1:8), Luke-Acts also displays a certain understanding of the structure of human history. For Luke the time of Jesus' ministry is the pivotal moment of human history when salvation dawns upon the world. The time of "the law and the prophets," the Epoch of Israel, preceded Jesus' activities (Luke 16:16), but after Jesus comes the Epoch of the Church (Acts 1:6-8), when news of salvation must be brought to all of humanity.

Luke-Acts also features a complementary geographical structure. The Gospel begins and ends in Jerusalem. Acts begins in Jerusalem, but Jesus commands the disciples to witness to him "in Jerusalem in Judea and Samaria, and to the end of the earth" (Acts 1:8). The end of the earth refers to the end of the book where the great apostle Paul is found preaching about Jesus "quite openly and unhindered" in the imperial capital of the known world — Rome (28:31). Thus, the goal of the Gospel is Jerusalem, while the goal of Acts is Rome. This structure dramatizes the principle that Jews must receive the Good News before Gentiles (Acts 13:46), but it also establishes that the mission of the church is no less than the salvation of the whole world.

A related Lucan purpose is the desire to convince Roman readers that the church poses no threat to imperial peace and ought to be granted legal status as a legitimate religion. The evangelist imparts this idea in several ways. The family of Jesus is portrayed as law-abiding Galilean peasants who dutifully comply with a Roman census (Luke 2:1-5). The adult Jesus responds to news about Pontius Pilate's latest atrocity, not by calling for revenge as Romans might expect of a native of troublesome Galilee,[27] but by calling in-

---

26. For an introduction to Lucan theology see Joseph A. Fitzmyer, *Luke the Theologian: Aspects of His Teaching* (New York/Mahwah: Paulist, 1989).

27. For a treatment of popular Jewish response to Roman rule see Richard A. Horsley with John S. Hanson, *Bandits, Prophets, and Messiahs* (San Francisco: Harper & Row, 1985). For an exploration of Jesus' ministry within this imperial sociological context see Horsley's *Jesus and the Spiral of Violence* (San Francisco: Harper & Row, 1987).

stead for repentance on the part of his fellow Jews (13:1-3). A centurion who has built a local synagogue asks through Jewish intermediaries that Jesus heal a sick slave — a request that Jesus honors (7:2-5). Pilate himself finds Jesus innocent of any crime (23:4, 14, 22). The centurion at the foot of the cross in Luke's Gospel declares, "Surely this man was innocent!" (23:47), unlike his cry in Mark and Matthew that Jesus was God's Son (Mark 15:39; Matt. 27:54).

In Acts, the Roman centurion Cornelius is the first Gentile to be baptized (Acts 10:1-48), the Roman proconsul Gallio refuses to judge a religious dispute involving Paul (18:12-16), and Roman soldiers save Paul from an irate Jewish mob in the Temple (21:30-32). They rescue him again from a contentious Jewish council (23:10), and a Roman tribune writes to the governor saying that Paul has done "nothing deserving death or imprisonment" (23:29), a verdict echoed by the Roman client-king Herod Agrippa and the Roman governor Festus (26:31).

These episodes tend to minimize the awkward fact that the founder of the Christian movement had been executed at the command of a Roman prefect as a pretender "King of the Jews" (Luke 23:38). This embarrassment is countered by picturing all the Romans who come into contact with Jesus or his followers as reacting favorably to them. It was the doing of the "chief priest, the leaders, and the people" (23:13) that a man declared to be guiltless by Roman authorities was crucified. Therefore, Rome should not hesitate to grant legal status to the movement begun by Jesus.

This positive portrayal of Romans has, what is for Luke, the welcome side-effect of distancing the church from those Jews who had rebelled against Rome in 66 C.E. This detachment is intensified by the frequent depiction of Jews as hostile to the church in Acts (e.g., Acts 9:23; 13:45, 50; 14:4, 19; 17:5-9; 18:12; 20:2, 19; 22:30; 23:1; 24:27; 25:9, 24). Thus, as part of his apologetic aimed at Rome, Luke takes pains to distinguish church members, whether Jew or Gentile, from non-Christian Jews, a distinction not always obvious to Roman eyes.

Luke's depiction of Jesus is consonant with his aims regarding Rome. The Lucan Jesus is the healing savior who brings reconciliation, forgiveness, wholeness, and peace. This is evident in several uniquely Lucan passages. It is foretold that John the Baptist will prepare for Jesus by being a guide "into the way of peace" (Luke 1:79). Angels proclaim Jesus' birth as the dawning of peace (2:10-11, 14). Old Simeon is gifted with peace by encountering the newborn infant (2:29-30). Jesus begins his ministry by referring to himself as the one anointed by the Spirit of God to announce Good News and to liberate the poor, the captive, the blind, and the oppressed (4:16-21). At the end of his ministry Jesus mourns for Jerusalem, which has not recognized "the things that make for peace" (19:42). Although all the Gospels report the severing of someone's ear in the garden when Jesus is arrested (Mark 1:47-50; Matt. 26:51-52; John 18:10-11), only the Lucan Jesus heals the injury (Luke 22:50-51). The mere presence of Jesus sparks a rapprochement between Pilate and Herod (23:12). Only the Lucan Jesus prays for forgiveness for his executioners (23:34) and only in Luke's Gospel does one of the men crucified with Jesus repent (23:39-43).

Another important aspect of the Lucan portrait of Jesus and the early church is his emphasis on their Jewish origins. In the Infancy Narrative all of those close to Jesus are pious, faithful Jews (Luke 1:6, 59; 2:21-22, 25, 27, 36-37, 39, 41). Jesus himself is devout and prayerful (3:21; 4:16; 5:16; 6:12-13; 9:18; 9:28; 11:1; 19:47; 22:32, 41-42; 23:34, 36-47). Similarly, the early church is composed of holy Jews who regularly pray at the Temple (Luke 24:53; Acts 1:14; 2:5, 4:2; 7:59-60; 21:26). Acts further indicates that great numbers of Jews responded to the apostles' preaching (e.g., Acts 2:41; 4:4; 5:14; 6:7; 9:42; 14:1).

The Jewishness of Jesus and of the early church underscores another Lucan theme. Jesus has actualized the promises God made to Israel in the Hebrew scriptures (e.g., Luke 1:54-55, 70-75; 4:21; 7:22; 18:31-33; 24:26-27, 44-46; Acts 3:18-26; 8:27-35; 10:43). Therefore, the death and raising of Jesus, the birth and spread of the church, the inclusion of Gentiles in the Christian community — all of these things have happened in accordance with the plan of God.

Although it is debated whether Luke is a Jew or a Gentile, the features of Luke-Acts are consistent with the idea that Luke is a Gentile "God-fearer." God-fearer was the name given to a Gentile who admired Judaism and had begun informally to observe certain dietary customs or celebrate the sabbath and Jewish feasts. There is archaeological evidence from the late second century C.E. that, by that time at least, God-fearers actually held some sort of official membership in diaspora[28] synagogues — their names appear in roughly equal numbers with the names of Jews who are memorialized as contributors to synagogue building projects.[29] It has been suggested that it is primarily such semi-Jewish Gentiles whom Luke depicts as becoming

---

28. "Diaspora" refers to Jews who are scattered around the Mediterranean world in contrast to Jews living in Judea or Galilee.

29. Joyce Reynolds and Robert Tannenbaum, *Jews and Godfearers at Aphrodisias* (Cambridge, England: Cambridge Philological Society, 1987).

members of the church, whereas pagan idolaters are avoided (see Acts 10:2, 22, 35; 13:16, 26; 15:28-29).[30]

Understanding Luke as a God-fearer explains his familiarity with Israel's scriptures, to which he frequently alludes, but it also accounts for his occasional misconstruing of Jewish practices such as in Luke 2:22-24 where he confuses several different Jewish customs.[31] Given the dietary norms for Gentile Christians which are established in Acts 15:28-29, Luke would appear to be a "Type Two" Christian. Circumcision is not demanded of Gentiles in the Lucan church (Acts 10:44-48), but certain basic Torah practices are required.

## B. Luke-Acts and Judaism

An exploration of the complex presentation of Jews and Judaism in Luke-Acts might begin by considering an important theme in Acts. A recurrent feature of the speeches in Acts is that Jews are blamed for the crucifixion of Jesus (Acts 2:22-23, 36; 3:15; 4:10; 4:27; 5:30; 7:53; 10:39; 13:27-29). Although in some of the passages Pilate or the Romans are mentioned as bearing some responsibility for Jesus' death, it is clear that the emphasis is primarily on the Jewish people's role. Similarly, while chief priests and rulers are occasionally singled out, the people at large are more often indicted. Luke issues blanket accusations against "the Jews" (Acts 10:39) for the execution of Jesus, even though historically this is untenable (see chapter 6). Why?

Two factors have already been mentioned: first, Luke's concern to portray Jesus as innocent of crimes against Rome causes him to tone down the fact that Roman authorities executed Jesus; second, a negative depiction of Jews harmonizes with negative Roman sentiments toward the Jews who had rebelled against imperial rule in the 66-70 C.E. war.

But the speeches also pertain to Luke's ideas about prophecy.[32] The Lucan Jesus is portrayed as the ideal model of a prophet who is rejected. From

---

30. Jacob Jervell, "The Church of Jews and Godfearers," in Joseph B. Tyson, ed., *Luke-Acts and the Jewish People* (Minneapolis: Augsburg, 1988), 11-20.

31. Joseph A. Fitzmyer, *The Gospel According to Luke, I–IX,* The Anchor Bible, vol. 28 (Garden City: Doubleday, 1981) 424-426.

32. It should be noted that the Bible understands prophecy as speaking on behalf of God, such speech usually exhorting the people to live in fidelity with the Covenant. Prophecy in the Bible does not primarily mean to predict the future as it does in colloquial English. The Lucan Jesus is God's ultimate spokesperson, not a mere soothsayer.

the programmatic scene in which Jesus is first accepted and then rejected by his townspeople because "no prophet is acceptable in his own country" (Luke 4:24), to his journey to the Holy City because "it cannot be that a prophet should perish away from Jerusalem" (13:33), to the last days in which "a prophet mighty in deed and word" (24:19) is not recognized in Jerusalem (19:44), Jesus is shown as the Ultimate Prophet who goes the way of all the prophets before him.

Seeing Jesus as the last and greatest of the slain prophets would obviously necessitate an emphasis on his own people's role in his death. It should be pointed out that the notion that Israel always abuses the prophetic messengers of God did not originate with Luke. The Chronicler, for example, believed that the rejection of the prophets caused the destruction of the first Temple (2 Chron. 36:15-16). Likewise, Luke attributes the Second Temple's demise to the rejection of the Great Prophet, Jesus (Luke 23:27-31).

This prophetic theme underlies the demand for repentance that often accompanies the accusation of guilt for Jesus' death (Acts 2:3; 3:19; 5:31; 10:43; 13:38). The pattern of condemning transgression and demanding a return to God is typical of Israelite prophetic utterances. Also typical is the harsh invective in which the cry for penitence may be couched. Indeed, in some prophecies there is no chance for repentance, but just a blunt decrying of the sins that have angered God (e.g., Ezek. 23). The Lucan apostolic prophets of Acts demand repentance from Israel in similarly harsh language.

The response to this call for repentance is notable. Acts often depicts Christian missionaries as successful in their preaching to Jews (2:4, 47; 4:4; 5:14; 6:1, 7; 9:42; 12:24; 13:43; 14:1; 17:11-12; 21:20).[33] This relates to Luke's emphasis on the Jewish origins of the church, and also to his conviction that "it was necessary that the word of God should be spoken first to [Jews]" (Acts 13:46).

Now there is no doubt that the author wishes to show how God's salvation has extended from Jerusalem to all Judea and Samaria and to the end of the earth (Acts 1:8). But the care taken to discuss the mission to Jews and its success among significant numbers of them makes it plain that for the author Gentiles have come to God *through* the witness of Jewish disciples of Christ. For Luke, Gentiles have not come to salvation by replacing Jews as God's Chosen People, but by entering into association with those noble Jews who have heard the word of God and believed it. The author also feels that the extension of salvation to Gentiles through repentant or faithful Israel

---

33. Jacob Jervell, *Luke and the People of God* (Minneapolis: Augsburg, 1972), 44.

is the fulfillment of the promises that God had made to Israel long ago (see esp. Luke 2:30-32). The coming of Jesus marks the time of salvation for the Gentiles and the moment of greatest glory for Israel, through whom that salvation comes.[34]

The presence of Jews in the church is thus of the utmost importance for Luke. In his eyes they are the faithful remnant who have heard the apostles' words and repented. Through them God not only fulfills the promises made to Israel but also extends salvation to the Gentiles. For Luke, the first believers in Jesus as Lord are the authentic Israel, sincerely repentant and ultimately faithful. They are the Jewish heart of the Lucan church.[35] This outlook suggests that the author of Luke-Acts wants to show that Christianity is the legitimate outcome of the preaching of faithful Jews. It is not some sort of falsification or aberration devised by Jewish apostates.[36] Although Jews are becoming more and more a minority in an increasingly Gentile church, Luke shows that their growing isolation is not a sign of God's disapproval. He does this by presenting them as the faithful Israel within the church, mediating salvation to the Gentiles.[37]

The author depicts the Jewish heart of the church, perhaps epitomized by his portrayal of Paul, as Torah-observing Jews (e.g., Acts 2:46-47; 3:1; 16:3; 21:17-26). Despite Stephen's attack on the Temple (7:48-50), Christian Jews continue to be Temple-goers (21:17-26). It is they who define the criteria for Gentile membership in the church (15:20; 21:25), and there is no evidence that Luke thinks them outdated.[38] The reasonable conclusion is that Luke honors Jewish believers in Christ both in his narrative of the early church and also in his own time period.

Since Luke conceives of baptized Jews as the faithful and authentic Israel of God, it is almost inevitable that those Jews who have not accepted the Christian message would be considered by him to be unfaithful and inauthentic. He holds that Jesus has caused a division between the faithful and unfaithful in Israel, an idea evident early in the Gospel (Luke 2:34, 35b). Israel's ultimate time of decision to be faithful to God is triggered, in Luke's view, by the apostles' witnessing to the raising of Jesus. Since

---

34. In this, incidentally, there is some affinity with Paul's perspective written decades earlier that with the raising of Jesus the time had come for Israel's light to be brought to the Gentile nations. See chapter 4.

35. Jervell, *Unknown Paul*, 41-43.

36. Fitzmyer, *Luke I–IX*, 178, 58-59.

37. Jervell, *Unknown Paul*, 39-43.

38. Jervell, *Unknown Paul*, 43.

theirs is the promise (Acts 2:39), Israel is given the opportunity to hear, repent, be baptized, and receive the Holy Spirit (2:38). Jews are urged to save themselves "from this crooked generation" (2:40) because "every soul that does not listen . . . shall be destroyed from the people" (3:23). Jews who heed the apostles are truly faithful and will receive the Spirit, but the evangelist concludes that unresponsive Jews are losing their status as Chosen People.[39] For Luke, Israel is in the process of being reconstructed out of the faithful Jews who hearken to the apostles' preaching and out of believing, God-fearing Gentiles.

Luke portrays "the [non-Christian] Jews" as increasingly opposing the spread of the church. A partial listing of such hostility includes Acts 9:23; 13:45, 50; 14:4, 19; 17:5-9; 18:12; 20:2, 19; 22:30; 23:12; 24:27; 25:9, 24. Associated with the theme of unrepentant Israel rejecting the prophets, these and other references convey the overwhelming impression that non-Christian Jews are the implacable foes of the church. This likely relates to the situation in Luke's day. By the mid-80s some synagogues had begun marginalizing the Christ-believing Jews in their ranks. By depicting Jewish rejection of the church as an opposition to God which deprives them of any claim to religious authority,[40] Luke seeks to counter any influence the synagogue might exert on his own church community.

In conclusion, the harsh language seen in Acts against "Jews" who are accused of killing Jesus and the portrayal of unbaptized Jews as the enemies of the church must be understood within their Lucan context. The evangelist Luke attempts to convince Jews outside of the church of the truth of the Christian message by patterning his apostolic speeches after the prophets of old. In the hope of sparking repentance and belief, he seeks to prod Israel's conscience regarding Jesus in a typically prophetic manner. His bitter words must be understood as originally rooted in the long tradition of rigorous Jewish self-criticism.

Nevertheless, such Jewish self-criticism was seen as more of an attack on Judaism itself once it was read in a totally Gentile church.[41] Luke-Acts readily

39. This conclusion is not reached without regret on the part of the evangelist. Luke's remorse about non-Christian Jews can be seen in the parable about an unfruitful fig tree that is to be fertilized for another year in the hopes of encouraging productivity (Luke 13:6-9), unlike Mark and Matthew who portray Jesus cursing and withering an unfruitful fig tree. It is also only Luke's Gospel that presents Jesus weeping over unperceptive Jerusalem (19:41-44).

40. Note the episode in Acts 19:13-16.

41. See Lloyd Gaston, "Anti-Judaism and the Passion Narrative in Luke and Acts," in Richardson, *Anti-Judaism*, 150-152.

lends itself to such an interpretation because the evangelist actually does believe that non-Christian Jews have "fallen,"[42] although it is not clear whether he feels that this fall is irrevocable. However, Luke's reverence for baptized Jews must be stressed. In Luke's context the edifying presence of Christ-believing Jews was critical evidence of the church's continuity with Judaism. This continuity assured, Luke could prophetically condemn non-Christian Jews, though not without remorse. Thus, Luke's presentation is in some ways both the most pro-Jewish and anti-Jewish of the synoptic Gospels.

## The Gospel of John

### A. General Background

This Gospel reached its final form in the 90s. It is quite different from the other three, which is probably because they were not in the authors' possession. Although Jewish, these writers were steeped in Greek culture and viewed the universe in a dualistic manner. They thought in binary terms. Such dualities as light/darkness, truth/falsehood, spirit/flesh, and life/death permeate the text. This dualism conceives of existence as divided into two realms: the world above and the world below. The world below is the world of earth and humanity, of darkness, fleshiness, and sin. The world above is the world of God and heaven, of light, spirit, and holiness.

For these authors, Jesus comes from the world above, has traversed the chasm which separates the world above from the world below, has testified to the truth from above, and has been "lifted up" (3:14; 8:28; 12:32) in order to return to his home above. He offers the chance for those who believe this to become animated by the life of the world above, and, ultimately, to abide in the world above with Jesus. This theme of the Son descending from heaven and ascending back there is encountered throughout the Gospel. Jesus tells Nicodemus that "no one has ascended into heaven except the one who descended from heaven, the Son of Man" (3:14). He tells the Pharisees that "you are from below, I am from above; you are of this world, I am not of this world" (8:23). At the Last Supper, he declares, "I came from the Father and have come into the world; again, I am leaving the world and am going to the Father" (16:28).

As the One from above, Jesus discloses the things of the world above to

---

42. As perhaps exemplified in Acts 3:23 and 19:13-16 and unlike Paul in Romans 11:11.

the ignorant world below. In particular, he reveals the Father so thoroughly that those who have seen Jesus have seen the Father (14:7). Through a series of rich metaphors, the writer exalts Jesus as the revealer who makes the Father accessible and is "the way, the truth, and the life" (14:6). Thus, Jesus is the "bread of life . . . that came down from heaven (6:35, 41); the "gate" (10:7, 9); the "good shepherd" (10:11, 14); the "light of the world" (8:12; 9:5); "the true vine" (15:1, 5); and "the resurrection and the life" (11:25).

Those who believe that Jesus has been sent by the Father are those who are "born from above" (3:3 — a wordplay on being "born again"). They are "born of the water [a baptismal reference] and the Spirit . . . which blows where it chooses" [3:5, 8]. "Out of the believer's heart shall flow rivers of living water," by which Jesus refers to the Spirit (7:38-39). This Spirit is unleashed at Jesus' death, as symbolically shown by the blood and water gushing from Jesus' side, a detail unique to John's Gospel (19:34). He is the "Lamb of God" (1:29, 35) who dies as the lambs are being sacrificed for Passover.

Believers perceive that Jesus and the Father are "in" each other (14:11). Consequently, the love which the Father has for Jesus comes into the hearts of believers (17:26). The Father and the Son (14:23) and the Spirit (14:17) come to dwell in believers. Thus, believers live according to Jesus' only commandment in this Gospel, "Love one another" (13:34; 15:12, 17). This is what John means by eternal life. It is a sharing in the love-relationship between the Father and the Son in the Spirit. It is a love/life which transcends human death. It is a relationship with the Father made possible because the Son came down from above and has returned to his home above "to prepare a place" and take believers there (14:3).

The main christological perspective in John, then, is that Jesus comes from above and brings the eternal life of the world above; namely, the love between the Father and the Son in the Spirit, to those who believe. Authentic discipleship, therefore, is defined by the bond of love which unites believers (13:35).

### B. John and Judaism

As the Gospel was being completed, the Johannine church was traumatized by the ouster of its Jewish members from the local synagogue (9:22; 12:42; 16:2). Angered by this expulsion, the author persistently uses the term "the Jews" in the Gospel, despite that fact that almost every character, including Jesus, is Jewish. This practice sarcastically conveys the alienation experienced by Johannine Jewish-Christians who have been uprooted from their Jewish heritage by so-called Jews.

The factor that precipitated the expulsion or shunning was probably what Johannine Jews were saying about Jesus. The exalted picture of Jesus as the One from above was understood in the synagogue as asserting the existence of two Gods: the Father and the Son (5:18; 10:33). Such a perceived breach of Jewish monotheism was intolerable to the synagogue and Christian theology had not sufficiently developed to precisely articulate the relationship between the Father and the Son so as to preserve monotheism.

The anger against "the Jews," who the author(s) believes ought to have known better, flashes throughout the entire narrative. For example, the Johannine Jesus is regularly depicted as personally surpassing major Jewish customs and feasts. He performs works that only God can perform on the Sabbath (5:16-18). He is the Bread from Heaven that is superior to the manna in the exodus from Egypt and to the Passover matzah (6:32-33, 53-58). He transcends the water and light ceremonies that accompanied Second Temple observance of the feast of Sukkot (7:37-39; 8:12). And during the festival of Hanukkah, Jesus is consecrated as Son of God (10:31-39).[43] This last scene in particular has the regrettable effect of reinforcing the anachronistic notion that Jesus engaged in debates with contemporary Jews over his claimed divine identity, a concept that did not arise before his disciples' experience of his transcendent exaltation after his crucifixion (see chapter 2).

Certain Johannine passages, stemming from the rift with the local synagogue in the 90s, have proven to be influential in promoting anti-Jewish attitudes among the Christians of later centuries. Most problematic is the heated argument between Jesus and "Jews who (had) believed in him" (8:31) over their respective paternities, during which Jesus declares "You belong to your father, the devil" (8:44). Such invective can be understood as the literary character of Jesus giving voice to the rage of the Johannine Jewish community, perhaps especially if directed at Jews who had once belonged to their ranks but who had renounced their faith in Jesus in response to the shunning by the mainstream Jewish community. However, in subsequent history this verse contributed to Christian associations of Jews with the satanic and to artistic portrayals of Jews with demonic features.[44]

43. So Raymond E. Brown *The Gospel According to John,* Anchor Bible Series (Garden City, NY: Doubleday, 1966), I, CXLI; 201-415.

44. See Heinz Schreckenberg, *The Jews in Christian Art: An Illustrated History* (New York: Continuum, 1996), chapter 8.

In sum, Hellenistic dualism refracted through the dispute between Johannine Jews and mainstream Jews over Jesus' status produced a defensive and polemical presentation of Jews and Judaism in this Gospel tradition. Ironically, the Gospel that powerfully expressed the meaning of Christian life in such phrases as "This is how all will know that you are my disciples, if you have love for one another" (13:35) is also the Gospel that unleashed intense polemic against the outsiders, especially "the Jews."

## Conclusion: Teaching the Gospels "Within Context"

This chapter began with the observation that contentious language in the Gospels has been used over the centuries to promote hostility toward Jews and Judaism. Reading the Gospels within their own contexts of dispute, exhortation, rivalry, and the need to fix clear boundaries in a new community explains the origins of such rhetoric. A contextual awareness discloses that this polemic is the product of human conflict and does not represent timeless truths about God.

While earlier generations read the Gospels in ways that absolutized and universalized polemical assertions, thereby fostering anti-Jewish behaviors among Christians, a sensitivity to the historical contexts of the evangelists averts a similar reading today. This leads to several suggestions about ways to read, preach, and teach the Gospel texts to minimize their anti-Jewish potentialities. (Chapter 6 provides a detailed examination of the passion narratives, which are especially neuralgic in terms of anti-Judaism.)

1. Promote a critical awareness of the Gospel texts. This can readily be done by noting their four distinctive portrayals of Jesus and their individual concerns and emphases. This would help readers or listeners to appreciate the Gospels as theological reflections on the significance of Jesus that were intended to address local needs.

2. Foster an understanding of the principles contained in the Pontifical Biblical Commission's "Instruction on the Historical Truth of the Gospels." By becoming familiar with the three stages of Gospel development, people would be enabled to understand the evangelists' individual contexts. They would also be less likely to regard the Gospels simply as transcripts of Jesus' ministry and come to appreciate better how divine inspiration can function in the life of ordinary people.

3. Highlight the real-life situations of the evangelists in order to show how

their attitudes about Jews and Judaism were molded by their contexts. This situates and de-absolutizes their polemical rhetoric. As the U.S. Bishops' Committee on the Liturgy advised in 1988:

> Many other elements, such as the crowds shouting "His blood be on us and on our children" in Matthew, or the generic use of the term "the Jews" in John, are unique to a given author and must be understood within the context of that author's overall theological scheme. Often, these unique elements reflect the perceived needs and emphases of the author's particular community at the end of the first century, after the split between Jews and Christians was well underway. The bitterness toward synagogue Judaism seen in John's gospel (e.g., Jn 9:22; 16:2) most likely reflects the bitterness felt by John's own community after its "parting of the ways" with the Jewish community, and the martyrdom of St. Stephen illustrates that verbal disputes could, at times, lead to violence by Jews against fellow Jews who believed in Jesus.[45]

4. Compare Gospel remarks about Jews and Judaism with modern understandings. Ecclesial statements that Jews cannot be held liable for the crucifixion[46] should be recalled when reading Luke's accusations against Jews or Matthew's attacks on the Pharisees. Similarly, John Paul II's words that Jews remain "the people of God of the Old Covenant, never revoked by God," ought to be cited when the Gospels could be construed to suggest that Judaism is obsolete or rejected by God. A comparison of the church's twenty-first-century context with those of the Gospels would also be worthwhile.

These strategies, adapted for different ages and backgrounds, would help to provide that "objective and rigorously accurate teaching of Judaism . . . [that leads] to an exact knowledge of the wholly unique 'bond' which joins us as a Church to the Jews and to Judaism."[47]

45. "God's Mercy Endures Forever: Guidelines on the Presentation of Jews and Judaism in Catholic Preaching" (1988), §24.

46. *Nostra Aetate,* 4. For an ecumenical collection of relevant Christian ecclesial documents see Franklin Sherman, ed., *Bridges: Documents of the Christian-Jewish Dialogue,* Volume One: *The Road to Reconciliation (1945-1985)* and Volume Two: *Building a New Relationship (1986-2013)* (New York/Mahwah: Paulist Press/Stimulus Books, 2011 and 2014).

47. John Paul II, "Address to the Jewish Community in Mainz, West Germany" November 17, 1980.

# CHAPTER 6

# The Passion Narratives and Christian-Jewish Relations Today

## Understanding the Passion Narratives

The previous chapter discussed how each of the four canonical Gospels treated the topic of Jews and Judaism. It paid special attention to the distinction between those traditions that originated in the life of Jesus himself ("Stage 1") and those that arose in the specific circumstances of each of the evangelists ("Stage 3"). This distinction is especially crucial when considering the "passion narratives" of each of the Gospels, those passages that describe the arrest and execution of Jesus. Regardless of what their authors' intentions might have been, it is inarguable that over the centuries, these texts, as Mary C. Boys has succinctly put it, "provided the raw materials for harsh depictions of Jews as enemies of Christ."[1] She further observes that:

> The charge that the Jews killed Jesus became a crucial component of the rhetoric of Christian identity formation. It was a key element in its rivalry with the synagogue in the complex and extended process by which Christianity ultimately separated from Judaism. As a fundamental part of the "us/them" binary, it stood at the center of the assertion that the Way of Christ, the crucified Savior, was the only faithful way to God and that

1. Mary C. Boys, *Redeeming Our Sacred Story* (New York/Mahwah: Paulist Press/Stimulus Books, 2013), 47.

---

This chapter adapts my "The Arrest and Sentencing of Jesus: A Historical Reconstruction," *Journal of Religion and Society* (2004), Supplemental Series I: http://moses.creighton.edu/ JRS/2004/2004-8.pdf.

the followers of Christ had become God's people. God now rejected the Jews, the former people of God, because of their infidelity in killing Jesus.[2]

The ongoing potential for anti-Jewish applications of the passion narratives has been a constant concern in the post–*Nostra Aetate* church, beginning with that conciliar declaration itself: "the Jews should not be spoken of as rejected or accursed as if this followed from Holy Scripture."[3]

Is there any historical basis for the recurrent blaming of Jews for the crucifixion of Jesus? The purpose of this chapter is to examine three scenes from the passion narratives according to Catholic biblical perspectives in order to assess what can be known about the Stage One events that lie behind them. The conclusions that will be reached are fairly widely agreed upon in contemporary scripture scholarship.

Another way of conceiving of this is to imagine that we are writing the script of a dramatization of the passion with a view to being as historically accurate as possible. At the conclusion of this chapter, I will offer some comments about the implications of our historical considerations for the preparations of "passion plays" or cinematic dramatizations, because these representations, when based on inherited interpretations, can subconsciously breed negative or hostile opinions toward the Jewish people. This was a highly publicized topic in the controversy in 2003-2004 over the Mel Gibson film, *The Passion of the Christ*.[4]

Before beginning, it is worthwhile to repeat a point made in the previous chapter about the three stages of Gospel tradition. Stage Three — the time of the composition of the Gospels — is the one most important for Christian faith. It testifies to the evangelists' inspired reflections on the meaning of Jesus' life, death, and resurrection. Christians believe that the inspiration of the Holy Spirit functioned in the minds and hearts of the Gospel writers, shaping

---

2. Boys, *Redeeming Our Sacred Story*, 76. On the consequences of the destruction of the Second Temple in 70 C.E. for this oppositional relationship, see Adam Gregerman, "'Have you despised Jerusalem and Zion after you had chosen them?': The Destruction of Jerusalem and the Temple in Jewish and Christian Writings from the Land of Israel in Late Antiquity," doctoral diss., Columbia University, 2007. UMI Publication Number 3266586.

3. *Nostra Aetate* (1965), 4. See also: PCRRJ, "Guidelines" (1974), II; PCRRJ, "Notes" (1985), 21, A; PBC, "Interpretation" (1988), IV, A, 3; BCL, "God's Mercy Endures Forever" (1988), 7, 21, 23-25; BCEIA, "Criteria" (1988).

4. For my analysis of that movie, see "A Challenge to Catholic Teaching" in Philip A. Cunningham, ed., *Pondering the Passion: What's at Stake for Christians and Jews?* (Franklin, WI, and Chicago: Sheed & Ward, 2004), 143-156.

their insights and individual presentations of the story and significance of Jesus. This inspiration did not include providing historical information to the evangelists, as the Gospels' differences in historical details demonstrate. By discerning their distinctive perspectives, modern readers gain insight into the inspired mind of each of the Gospel writers as they encouraged faith in Jesus Christ. As seen in the previous chapter, it is also possible to detect their concerns and biases.

This means that the goal of this chapter, to reconstruct briefly the historical circumstances of Jesus' death, is to seek of the Gospels something they were not really meant to provide. Questions such as "What is the meaning of Jesus?" or "Why is Jesus important?" are more appropriate to ask of the evangelists' writings. Nevertheless, since modern Western readers have a consciousness that history shapes our perceptions and expressions and in particular tend to collapse truth to what is empirically verifiable, they will inevitably pose historical questions to the Gospels such as "What really happened at the execution of Jesus?" However, they should bear in mind that the biblical authors do not share our mental horizons and linguistic conventions.

## The Land of Israel in Roman Times

In the process of asking historical questions of the Gospels, certain facts about life in Roman times are important. Ancient societies did not make modern distinctions between religion, politics, or economics. "Religion" was imbedded with politics and economics in the concrete social forms of family and local community authority structures. For example, the Temple in Jerusalem was the spiritual center of Judaism *and* a military fortress *and* the economic lifeblood of the city. Similarly, Jesus' proclamation of the coming Reign of God was not simply a religious or spiritual message. It also had political consequences since the arrival of God's Reign would mean the replacement of earthly realms, including the Roman Empire.

The Roman prefect over Samaria and Judea (including Jerusalem), Pontius Pilate, effectively appointed the Temple's high priest. While Pilate was prefect (26-36 C.E.), the high priest was Joseph Caiaphas. Pilate could remove an uncooperative priest by refusing to give him the sacred vestments worn to enter the Holy of Holies on Yom Kippur. Since Caiaphas remained high priest during Pilate's entire tenure as prefect, it seems clear that they had a good working relationship.

Also of historical importance in reconstructing the circumstances of

Jesus' death is the fact that Passover in Jerusalem could be a volatile time. Thousands of Jewish pilgrims streamed to Jerusalem from all over the Mediterranean world to celebrate the festival of freedom from foreign domination, but upon arriving they would see many signs of Roman supremacy. The first-century writer Flavius Josephus tells of the regular Roman practice of stationing troops to maintain public order in the Temple precincts (*Jewish Wars*, 2.12.1). The inflamed mood of the Jewish populace at Passover was probably why Pilate was in Jerusalem, instead of at his headquarters in Caesarea Maritima, when Jesus entered the city.

If, as the synoptic Gospels relate, Jesus caused a disturbance in the Temple after his arrival, this would certainly alarm both Jewish and Roman authorities: a Galilean troublemaker might be planning to start a Passover riot. Pilate would want to keep the peace. So would Caiaphas, who could reasonably fear that violence could lead to the destruction of the Temple, as indeed eventually occurred in 70 C.E. (see John 11:48-50).

## Analysis by Scene

With this background, let us turn to three scenes in the passion narratives: the Arrest of Jesus, Jesus before the Temple Priests, and Jesus before Pilate. Although it is possible to devise a minimalist reconstruction (for instance some have suggested that Jesus and Pilate never directly encountered each other), we will follow the main lines of the passion narratives and draw cautious conclusions after comparing some of the distinct elements of the four Gospel accounts.

### A. The Arrest of Jesus

The four Gospels share many common features in this scene, probably because it was an event in which some followers of Jesus were participants. Nonetheless, there are notable differences as well.

In Mark's Gospel, Jesus prays three times for "this cup to pass me by," but he will do his Father's will. Three times he returns to a group of his disciples and finds they cannot keep awake. When an arresting party arrives, someone draws a sword and slices off an ear of someone in the arresting party. Mark is very blunt, "All of them abandoned him and fled" (14:50). In Mark's Gospel, Jesus is left utterly alone.

Then follows an episode that is unique to Mark: "A certain young man was following him, wearing nothing but a linen cloth. They caught hold of him, but he left the linen cloth and ran off naked" (14:51-52). Most commentators understand this not as a historical incident, but as related to Mark's pattern of showing that no human being realizes that Jesus is Son of God before the crucifixion. He portrays the disciples especially negatively, as their sleepiness illustrates. Many see this incident as referring to a scene at the beginning of the Gospel, as Raymond E. Brown explains: "[T]he disciple fleeing naked is symbolic simply of the total abandonment of Jesus by his disciples. The first [Marcan] disciples to be called left nets and family (1:18, 20), indeed everything (10:28), to follow him; but this last disciple, who at first sought to follow Jesus, ultimately leaves everything to get away from him."[5]

Mark's purpose in having characters fail to understand Jesus' full identity throughout his Gospel becomes clearer later in the passion narrative when Jesus dies, having been totally forsaken by everyone. "Now when the centurion . . . saw that in this way he breathed his last, he said, 'Truly this man was God's Son!'" (15:39). This individual is the first human character in Mark's Gospel to perceive accurately Jesus' identity and this is because he discerned the love of God made manifest in Jesus' death. This for Mark is authentic faith, faith that endures even when threatened by violence and death — a crucial pastoral message if the Marcan church has been the victim of persecution, possibly in Rome between 64 and 70 C.E.[6]

Matthew's presentation of the arrest scene mostly follows Mark, but in Luke's account Jesus prays for the cup to pass him by only once. "When he got up from prayer, he came to the disciples and found them sleeping because of grief" (22:5). If Luke had a version of Mark before him, as most scholars think, then he clearly has toned down the negative Marcan portrayal of the disciples.

In addition, the scene depicting the cutting of the ear has a characteristically Lucan feature: "Then one of them struck the slave of the high priest and cut off his right ear. But Jesus said, 'No more of this!' And he touched his ear and healed him" (22:51). In all the other Gospels, the severed ear is presumably left lying on the ground. However, as can be seen throughout Luke's Gospel, Jesus is conceived by this evangelist as the one who brings

---

5. Raymond E. Brown, *A Crucified Christ in Holy Week: Essays on the Four Gospel Passion Narratives* (Collegeville: Liturgical Press, 1986), 23. See also his *The Death of the Messiah* (New York: Doubleday, 1994), 302-304.

6. See, e.g., the discussion in John R. Donahue and Daniel J. Harrington, *The Gospel of Mark*, Sacra Pagina Series (Collegeville: Liturgical Press, 2002), 41-46.

healing, wholeness, and reconciliation. It would be unthinkable for him to portray Jesus as failing to heal someone of such an injury.

John's Gospel has several notable differences from the three synoptic Gospels. Roman soldiers are in the arresting party, for instance. Most importantly, there is no prayer of Jesus wishing that his imminent suffering could be avoided:

> Then Jesus, knowing all that was to happen to him, came forward and asked them, "Whom are you looking for?" They answered, "Jesus of Nazareth." Jesus replied, "I am he." . . . When Jesus said to them, "I am he," they stepped back and fell to the ground. Again he asked them, "Whom are you looking for?" And they said, "Jesus of Nazareth." Jesus answered, "I told you that I am he." (18:4-7)

In the Gospel of John, Jesus is in total control of every scene. He knows what is going to happen. This writer(s) stresses Jesus' divine status. That is why when he says, "I AM," recalling the holy name revealed to Moses in the burning bush, his arrestors all swoon in his divine presence. This would surely be a difficult scene to dramatize without making the arrestors seem clownish.

Moreover, after Peter cuts off the servant's ear, Jesus says, "Put your sword back into its sheath. Am I not to drink the cup that the Father has given me?" (18:11). Not only is there no prayer of avoidance in John, but the image of "the cup" is here treated as something that Jesus would drink without question or hesitation: "There is no question that I am going to drink the cup the Father has given me!" This is because of this Gospel's stress on Jesus as divine and in total control.

### Historical Conclusions about the Arrest of Jesus

Clearly, authors of passion dramas today have to choose from among very different portraits of Jesus in presenting his arrest. To peer past these Stage Three portrayals to their Stage One bases, the following would seem to be reasonable historical conclusions.

Jesus was quietly arrested at night on the Mount of Olives. This means that his foes were concerned about his general popularity and feared taking him into custody publicly (cf. Mark 14:2). The composition of the arresting party is unclear, but given the good working relationship of the prefect and the high priest, this may not really matter. Furthermore, although Jesus did not resist arrest, there was some swordplay that Jesus stopped.

## B. Before the Temple Priests

Not surprisingly, the Gospels are not consistent in presenting this "behind closed doors" scene. In Mark and Matthew "the chief priests and whole council" convene on the first night of Passover to judge Jesus' fate. This scene has always caused difficulties for historians who question how it would be possible to convene a formal council on the night that Jews are eating the Passover Seder (as both Mark 14:12 and Matthew 26:17 had indicated earlier, though John 19:31 has a different timetable). Luke only has a morning "assembly of the elders of the people" (22:6), while John depicts no council meeting at all at this point, but only a questioning of Jesus by Annas about his disciples and teaching (18:13, 19).

The Marcan episode of Jesus before the high priest contains this famous scene:

> Again the high priest asked him, "Are you the Messiah, the Son of the Blessed One?" Jesus said, "I am; and 'you will see the Son of Man seated at the right hand of the Power,' and 'coming with the clouds of heaven.'" Then the high priest tore his clothes and said, "Why do we still need witnesses? You have heard his blasphemy!" (14:61-64)

Several important points need to be made about this passage. First, the words of Jesus are a blending of Daniel 7:13 and Psalm 110:1, strongly suggesting that they are a result of later Christian reflection on the identity of Jesus. This is confirmed by the question of the high priest about whether Jesus is God's divine Son. Recalling the three stages of Gospel development, this question presupposes the resurrection experience, something that of course has not yet occurred in the Gospel narrative. Indeed, since, as we have earlier seen, Mark emphasizes that no one really understands Jesus' identity until the crucifixion, this premature insight on the part of a character hostile to Jesus is quite peculiar. The conclusion is that debates about Jesus' divine Sonship that occurred in Stage Three between Jewish and Gentile believers in Jesus as the Crucified and Raised Lord and disbelieving Jews who do not share this belief have been retrojected by Mark back into this scene that will lead to Jesus' execution.

Likewise, the "blasphemy" charge can be understood in Stage One and Stage Three layers. In Stage Three, the Christian claim that Jesus is divine sounds to Jewish ears as if a second "god" is being proposed, something that of course is unacceptable. However, in Stage One, the charge of blasphemy could be leveled against anyone arrogantly claiming to have the authority to criticize God's anointed priests.[7] If Jesus did indeed accuse the Temple leaders of being corrupt stewards as some parables suggest, then his targets might well have viewed his remarks as blasphemous preludes to violence against them.

If Christological issues color the Marcan account, it is fascinating that they are absent from the Johannine version given the Fourth Gospel's emphasis on Jesus' divinity:

> The high priest questioned Jesus about his disciples and about his teaching. Jesus answered him, "I have spoken publicly to the world. I have always taught in a synagogue or in the temple area where all Jews gather, and in secret I have said nothing. Why ask me? Ask those who heard me what I said to them. They know what I said." When he had said this, one of the temple guards standing there struck Jesus and said, "Is this the way you answer the high priest?" Jesus answered him, "If I have spoken wrongly, testify to the wrong; but if I have spoken rightly, why do you strike me?" Then Annas sent him bound to Caiaphas the high priest. (18:19-24)

In addition to the lack of any council meeting at this juncture, it is noteworthy that Annas asks Jesus only about his disciples and teaching. There is considerable plausibility that these would be the topics of concern in a Stage One context. Has Jesus' teaching been aimed at provoking Passover violence? Might his disciples be poised to incite violence if Jesus were to be removed?

One of the facts about Jesus' death that should be considered is that his followers were permitted to scatter. They were not also taken into custody. If Jesus' foes were motivated by a fear that a Passover riot was being plotted, they would have to determine if Jesus' disciples had instructions to launch violence even if their master were imprisoned or killed. Perhaps this reasoning lies behind the Johannine element of Annas interrogating Jesus about his followers.

The content of Jesus' teaching would also relate to a concern about Passover violence, especially given the lack of a christological tone to the questioning.

---

7. Brown, *Death of the Messiah*, 520-527.

*Historical Conclusions about Jesus before the Priests*

For a variety of reasons, a formal legal proceeding before a Sanhedrin on the first night of Passover is implausible. Whether or not there was a council meeting prior to Jesus' arrest (as in John 11:45-53), a large debate would not be in the interests of hurried authorities who had already determined that Jesus was a threat to public order on Passover. His questioning, therefore, is most likely restricted to the high priests and their inner circle. This questioning may have largely focused on whether the disciples posed a threat.

## C. Before Pilate

Again, there are many inconsistencies among the Gospels in this private scene. Among their common features are care in the portrayal of Roman justice, Jesus being asked if he is "the king of the Jews" (likely enough based on the eventual crime posted on Jesus' cross), and a "crowd" demanding Barabbas's release and Jesus' execution. I put "crowd" in quotation marks because no Gospel specifies the size of this group. Creators of passion dramas are therefore free to depict a group of anywhere from a dozen people up to a Cecile B. DeMille–like cast of thousands. However, the Barabbas incident has several peculiar aspects, and needs to be discussed as a distinct category.

In the synoptic Gospels Pilate has a custom to release a prisoner to honor the Passover festival, whereas in John it is a Jewish custom that Pilate observes. In either case, there is little or no extra-biblical evidence for such practices in areas under Roman rule. Furthermore, is it likely that Pilate would release a murderer or an insurrectionist as he is described in Mark and Luke?

Questions mount when one realizes that the name Bar-abbas means "son of the father," an excellent soubriquet for Jesus of Nazareth. In fact, in certain texts of Matthew's Gospel, Barabbas's surname is Jesus and so Pilate asks whether he should release Jesus son of the father or Jesus the messiah (Matt. 27:17)!

Clearly there are theological factors at work in this incident that date from before Stage Three, most likely from early in Stage Two, that are difficult to discern clearly. Raymond E. Brown has offered what still seems to be the best theory to explain these puzzles:

A man with the name Barabbas was arrested after a riot that had caused some deaths in Jerusalem. Eventually he was released by Pilate when a feast brought the governor to Jerusalem to supervise public order. Presumably this took place at the same time that Jesus was crucified, or not far from it, or on another Passover. In any case, this release struck Christians as ironic: The same legal issue was involved, sedition against the authority of the emperor. Although they knew Jesus was innocent, he was found guilty by Pilate, while Barabbas was let go. The storytelling tendency to contrast the released Barabbas and the crucified Jesus by bringing them together at the same moment before Pilate's 'justice' would have been enhanced if both had the same personal name, Jesus.[8]

Given the difficulties and uncertainties associated with the Barabbas incident, it will not be assigned a high degree of historicity in this reconstruction of Jesus' death. This has implications for the portrayal of the "crowd" in general.

Matthew's Gospel at this scene contains some unique phrases that have been especially destructive toward Jews over Christian history:

> Now the chief priests and the elders persuaded the crowds to ask for Barabbas and to have Jesus killed. . . . So when Pilate saw that he could do nothing, but rather that a riot was beginning, he took some water and washed his hands before the crowd, saying, "I am innocent of this man's blood; see to it yourselves." Then the people as a whole answered, "His blood be on us and on our children!" (27:20, 24-25)

In interpreting this passage it is important to note that the chief priests and elders are shown to mislead the people into calling for Jesus' death. This relates to two parables presented a few chapters earlier in Matthew:

> Once more Jesus spoke to them in parables, saying: "The kingdom of heaven may be compared to a king who gave a wedding banquet for his son. He sent his slaves to call those who had been invited to the wedding banquet, but they would not come. Again he sent other slaves, saying, 'Tell those who have been invited: Look, I have prepared my dinner, my oxen and my fat calves have been slaughtered, and everything is ready; come to the wedding banquet.' But they made light of it and went away, one to his farm, another to his business, *while the rest seized his slaves, mistreated them, and killed them. The king was enraged. He*

---

8. Brown, *Death of the Messiah*, 819-820.

*sent his troops, destroyed those murderers, and burned their city."* (22:1-7, emphasis added)

There is a parallel version of the same parable in Luke 14:16-24. However, the italicized words above, undoubtedly referring to the Roman destruction of Jerusalem in the year 70, are not present in Luke.

Matthew is relating the destruction of the Temple to those who should have known better but yet declined the invitation of God's messengers and even killed them. A similar pattern can be seen in another Matthean parable:

> Jesus said to the chief priests [concluding a parable he tells], ". . . But when the tenants saw the son, they said to themselves, 'This is the heir; come, let us kill him and get his inheritance.' So they seized him, threw him out of the vineyard, and killed him. Now when the owner of the vineyard comes, what will he do to those tenants?" They said to him, "He will put those wretches to a miserable death, and lease the vineyard to other tenants who will give him the produce at the harvest time." Jesus said to them, ". . . Therefore I tell you, the kingdom of God will be taken away from you and given to a people that produces the fruits of the kingdom." (21:23, 38-43)

In this Matthean scene, Jesus tells the chief priests a parable about tenants working a vineyard for a landowner. Since a vineyard is a standard biblical symbol for Israel (Isa. 5:7), it is clear that the story is a pointed one about corrupt rulers of God's people. These rulers kill the landowner's son and so will lose their authority. Obviously, comparisons to God's Son Jesus being killed outside the vineyard/city are being drawn.

How do these three Matthean passages interrelate? After the Temple was destroyed by the Romans in 70 C.E., different groups of Jews blamed one another for its demise, Matthew among them. He blames the Temple priests for leading the people of Jerusalem astray in demanding Jesus' death. They and their children, in Matthew's view, were destroyed by the Romans in 70 C.E. for this crime.

Now, Matthew argues, leadership in the Jewish community is given to "another group," namely, Matthew's church, which follows the Torah definitively interpreted by Jesus at the Sermon on the Mount. Matthew warns his readers not to follow the leaders he considers corrupt in his day, the Pharisees. He characterizes them as blind guides (Matt. 23:16 and, indeed, the whole chapter) who will lead the people to destruction just as the Temple priests did. The "blood curse" in 27:25 is thus not a Stage One historical event, but is part of Matthew's Stage Three polemic against Jewish rivals.

Luke also has some unique verses when Jesus is presented to Pilate: "Then the assembly rose as a body and brought Jesus before Pilate. They began to accuse him, saying, 'We found this man perverting our nation, forbidding us to pay taxes to the emperor, and saying that he himself is the Messiah, a king'" (23:1-2).

These three charges are only found in Luke; however, they have some degree of historical plausibility in connection with Jesus. The charge of "perverting the nation" is usually understood to mean teaching falsely. Jesus' proclamation of God's imminent intervention in establishing his Reign and/or his critique of the Temple leaders could both be deemed falsehoods by his accusers. Jesus' riddling response to the question of paying taxes to Caesar (20:22-25) could be interpreted as meaning that God is owed everything and Caesar nothing. The charge of calling himself a king, while not attested explicitly in the New Testament, is not without basis given Jesus' constant activities on behalf of God's Reign or Kingdom.

It is therefore unsurprising when Pilate next asks, "Are you the king of the Jews?" Jesus gives a smart-alecky response, "You say so" or "You're the one who used the word" (23:3). This is a particularly risky reply given the Roman legal norm that one is guilty until proven innocent. One would therefore expect that having been confronted with plausible accusations against a Galilean at a volatile time and hearing a disrespectful or defiant reply, Pilate would quickly decide that Jesus was at least a troublemaker.

Instead the Lucan Pilate states, "I find no basis for an accusation against this man" (23:4) — an astonishing reversal of the flow of the narrative to that point. Luke gives no reason for Pilate's pronouncement, but it is only the first of three such exclamations from him (23:4, 14, 22). The answer to this logical puzzle is found in this Gospel's apologetic (and theological) interests: Roman characters in Luke constantly testify to Jesus' righteousness.

This agenda is again seen in the words declared by the centurion at the foot of the cross in Luke's Gospel ("Surely this man was innocent!" — 23:47) in contrast to the Marcan centurion's pronouncement of Jesus' divine Sonship. Additionally, Jesus as the suffering righteous prophet is one of Luke's principal Christological themes.

Luke is probably also motivated by his desire to win the church legal status in the Roman Empire. It would not do to explicitly show Jesus found guilty of sedition by a Roman prefect. As a result, Pilate and indeed all the Roman characters in his Gospel and in Acts of the Apostles are positively portrayed and Jesus' innocence is constantly repeated.

Another unique Lucan episode is Jesus being brought to Herod Antipas, who is in Jerusalem for the Passover. The story ends with, "That same day Herod and Pilate became friends with each other; before this they had been enemies" (23:12). For Luke, no one can enter the healing presence of Jesus without being affected; hence, Pilate and Antipas become friends.

Likewise, one of the two men crucified alongside Jesus is affected by his proximity to him. Unlike the other Gospels, this individual repents and expresses confidence in Jesus (23:39-43). Perhaps also related to the aura cast by the Lucan Jesus is that after he dies, the spectators return home beating their breasts in sorrow (23:48).

As is the case throughout John's Gospel, Jesus remains fully in control during his encounter with Pilate. He and Pilate engage in philosophical discussions about kingship and authority. Again, asserting a theme that spans this Gospel, Jesus' divine identity is stressed. For example, Jesus tells Pilate his kingdom is "not from this world" (18:36).

John's Gospel uses the phrase "the Jews" in a sweeping collective sense that has contributed to the Christian "Christ killer" charge against Jews in all times and places. As explored in the previous chapter, most researchers see a Stage Three origin for this practice. John's church community has recently been involved in a painful break with the local Jewish community (see 9:22; 12:42; 16:2). In his anger, the author refers sarcastically to "the Jews" who expelled Jewish believers in Christ, even though he feels that they have in a sense forsaken their Jewish heritage by doing so.

A unique aspect of John's account is that Pilate shuttles inside and outside the praetorium, reflecting his inner confusion. As part of his perplexity, Pilate orders Jesus scourged in a futile effort to release him. This is the only Gospel to posit this reason for the scourging. In the synoptics, scourging is simply part of the Roman crucifixion process. The entire scene is carefully organized to form a chiasm in which episodes are inversely parallel to each other, with the scourging being the central pivot to the structure (see the diagram on p. 122).[9]

Why should the writer make the scourging of Jesus so central to his presentation? One plausible suggestion is that it is an effort to ensure that

---

9. Raymond E. Brown, *The Gospel According to John,* Anchor Bible Series (Garden City, NY: Doubleday, 1966), 859.

## The Trial Before Pilate in John

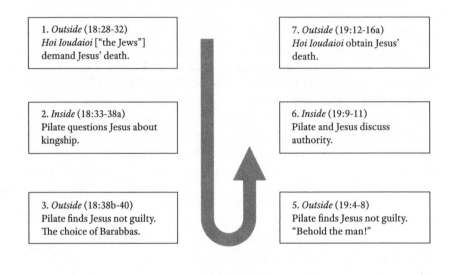

1. *Outside* (18:28-32)
*Hoi Ioudaioi* ["the Jews"]
demand Jesus' death.

7. *Outside* (19:12-16a)
*Hoi Ioudaioi* obtain Jesus'
death.

2. *Inside* (18:33-38a)
Pilate questions Jesus about
kingship.

6. *Inside* (19:9-11)
Pilate and Jesus discuss
authority.

3. *Outside* (18:38b-40)
Pilate finds Jesus not guilty.
The choice of Barabbas.

5. *Outside* (19:4-8)
Pilate finds Jesus not guilty.
"Behold the man!"

4. *Inside* (19:1-3)
Soldiers scourge Jesus.

despite the Gospel's emphasis on Jesus' divinity, his true humanity and the reality of his suffering will not be forgotten. In any case, it is evident that the decision to have Pilate scourge Jesus in an attempt to free him arises from literary, structural, and theological concerns, and not from a preserved historical memory.

### Historical Conclusions about Jesus before Pilate

Given the above considerations, the following would seem to be reasonable conclusions about the encounter of Jesus with Pilate, assuming that such an encounter indeed occurred.

The role, composition, and size of the early morning "crowd" is very unclear, especially if the Barabbas episode did not occur simultaneously with the proceedings against Jesus of Nazareth. The most plausible picture of the "crowd" is a group of priests or Temple staff who had escorted Jesus from his questioning by the high priest to Pilate.

It is impossible to discern Pilate's opinions or motives, although some extra-biblical sources portray him as a ruthless governor.[10] Whether enthusiastically or apathetically, Pilate commands that Jesus be executed as a seditious "king of the Jews" and Jesus is scourged as part of the Roman crucifixion process.

A final point should be made here. For several reasons it is significant that Jesus is killed by crucifixion, a Roman method of terrorizing subjugated peoples. For those concerned that Jesus might have been planning Passover violence, he could have been exiled or quietly assassinated. It seems someone wanted to make an example of him to deter anyone opposed to the status quo. This would seem primarily to be a Roman calculation.

## Summary and Implications for Passion Plays

1. Pilate and Caiaphas colluded in the death of Jesus. Which of the two initiated his arrest is impossible to determine. Jesus' words and deeds on behalf of a coming "Reign" or "Kingdom of God" were enough to convince Pilate that Jesus should be preemptively and publicly dispensed with as a warning to the thousands of Jewish pilgrims in Jerusalem for Passover. Jesus' Kingdom preaching and criticisms of the priestly leadership were enough to persuade Caiaphas that this popular Galilean could incite anti-Roman agitation and thus prompt the Romans to act against the people and destroy the Temple that he was responsible to protect. The high priest was not necessarily personally popular with the people, so he had additional reasons to move carefully in his efforts to maintain the peace.

2. Caiaphas orchestrated Jesus' nighttime arrest out of sight of the general public. Perhaps together with a few priestly colleagues, he questioned him and determined his disciples were not a threat. Possibly at dawn, he dispatched Jesus to Pilate for execution. This outcome was likely determined in advance, but the precise content of conversations or disagreements between Pilate and Caiaphas, or their subordinates, is inaccessible to contemporary historians. Mark 15:25 depicts Jesus be-

10. Warren Carter offers a convenient survey of the extra-biblical material in *Pontius Pilate: Portraits of a Roman Governor* (Collegeville, MN: Liturgical Press, 2003), 13-17. His conclusion after examining the four Gospel depictions is: "Pilate's truth or loyalty or faithfulness was to an empire that in its very structures established, protected, maintained, and advocated injustice to the huge detriment of most of its subjects" (159).

ing crucified at 9 a.m., before most of Jerusalem would have even been aware of Jesus' arrest, and this indicates a desire for haste before the Passover and/or the Sabbath.

3. Given all of these complexities, it is obvious that authors of passion dramatizations face several challenges. They have to deal with the apologetic and polemical aspects of passion accounts that originated decades after the events being depicted. They also have to negotiate the multi-layered historical and theological contexts, even within one specific Gospel and convert them into a dramatic medium that tends to flatten these layers down to one historical dimension. Since the Gospel narratives are fairly sparse, passion play authors also have to decide how and with what sources to supplement them.

4. In addition, they must select from among the diverse and distinctive narrative elements in the four passion narratives. Everyone who understands the Gospels to be theologically driven narratives would likely agree with the Roman Catholic instruction issued by the Bishops' Committee on Ecumenical and Interreligious Affairs that urged "the greatest caution . . . in all cases where 'it is a question of passages that seem to show the Jewish people as such in an unfavorable light.' "[11]

5. In the past, passion plays have combined the most dramatic features from the four Gospels and in the process have intensified their polemical anti-Jewish aspects:

   a. A night trial of Jesus before the entire Sanhedrin, at which the high priest declares Jesus blasphemous for claiming divine authority (Matthew and Mark).

   b. Herod Antipas being unwilling to condemn Jesus despite the chief priests' insistence (found only in Luke).

   c. Pilate having Jesus scourged in a vain attempt to placate the demands of "the Jews" (found only in John).

   d. Pilate washing his hands of responsibility for condemning Jesus before the Jewish mob that accepts guilt for his blood on themselves and their children (found only in Matthew).

6. On the other hand, one could easily combine scenes that reduce the risk of reinforcing the notion of Jewish collective guilt for Jesus' death. Specifically:

   a. Because Jesus is popular with the (Jewish) people at large, he is arrested clandestinely at night to avoid a riot (Mark 14:2).

11. BCEIA, "Criteria," C, 1, d.

b. Caiaphas fears that a riot could provoke the Romans to destroy the Temple (John 11:48).

c. Jesus is arrested by Temple guards and Roman soldiers (John 18:3).

d. Jesus is questioned about his teaching and disciples by Annas and Caiaphas and taken to Pilate (John 18:19, 24, 28).

e. Pilate was known to use violence to enforce Roman rule (Luke 13:1).

f. Jesus is charged with misleading the people, opposing the Roman tribute, and calling himself a king (Luke 23:3).

g. The "crowd" demanding Barabbas's release is prompted by the chief priests (Mark 15:11). (Note that "crowd" is not quantified. Generally, the greater its association with the priests, the less it is a sizable portion of the Jewish populace generally.)

h. Jesus was scourged as part of the Roman crucifixion procedure once Pilate ordered his execution (Mark 15:15, as against John 19:1-16).

i. Jesus was executed as a seditionist king (Mark 15:16 and parallels).

j. "A great multitude of the people" (Luke 23:27) and "all the multitudes" (Luke 23:48) of Jews are sorrowful about Jesus' crucifixion.

k. Jesus' execution was done in haste (Mark 15:25; John 19:31).

7. Both of the above lists could equally claim to be "faithful to the New Testament." But the first one amplifies Jewish culpability for the crucifixion beyond what any single Gospel account presents. Collective guilt interpretations are obviously made more likely. It could well be, then, that a particular dramatization is true to the Gospels, but that does not necessarily mean that the diverse New Testament episodes have been selected and organized responsibly.

8. From a Catholic perspective, again quoting from the U.S. Bishops' Committee on Ecumenical and Interreligious Affairs:

> A clear and precise hermeneutic [method of biblical interpretation] and a guiding artistic vision sensitive to historical fact and to the best biblical scholarship are obviously necessary. Just as obviously, it is not sufficient for the producers of passion dramatizations to respond to responsible criticism simply by appealing to the notion that "it's in the Bible." One must account for one's selections.[12]

In 1997, Saint John Paul II explicitly declared that "In the Christian world . . . erroneous and unjust interpretations of the New Testament regarding the

---

12. BCEIA, "Criteria," C, 1, c.

Jewish people and their alleged culpability [for the crucifixion] have circulated for too long, engendering feelings of hostility towards this people."[13] All preaching and teaching about the death of Jesus in a post–*Nostra Aetate* church must therefore counteract the inherited habit of attributing his execution to a collective and timeless artificial construct known as "the Jews."

13. John Paul II, "Address to Participants in the Vatican Symposium on 'The Roots of Anti-Judaism in the Christian Milieu'" (October 31, 1997), §1.

# CHAPTER 7

# Matthean Christology in a Post–*Nostra Aetate* Church

## Rereading the New Testament to Replace Replacement Theology through Contextual Rereading

This chapter, a tribute to the late Anthony J. Saldarini, provides a fitting conclusion to the first part of this book because it begins to develop a biblical theology of Christian-Jewish relations, the subject of Part Two.

On April 14, 1999, in Chicago, Anthony J. Saldarini offered one of his last public addresses, the annual Joseph Cardinal Bernardin Jerusalem Lecture. Entitled "Christian Anti-Judaism: The First Century Speaks to the Twenty-first Century,"[1] it concerned two subjects that were major features of his professional career: the Matthean community and present-day relations between Christians and Jews. He argued forcefully that Christianity has only just begun the enormous task of building a new relationship with Judaism and the Jewish people:

> Christians need to rethink and reform their theological tradition. A negative evaluation of Judaism has dominated Christian theology since the second century. This authoritative theological tradition goes by the names

---

1. In Thomas A. Baima, ed., *A Legacy of Catholic-Jewish Dialogue: The Joseph Cardinal Bernardin Jerusalem Lectures* (Chicago: Liturgy Training Publications, 2012), 75-90.

---

Adapted from "Actualizing Matthean Christology in a Post-Supersessionist Church" in Alan J. Avery-Peck, Daniel J. Harrington, and Jacob Neusner, eds., *When Judaism and Christianity Began: Essays in Memory of Anthony J. Saldarini* (Leiden and Boston: E. J. Brill, 2004): 563-576. The late Anthony J. Saldarini, a professor at Boston College, was a member of the author's dissertation committee.

supersessionism, substitution, fulfillment, and replacement. The Christian church, according to this view, is the new people of God and the true Israel founded by a new covenant. Most Christians understand this view in a fairly crass fashion. Christians have superseded Jews, that is, Christians have set aside or forced out as inferior or taken the place of Jews. The old covenant is no longer valid because it has been replaced by a new covenant. The new covenant has completed, fulfilled, or perfected the preparatory, preliminary, temporary, imperfect, limited, defective old covenant. . . .

I concede immediately that this Christian supersessionist outlook has been seriously criticized by many Christian writers and teachers since World War II. But I emphasize to you that replacement theology has not been replaced. Despite thousands of dialogues, uncounted pages of criticism and frequent ecclesiastical pronouncements, Pharisees are still hypocrites to most Christians because Matthew says so (Matt. 23) and Jews are still legalistic because Paul criticized the law. For most Christians and in most educational textbooks and ecclesiastical documents, including the recent *Catechism of the Catholic Church,* Israel has value only insofar as it has provided the foundations for the Christian church. In the view of most Christians what is good in Jewish teachings and practices has been absorbed by, integrated into and subsumed under the new, final, and fully adequate revelation from God in Jesus Christ. To put the matter bluntly, for most Christians Judaism doesn't matter after Jesus Christ.[2]

In his lecture, Professor Saldarini went on to make a number of suggestions about pursuing this needed theological reform. First, he saw a parallel between the first-century church, especially as represented by the Matthean community, and the church today. In both eras Jews and Christians "rub shoulders" on a regular basis. In the intervening centuries Christians who never met Jews were taught contempt for them on the basis of abstract religious claims. But today, when Christians and Jews (especially in the United States) actually live together, "Real conflicts can be solved and real relationships can be worked out in contrast to universal, eternal prejudices which resist reason and experience."[3] Thus, Professor Saldarini concluded that, "We may make more progress by speaking of the actual relationships of our communities in the first century as well as in the twentieth."[4] Such progress,

2. Saldarini, "Christian Anti-Judaism," 76-77.
3. Saldarini, "Christian Anti-Judaism," 84.
4. Saldarini, "Christian Anti-Judaism," 88.

he felt, was demanded because of his Catholic faith conviction that "God has called the Jewish and Christian communities to be his people in some sort of relationship with one another."[5]

Second, Professor Saldarini proposed that "the New Testament, read in context, may subvert the anti-Jewish theology which it spawned and suggest new avenues of thought." In other words, the tremendous and diverse creativity of the New Testament authors may offer insights to today's church, which is also confronted with a need for theological creativity. As Professor Saldarini explained:

[T]he flexibility and openness of the New Testament has the potential to shake Christians loose from the overdetermined traditions, attitudes and institutions which subordinate or annihilate the Jews. We need a robust, nuanced theology of Jews and Christians which grapples with the tensions and anguish of our history without the first-century polemics and the nineteen hundred years of theological anti-Judaism and social anti-Semitism.[6]

Third, Professor Saldarini cogently observed that the Christian Trinitarian tradition must be emphasized while constructing post-supersessionist theologies:

The triune Christian God is one reality with inner relations among three subsistents, the begetter, the begotten and the spirated one. [. . .] In all else, in all activity, in all relationships with humans, God is, acts, loves and saves as one, indivisibly. To say that God saves humans means that the Father saves as do the Son and the Spirit. To say that Jesus the Son of God saves is to say that God saves. When God saves Israel, in the Christian understanding of God, the Spirit of God and the Son of God as well as God the Father save Israel. God has acted and acts today in and for Israel and the church. [. . .] At the most fundamental level of theology Christians need to emphasize God more than they have and Jesus Christ as savior within the context of God's relationship to humanity. Christians too frequently center everything on Jesus to the detriment of the God who sent him, guided him and sustained him.[7]

---

5. Saldarini, "Christian Anti-Judaism," 78.
6. Saldarini, "Christian Anti-Judaism," 85.
7. Saldarini, "Christian Anti-Judaism," 89-90. Cf. my *A Story of Shalom* (New York/Mahwah: Stimulus Foundation/Paulist Press, 2001), 10, 65.

This caution against so emphasizing the salvific work of the Son that the Tri-unity of God is eclipsed (known as "Christomonism") has implications for how salvation is understood and also bears on Professor Saldarini's repeated references to "relationships," both among first- and twenty-first-century Jews and Christians, and in terms of the Triune God's interactions with humanity. They suggest that a theological emphasis on inter-relationships is necessary for the "radical intervention"[8] in the Christian religious imagination that Professor Saldarini felt is urgently required today.

## Matthean Christology

In many writings, Professor Saldarini persuasively argued that the Gospel of Matthew arose in a predominately Jewish church that was competing for influence in a Jewish world traumatized by the destruction of the Temple in 70 C.E. He claimed that this could be seen both in the harsh polemic that the evangelist directs at Pharisaic rivals and in the thoroughly Jewish categories of thought in which the Gospel operates. As he noted in the Bernardin lecture: "Matthew's Jesus fits comfortably within first-century Jewish understandings of how God guides human affairs and acts through divinely empowered agents. Typological associations of Jesus with Moses, personified Wisdom and the prophets resonate deeply with first-century Jewish understandings of history and its heroes."[9]

Indeed, a case could be made that in the Gospel of Matthew, Jesus is seen as a sort of personal reprise and culmination of preceding Jewish history (see chapter 5). Let me quickly sketch this out on the basis of fairly widespread opinions among Matthean scholars.

Matthew's infancy narrative commences with a tripartite list of Jesus' descent from Abraham that is partitioned at the reign of David (1:6) and at the Babylonian exile (1:11, 12). The evangelist explicitly draws his readers' attention to this organization of the genealogy, "So all the generations from Abraham to David are fourteen generations; and from David to the deportation to Babylon, fourteen generations; and from the deportation to Babylon to the Christ, fourteen generations" (1:17). This deliberate structure suggests that Jesus, son of Abraham, son of David, is being born "in the fullness of time," at the end of the exilic epoch. The Davidic link is very strong if, as

8. Saldarini, "Christian Anti-Judaism," 88.
9. Saldarini, "Christian Anti-Judaism," 83.

many scholars suspect, gematria was at work in the organization of three groups of fourteen generations. Thus, the name David = $d + w + d = 4 + 6 + 4 = 14$.[10] The birth of Jesus, then, represents the coming of an eschatological Davidic reign, culminating all of Israel's hopes.

As is well known, the Matthean genealogy also features five notable women who have in common unusual sexual histories. Thus, Tamar (Matt. 1:3) disguises herself as a prostitute to become pregnant by her father-in-law (Gen. 38). Rahab (Matt. 1:5) is a prostitute in Jericho who assists Joshua's spies (Josh. 2). Ruth (Matt. 1:5) is a pagan who in effect seduces her future husband (Ruth 3–4), while the wife of Uriah (Bathsheba, Matt. 1:6) commits adultery with King David (2 Sam. 11:2-5). Finally, Mary, the mother of Jesus, is found by her fiancé to be pregnant before their marriage (Matt. 1:18-25). The point of so mentioning these particular five women would seem to be that despite, or even because of, the extraordinary circumstances of their stories, God worked through them to advance divine plans for Israel. The coming of Jesus draws together and culminates the story of his people, whom he will save (1:21).

A further feature of Matthew's Gospel is that there are the numerous "fulfillment passages" that explicitly relate Jesus to the Hebrew prophets (1:22-23; 2:5-6, 14-15, 17-18, 23; 4:14; 8:17; 12:17; 13:14, 35; 21:4; 26:54, 56; 27:9). While these verses are often simply read as predictions made in Israel's past being realized in the life of Jesus, Matthew's sophisticated use of Hosea in the infancy narrative manifests a more complex engagement with Israel's scriptures. Hosea 11:1, "When Israel was a child, I loved him, and out of Egypt I called my son," is obviously referring to Israel's defining experience of God in the exodus, an event centuries in Hosea's past. Matthew is assuredly aware of this, but describes the verse as "fulfilled" centuries after the time of Hosea in the flight of the newborn Jesus to Egypt (Matt. 2:15). Since Matthew surely realized that Hosea was not making a prediction for the future by evoking Israel's foundational story from the past, it is better to understand Matthew's use of him as expressing the Matthean conviction that God's historical interactions with Israel were reprised in an intensified individual form in the life of Jesus. The same pattern can be seen in other "fulfillment passages," such as Matthew's citation of Jeremiah 31:15-17, a non-predictive lament of Israel's sufferings at the hands of the Babylonians, but which Matthew sees as "fulfilled" (i.e., recapitulated) in the grief that attends Herod's slaughter of infants (Matt. 2:17-18).

---

10. W. D. Davies and Dale C. Allison, *A Critical and Exegetical Commentary on the Gospel According to Saint Matthew,* vol. 1 (Edinburgh: T&T Clark, 1988), 161-165.

This latter passage is an example of another Matthean device; namely, allusions in his telling of the story of Jesus to famous Hebrew persons or events of the past. Thus, Jesus, like Moses, was rescued as an infant from a murderous king [2:16-18]. Joseph, his mother's husband, receives dream-messages like his biblical forebear (1:20; 2:13, 22). And perhaps most importantly, Jesus' ministry begins with three temptations in the desert that correspond to the experiences of Israel in the desert after the exodus (cf. Exod. 16:1-3; 17:1-2, 7; 32:1-4; and Matt. 4:3-10). However, where Israel son of God failed, Jesus Son of God succeeds. He is, in effect, presented as the perfect Son of Israel, the perfect Jew, doing God's will perfectly.

Beginning with B. W. Bacon,[11] some have suggested that Matthew's Gospel is organized for instructional purposes and note that it contains five sermons of Jesus (5:1–7:29; 9:36–10:42; 13:1-52; 17:22–18:35; and 23:1–25:46), possibly recalling the five books of the Torah. In the first of these — the "Sermon on the Mount" (which in Luke 6:17ff. occurs on a level place) — Jesus is depicted as a new Moses, presenting the definitive, eschatological teaching about the Torah. After stating that Jesus has come not to abolish the law or the prophets but to fulfill them (Matt. 5:17), the sermon goes on to present six pericopes in which Jesus employs the recurrent formula, "you have heard it said of old . . . but I say to you . . ." (5:21, 27, 31, 33, 38, 43). The formula indicates the superlative personal authority of the one whom Matthew has consistently portrayed as embodying and climaxing Israel's historical experience of God.

Jesus' personal authority is further illuminated in the middle of the Gospel. The Matthean Jesus is linked to the figure of the Wisdom of God who is vindicated by her deeds (11:19). She, like the Matthean Jesus, is the one whose yoke is easy and whose burden is light, and who gives comfort to those who come to her (cf. Matt. 11:19, 28-30; Sirach 6:18-37; 24:19-24; 51:23-27). There is some debate in Matthean scholarship as to whether the evangelist thinks of Jesus as the Wisdom of God personified or simply wishes to associate him with Wisdom to the ultimate degree. However, there is little doubt that he bears the authority of the Wisdom of God — that same Wisdom who in the books of Proverbs and Sirach was with God at the creation, took up her abode in Israel, dwelt in the Temple, and was enshrined in the Torah. This explains why in the Sermon on the Mount the Matthean Jesus is able on the basis of his personal authority ("*I* say to you . . .") to teach the Torah definitively. If the Torah expresses God's Wisdom in written form, then

---

11. Benjamin Wisner Bacon, *Studies in Matthew* (New York: H. Holt, 1930).

who better to define its meaning than the one who virtually makes Wisdom present as the perfect son of Abraham? As Matthew puts it in chapter 12, in Jesus is something greater than the Temple (12:6, where according to Sirach 24:10 Wisdom has taken up her abode). The Matthean Jesus is greater than the prophet Jonah who caused the pagan superpower of his day to repent (12:41), and he is greater than Solomon, famed for the depth of the wisdom he had received from God (12:42).

To sum up, Matthew's portrayal of Jesus shows him as both the recapitulation and climax of Israel's long history of relationship with God, and also as one with divine authority to teach God's will conclusively. Jesus' disciples, Matthew's church, are to carry this teaching everywhere with the assurance that the one who has been given all authority in heaven and on earth will be with them always until the eschaton is established in its fullness (Matt. 28:18-20).

## Actualizing Matthean Christology Today

Matthew's exposition of the significance of Jesus Christ was naturally shaped by his social circumstance of competition for influence in the post-Temple Jewish world. As Professor Saldarini observed, the Matthean "Jesus is presented as a divinely warranted teacher who is messianic ruler and eschatological judge. Jesus' status and access to God, according to Matthew, transcend any authority found elsewhere in the Jewish community."[12]

Christianity is not in the same historical situation today. As a distinct, even if related, religious tradition, the overwhelming majority of Christians are not competing with Jewish leaders for influence over Jewish communities.[13] Nor do Christians today share Matthew's imminent eschatological

---

12. Anthony J. Saldarini, *Matthew's Christian-Jewish Community* (Chicago/London: University of Chicago Press, 1994), 178.

13. I include the caveat "overwhelming majority," to acknowledge the existence of self-identified "messianic Jews" or "Jews for Jesus" who can be understood as competing with today's rabbinic authorities for the hearts and minds of Jews, seemingly especially those who are not well educated in the rabbinic tradition. Their understanding of Christianity can deny religious legitimacy to rabbinic Judaism whose adherents are not "saved" unless they acknowledge Jesus as their messiah. The ongoing vitality of rabbinic Judaism is absorbed into various eschatological scenarios that often include an ingathering of Jews into the modern State of Israel. In this they differ from major Christian denominations that are coming to a deeper appreciation of rabbinic Judaism in terms of its own religious experience.

expectations, which, even if not as intense as some other New Testament writers, hardly anticipated that untold millennia would transpire before the establishment of the Age to Come. Thus, Christians today can encounter a dynamic Jewish tradition that has evolved over time from roots in rabbinic traditions that were not written until after Matthew's generation. Finally, most churches today have begun to grapple with the awful legacy of the Shoah, a horror that was made possible by Christian anti-Jewish theologies. Those replacement or supersessionist theologies made use of Matthew's polemics in ways that the evangelist who wrote, "by their fruits you shall know them" (Matt. 7:16, 20) would presumably disavow if he could.

This brings us to the question of actualization. How should Christians bring the Matthean scriptures to life in our world today? Can we, as Professor Saldarini suggested, creatively develop "new avenues of thought" by re-reading the New Testament in context?

A word about the meaning of "actualization" is in order here. In my own Roman Catholic tradition, biblical interpretation is understood to involve a dialogue between present-day faith communities and those communities of long ago in which the biblical texts were composed. As the Pontifical Biblical Commission describes it, "Such dialogue will mean establishing a relationship of continuity. It will also involve acknowledging differences. Hence the interpretation of Scripture involves a work of sifting and setting aside; it stands in continuity with earlier exegetical traditions, many elements of which it preserves and makes its own; but in other matters it will go its own way, seeking to make further progress."[14]

Therefore, how is the Matthean context of rivalry with his Jewish contemporaries to be "set aside" in the Christian community of the twenty-first century? How do Christians preserve and make Matthew's christological insights their own without perpetuating its associated polemic? Is it possible to disentangle the two? Frankly, it must be if Christianity is to be ethically credible in a post-Shoah world.

In the Roman Catholic tradition, which has officially rejected the idea that God had cursed the Jewish people for the eternal blood guilt of the crucifixion (a perennial construal of Matt. 27:25), the challenge has been put very pointedly by the Pontifical Biblical Commission:

Particular attention is necessary, according to the spirit of the Second Vatican Council (*Nostra Aetate,* 4), to avoid absolutely any actualization

14. PBC, "The Interpretation of the Bible in the Church" (1993), III, A.

of certain texts of the New Testament which could provoke or reinforce unfavorable attitudes toward the Jewish people. The tragic events of the past must, on the contrary, impel all to keep unceasing in mind that, according to the New Testament, the Jews remain "beloved" of God, "since the gifts and calling of God are irrevocable" (Rom. 11:28-29).[15]

In his Bernardin lecture, Professor Saldarini asked, "So how shall Christians speak of God, Jesus Christ, Israel and the church?"[16]

If Christian theological teaching does not change, then Christian thought and attitudes will not change and, inevitably, the traditional anti-Jewish teachings will reappear in new ways and anti-Semitism will go on and on. The problem of anti-Semitism in the Christian community and of anti-Judaism in Christian theology is rooted in the New Testament, has flourished in almost all Christian theologies and societies for centuries and is alive and well today despite massive efforts by Jews and Christians since World War II. Radical intervention is required.[17]

For the purposes of this chapter, allow me to focus the question this way: can Matthew's christological approach be actualized in a post-supersessionist church so as to theologically ground an affirmative relationship between the present-day Jewish and Christian communities? Can Christians today conceive of Christ Jesus in ways that are predicated on respect for the dynamism of Jewish covenantal life over the intervening centuries since Matthew's day?

Taking a cue from Matthew's depiction of Jesus as the embodiment of Israel's experience of God, as the perfect Jew, and as the human expression of God's divine Wisdom, I would suggest that today we articulate the church's christological traditional in relational terms. By this I mean an approach to the "being-ness" or ontological nature of some existing thing which stresses its interrelationships with other things that exist. Being "human," for example, is largely determined by an individual's interactions with others over the course of a lifetime. This is so much the case that children raised with little or no human contact develop grave personality impairments.

So, too, the human Jesus was "formed" in his humanity through his upbringing and life in the rich heritage of the Jewish people of the late Second

---

15. "Interpretation of the Bible in the Church," IV, A, 3.
16. Saldarini, "Christian Anti-Judaism," 88.
17. Saldarini, "Christian Anti-Judaism," 87-88.

Temple period. Christian faith understands Jesus also as the divine *Logos* of God incarnate, but that "Word" is defined through interrelationship with the other subsistents of the Triune One. A relational approach to the divine *Logos* leads to a more dynamic understanding of the *Logos*. God's revealing Word is not so much disclosing factual data to the human beings it inspires, as it is inviting human beings into relationship with God.

Thus, it is the church's experience that Jesus Christ incarnates both Israel's covenantal relationship with God and God's constant divine self-revealing Word that brings people into relationship with the Triune God.

By embodying Israel's covenantal life with God, Jesus, the faithful Son of Israel, epitomized what life in covenant was and is all about. Covenant is a sharing, a walking in life together that brings mutual responsibilities to the participants in it. Israel's experience of being in covenant with God and of trying to walk in God's Way has included times of disaster and suffering that were brought about by a combination of internal failings and external Gentile hostility. However, the People of Israel have also experienced restorations and revivals after these calamities.

For Christians, Jesus walked God's Way with perfect fidelity and epitomized the perfect Jewish covenantal partner. Like Israel, he suffered for his faithfulness to God. He also experienced a divine covenantal restoration after his suffering that was uniquely eschatological in nature, a raising up to transcendent life that showed that death itself would be defeated in the inevitable Reign of God. The revelation of this exaltation discloses to the church the identity of Jesus as the Triune God's Word that invites people into relationship. Through Christ, through the Crucified and Raised Jew, the church continuously encounters God's sustaining invitation to and empowerment of covenantal life. Jesus Christ brings the church into an ongoing covenant with Israel's God. God's will for the church, now having become a Gentile assembly with deep roots in Israel's story, is made known through its Christ-shaped encounter with God.

If Jesus Christ is understood as personifying Israel's covenanting with God, and thereby making possible a similar if distinctive life for the church, then Israel's covenanting with God in biblical times and down to the present must be permanent and vital. This would explain why the church knows its own covenanting with God through Christ to also be permanent and vital. If Israel's covenanting could be obsolete or inert, then Christ would be mediating and inviting the church to a relationship with God that is also susceptible to being rendered outmoded by God. This is unimaginable. It would be contrary to the character of the God of Israel and of Jesus to establish a covenantal bonding that was not founded upon divine fidelity and empower-ment.[18] A Matthean Christology actualized in a post-supersessionist church can affirm Jesus as epitomizing and mediating Israel's covenanting life, and would thereby necessarily affirm the "covenant of eternal love which was never revoked"[19] between God and the Jewish people.

This relational approach to Matthew's Christology, namely, understand-ing Jesus Christ as embodying Israel's covenantal life and experiences, pro-duces helpful (and necessary) interconnections with the Christian Trinitar-ian tradition, especially if that is also understood relationally. As Professor Saldarini noted in his Bernardin lecture using classical Christian terms, "The triune Christian God is one reality with inner relations among three subsis-tents, the begetter, the begotten and the spirated one, or more familiarly, the Father, Son and Holy Spirit. In all else, in all activity, in all relationships with humans, God is, acts, loves and saves as one, indivisibly." But if everything that God does is done "as one, indivisibly," then that must also be true for divine interactions with humanity.

Expressing this relationally, the church knows God as constantly and simultaneously creating-sustaining, inviting into relationship, and empow-ering that invitation's acceptance. Everything that God is and does the three "subsistents" participate in utterly and totally. If that "subsistent" tradition-ally called the *Logos* is conceived relationally as the constant divine invitation into covenanting relationship, then humans are being invited into a sharing in life with God that mirrors on a mortal scale the inner relationality of the Triune God. Christians might say that the divine invitation to relationship that the church finds embodied in Jesus Christ draws people into the very way of life of the Triune God.

Without excessively developing an aspect of the Johannine tradition in a chapter devoted to Matthean thought, this concept is essentially the mutual indwelling *(perichoresis)* formulation of the Gospel of John. That text por-trays the Father, Son, and Spirit as "abiding in" one another. In Johannine terms eternal life is a sharing in the love-relationship between the Father and the Son in the Spirit. It is a love-life that transcends human death.

Thus one can say that the *Logos,* God's constant outreach for relation-

18. See BCL, "God's Mercy Endures Forever" (1988), 8: "[F]alse or demeaning portraits of a repudiated Israel may undermine Christianity as well. How can one confidently affirm the truth of God's covenant with all humanity and creation in Christ (see Rom 8:21) without at the same time affirming God's faithfulness to the Covenant with Israel that also lies at the heart of the biblical testimony?"

19. John Paul II, "Address to Jewish Leaders in Miami" (Sept. 11, 1987).

ship, brings into human history the very covenanting life of the Trinity. The immanent Trinity, the essential relationality of God within Godself, therefore necessarily coheres with the relational actions of the economic Trinity in human history. Both the People of Israel and the people of Christ are covenanting in their distinctive yet analogous ways with the One who summons humanity to live in the divine image. They experience and define their relationship with God differently, one through Torah and the other through Christ. However, Christians would say that both communities have entered into covenant with God through the agency of the divine *Logos,* whose invitation to divine relationship is sustained and enabled by the continuous actions of the other subsistents of the Triune One.

Jews and Christians are thus co-covenanting partners with God. It stands to reason that covenantal partners with the same relational One would be obligated to be partners with one another. For Christians, our covenant with the Triune One impels us to be open to sharing-in-life with others in covenant with that One, even if their covenanting is not Christ-shaped as ours is.

This theological approach to Christian self-understanding, significantly inspired by Matthean perspectives, understands Christ as embodying and mediating Israel's covenanting with God and apprehends the Triune One's innate relationality as defining all of God's actions in human history. It precludes hostility to the Jewish people and tradition since they are co-covenanting with the same God. It corroborates and justifies the conviction expressed by Anthony J. Saldarini that "God has called the Jewish and Christian communities to be his people in . . . relationship with one another."[20]

---

20. Saldarini, "Christian Anti-Judaism," 78.

# PART TWO

# THEOLOGY

# CHAPTER 8

# Nostra Aetate and the "Beginning of a New Beginning"

## Introduction

Part One of this volume explored the renaissance in Catholic biblical scholarship in the second half of the twentieth century, paying particular attention to its implications for new ways of understanding the church's relationship with the Jewish people. Naturally, since "all the preaching of the Church must be nourished and regulated by Sacred Scripture,"[1] new scriptural insights into the Christian and Jewish relationship automatically produce consequences for Christian theology. That was evident in chapter 7, but here in Part Two theological topics will receive extended treatment. We begin by examining the other relevant post–World War II "trajectory" of Catholic thought first noted in chapter 1, namely, the church's unprecedented exploration of its understanding of Jewish covenantal life. By this phrase and similar ones throughout this book, such as "Israel's covenanting," I intend to assert both that the covenantal bond between God and the Jewish people has never been revoked *and* that this bond is organically related to the church's covenanting in Christ.

In terms of authoritative ecclesial teaching, this trajectory began with the Second Vatican Council's 1965 Declaration on the Relationship of the

---

1. Second Vatican Council, *Dei Verbum:* The Dogmatic Constitution on Divine Revelation (1965), VI, 21.

---

This chapter expands and updates my "How *Nostra Aetate* Transformed the Jewish-Catholic Relationship: 'The Beginning of the Beginning,'" in Eric J. Greenberg, ed., *Transforming the Catholic-Jewish Relationship:* Nostra Aetate *on Its Fortieth Anniversary* (New York: Anti-Defamation League, 2005), 33-45.

Church to Non-Christian Religions, known by its opening Latin words, *Nostra Aetate*, "In our time" or "In our age." It is rightly described as a revolutionary document. Although it was the first authoritative conciliar and magisterial statement in history to address the Catholic Church's relations with the Jewish people and tradition, it effectively reversed centuries and centuries of standard Christian presuppositions and teachings about Jews. It launched a process of unprecedented Catholic reform and creativity, as will be considered in the following chapters. Its impact continues to be felt as we observe the declaration's fiftieth anniversary, even though — in the words of Cardinal Walter Kasper, past president of the Pontifical Commission for Religious Relations with the Jews — we are probably still only at "the beginning of a new beginning"[2] of a deep-seated process of reform.

Indeed, the renewal catalyzed by *Nostra Aetate* can properly be described by the Greek word *metanoia*, in Hebrew *teshuvah*, a complete "turning," a total reorientation of attitude or action. This can be demonstrated by considering Catholic perspectives before 1965, the story of the composition of the document, and how its key points have developed over the past five decades. This chapter will concentrate on the declaration's importance for Catholic-Jewish relations, the original concern from which eventually emerged the final version that discussed all the world's religions.

## The Catholic Theological Stance toward Jews and Judaism before *Nostra Aetate*

The *metanoia*, the turnaround represented by *Nostra Aetate*, becomes strikingly clear if one contrasts pre–Vatican II Catholic understandings with those that began to arise subsequently. In 1938, Pope Pius XI commissioned the preparation of an encyclical letter that ultimately was never promulgated. To be titled *Humani Generis Unitas* ("The Unity of the Human Race"), this letter was intended to condemn racism in the wake of Hitler's rise to power in Germany. A section of the draft of the encyclical dealing with antisemitism provides a convenient synopsis of pre–Vatican II Catholic theological perspectives on Jews and Judaism.[3]

2. Walter Cardinal Kasper, "Foreword," in Philip A. Cunningham et al., eds. *Christ Jesus and the Jewish People Today* (Grand Rapids: Eerdmans, 2011), p. xiv.

3. See Georges Passelecq and Bernard Suchecky, *The Hidden Encyclical of Pius XI* (New York: Harcourt, Brace, and Co., 1997). For new insights into the fate of the draft, see also

While rebuking Nazi policies through which "millions of [Jewish] persons are deprived of the most elementary rights and privileges of citizens,"[4] the draft goes on to state that there is an "authentic basis of the social separation of the Jews from the rest of humanity."[5] This "authentic" reason for discrimination was not because of race but because of religion: "The Savior . . . was rejected by that people, violently repudiated, and condemned as a criminal by the highest tribunals of the Jewish nation. . . . [However,] the very act by which the Jewish people put to death their Savior and King was . . . the salvation of the world."[6]

Having asserted that the "Jewish nation" bore a collective responsibility for the death of Jesus, the draft claims that Jews were doomed "to perpetually wander over the face of the earth . . . [were] never allowed to perish, but have been preserved through the ages into our own time."[7] The draft went on to opine that there exists "a historic enmity of the Jewish people to Christianity, creating a perpetual tension between Jew and Gentile."[8] Therefore, it alleges that the church has constantly had to be on guard against "the spiritual dangers to which contact with the Jews can expose souls."[9] This danger, which "is not diminished in our own time,"[10] was "the authentic basis of the social separation of the Jews from the rest of humanity."[11]

It must be stressed that this draft was never promulgated. Clearly, the drafters of this text operated with theological ideas about Jews that undermined their ability to condemn the racist policies of the Nazis. Indeed, the "social separation of the Jews from the rest of humanity" was a goal that Hitler could claim he was merely implementing.

The draft's main theological positions about Jews — that they had killed Christ, that they were doomed to eternal wandering, and that they posed a constant danger to Christian souls — were simply restatements of elements of the perennial Christian "teaching of contempt"[12] that had persisted for

---

David I. Kertzer, *The Pope and Mussolini: The Secret History of Pius XI and the Rise of Fascism in Europe* (New York: Random House, 2014), 287-289, 291, 332, 363-364, 369, 373, 491 n. 31.

4. Passelecq and Suchecky, *The Hidden Encyclical*, 246.

5. Passelecq and Suchecky, *The Hidden Encyclical*, 247.

6. Passelecq and Suchecky, *The Hidden Encyclical*, 248-249.

7. Passelecq and Suchecky, *The Hidden Encyclical*, 249.

8. Passelecq and Suchecky, *The Hidden Encyclical*, 251-252.

9. Passelecq and Suchecky, *The Hidden Encyclical*, 252.

10. Passelecq and Suchecky, *The Hidden Encyclical*, 252.

11. Passelecq and Suchecky, *The Hidden Encyclical*, 247.

12. The phrase was coined by the French historian Jules Isaac in his book *The Teaching of Contempt: Christian Roots of Anti-Semitism* (New York: Holt, Rinehart & Winston, 1964).

over 1500 years.[13] In the words of Cardinal Edward Cassidy, president of the Pontifical Commission for Religious Relations with the Jews from 1989-2000, "preaching accused the Jews of every age of deicide."[14] While this anti-Jewish theology was never defined by a church council or pope as formal doctrine, it pervaded Christian thought so thoroughly and for so long that it unquestionably is an expression of what is called the ordinary magisterium of the church.[15]

However, one long-standing Christian belief did not appear in the draft of *Humani Generis Unitas*. This is the notion that God's covenant with the Jewish people, and hence their calling as God's Chosen People, had ended because of the crucifixion of Jesus and had been transferred to the church.[16] Notably, the draft asserted:

> Israel remains the chosen people, for its election has never been revoked. Through the ineffable mercy of God, Israel may also share in the redemption that Israel's own rejection has made available to the Gentiles, who had themselves been unbelievers.[17]

> [St. Paul] holds out still the possibility of salvation to the Jews, once they are converted from their sins, and return to the spiritual tradition of Israel, which is properly theirs by their historic past and calling. . . .[18]

Key to analyzing these comments theologically is the phrase, "return to the spiritual tradition of Israel." The authors of the draft apparently believed that their Jewish contemporaries had departed from Israel's heritage by failing to enter the church. Israel here is understood as biblical Israel, whose traditions are significant to the authors only because they prepared for the

13. See the quotations from Justin, Melito, and Origen provided in chapter 3 above for pivotal expressions of the teaching of contempt during the church's formative centuries.

14. Cassidy, Edward Idris Cardinal, "Reflections: The Vatican Statement on the Shoah," *Origins* 28/2 (May 28, 1998): 31.

15. Which is why one of the theological experts who helped draft *Nostra Aetate* could say that the declaration represented the Second Vatican Council's most radical revision of the ordinary magisterium. See Gregory Baum, "The Social Context of American Catholic Theology," *Proceedings of the Catholic Theological Society of America* 41 (1986): 87, cited by John Pawlikowski, "Historical Memory and Christian-Jewish Relations," in Cunningham et al., eds., *Christ Jesus and the Jewish People Today,* 16.

16. As in Origen, *Contra Celsum,* IV, 22.

17. Passelecq and Suchecky, *Hidden Encyclical,* 251.

18. Passelecq and Suchecky, *Hidden Encyclical,* 250.

coming of Christ and the church. Thus, their argument is that while Jews remain the Chosen People, they have betrayed their own spiritual heritage because of their rejection of the Christian message. In this wayward state, they stand outside of salvation despite their chosen status.

## The Conception and Gestation of *Nostra Aetate*

Such was the Catholic theological landscape when a papal conclave elected Pope John XXIII on October 20, 1958. As a Vatican diplomat during the Second World War, Angelo Roncalli had facilitated the escape of thousands of Jews from the Nazis. His experiences surely motivated him when he became pope. On March 21, 1959, only two months after announcing that a great council would be held, he ordered the removal of the word *perfidus* from the Good Friday prayer for the Jews. The next year, John XXIII greeted a delegation of American Jews with the biblical words, "I am Joseph your brother," suggesting that reconciliation between Catholic and Jews — something akin to the Genesis reconciliation between the biblical Joseph and the brothers who had subjugated him — was imaginable. Most importantly, on September 18, 1960, he directed Cardinal Augustin Bea, S.J., president of the Secretariat for Promoting Christian Unity, to prepare a draft declaration for the upcoming council that would address the relations between the church and the People of Israel.

However, the process of bringing *Nostra Aetate* to birth was a prolonged and difficult labor. Despite John XXIII's desire, it was not clear whether the proposed statement should be a free-standing document, part of the planned constitution of the church, part of an ecumenical text on Christian unity, or, as ultimately happened, be contained within a declaration on the church's relations with the other religions of the world. After all the bishops assembled in 1962, it became clear that there was opposition to the endeavor from both inside and outside the Council. Some bishops recoiled at the thought of changing long-standing teachings, while others feared for the safety of Christians in Arab countries. The press offices of various Middle-Eastern countries publicly campaigned against any statement that absolved "the Jews" of the crime of crucifying Jesus. Various procedural maneuvers were employed in an effort to stymie the document.[19]

19. For further details see Giovanni Miccoli, "Two Sensitive Issues: Religious Freedom and the Jews," in Giuseppe Albergio and Joseph A. Komonchak, eds., *History of Vatican II*, vol. 4, *Church as Communion: Third Period and Intersession, September 1964–September 1965*

The eventual decision to address Judaism within the larger context of all the world's religions was a compromise that weakened the text's stress on the unique relationship between the church and Judaism, but was necessary, in the colorful imagery of Cardinal Kasper, "in order to save the furniture from the burning house."[20] Despite these travails, on October 28, 1965, the declaration was officially promulgated after a final, overwhelmingly favorable vote of 2,221 bishops for and 88 against.[21] For the first time in its almost two thousand year history, a formal council of the Catholic Church had issued an authoritative declaration on the Catholic-Jewish relationship.

## The Teaching of *Nostra Aetate*

Although chapter 4 of the declaration, the section concerning Jews and Judaism, is fairly brief, over the ensuing five decades it has proven to be tremendously influential. While the following chapters in this book will detail the developments in subsequent ecclesial documents, the seven items below summarize *Nostra Aetate*'s main points and also briefly note in passing some important later elaborations. Some continuing questions and issues will also be sketched (see chapter 9 for a fuller treatment of the later developments).

A. *Nostra Aetate* **repudiated the long-standing "deicide" charge** by declaring that "Jews should not be spoken of as rejected or accursed as if this followed from holy scripture." This refutation of any notion of a divine curse upon Jews for "killing God" was an explicit reversal of a presupposition held universally by Christians for more than a millennium. No longer was it permissible for "preaching [to] accuse the Jews of deicide," as Cardinal Cassidy had put it. This fact alone justifies describing the declaration as revolutionary.

---

(Maryknoll, NY, and Leuven, Belgium: Orbis Books and Peeters, 2003): 95-193; John W. O'Malley, *What Happened at Vatican II* (Cambridge, MA: Harvard University Press, 2008), 218-226, 250-252, 275-277; Alberto Melloni, "*Nostra Aetate* and the Discovery of the Sacrament of Otherness," in Philip A. Cunningham, Norbert J. Hofmann, SDB, and Joseph Sievers, eds., *The Catholic Church and the Jewish People: Recent Reflections from Rome* (New York: Fordham University Press, 2007), 129-151.

20. Walter Kasper, "The Commission for Religious Relations with the Jews: A Crucial Endeavour of the Catholic Church," address delivered at Boston College, Nov. 6, 2002.

21. See John M. Oesterreicher, *The New Encounter between Christians and Jews* (New York: Philosophical Library, 1986), for the story of the development of *Nostra Aetate*.

B. *Nostra Aetate* **stressed the religious bond and spiritual legacy shared by Jews and Christians.** It acknowledged the Jewishness of Jesus, his mother, and the apostles, and recognized Christianity's debt to biblical Israel. This has become foundational for subsequent Catholic ecclesiastical and theological writings. To offer just one illustration, Saint John Paul II would later write movingly that "Jesus also came humanly to know [Israel's scriptures]; he nourished his mind and heart with them, using them in prayer and as an inspiration for his actions. Thus he became an authentic son of Israel, deeply rooted in his own people's long history."[22]

To reflect on the subject of the Jewishness of Jesus as understood in the Catholic community today, it seems to me to be an open question whether most Christians in their religious imaginations really picture Jesus as "fully a man of his time, and of his environment — the Jewish Palestinian one of the first century, the anxieties and hopes of which he shared,"[23] or if they envision of him purely in terms of later Christian concepts. Lingering habits of imagining Jesus as adverse to an alleged heartlessness or legalism among contemporary Jews inhibit a full appreciation of Jesus' Jewishness.[24] Likewise, understanding what could be called the Jewishness of the early church — in other words, that the church was for many decades a movement *within* the diverse late Second Temple period Jewish world — has not really penetrated Christian thinking at large, which is more comfortable thinking of a church cleanly and distinctively separated, and even opposed to "Judaism" from as early as Pentecost, if not from Jesus' ministry itself.

On the other hand, the spiritual connectedness between the two traditions has been strongly emphasized since *Nostra Aetate,* perhaps most powerfully during John Paul II's historic visit to the Great Synagogue of Rome: "The Jewish religion is not 'extrinsic' to us, but in a certain way is 'intrinsic' to our own religion," he declared. "With Judaism therefore we have a relationship which we do not have with any other religion. You are our dearly beloved brothers and, in a certain way, it

---

22. John Paul II, "Address to the Pontifical Biblical Commission," April 11, 1997.

23. Vatican, "Notes" (1985), III, 1.

24. For important explorations of this topic, see Hans Hermann Henrix, "The Son of God Became Human as a Jew: Implications of the Jewishness of Jesus for Christology," and Barbara U. Meyer, "The Dogmatic Significance of Christ Being Jewish," in Cunningham et al., eds., *Christ Jesus and the Jewish People Today,* respectively 114-143 and 144-156. In the same volume see the response by Edward Kessler, "A Jewish Response to Hans Hermann Henrix and Barbara Meyer," 157-163.

could be said that you are our elder brothers."[25] This familial attitude has been widely disseminated and reiterated by Popes Benedict XVI and Francis.[26]

C. *Nostra Aetate* **strongly implied that God and Jews abide in covenant.** Following logically from its rejection of the idea that the Jewish people lay under a divine curse, the Council Fathers cited Romans 11:28 to observe that "the Jews remain very dear to God, for the sake of the patriarchs, since God does not take back the gifts he bestowed or the choice he made." This was reinforced, as Eugene J. Fisher has pointed out,[27] when *Nostra Aetate* rendered an ambiguous Greek verb in Romans 9:4-5 in the present tense: "They *are* Israelites and it is for them *to be* sons and daughters, to them *belong* the glory, the covenants, the giving of the law, the worship, and the promises; to them *belong* the patriarchs, and of their race according to the flesh, is the Christ."

*Nostra Aetate*'s implicit recognition that Israel abides in a perpetual covenantal relationship with God has subsequently been made fully explicit. John Paul II repeatedly taught that Jews are "the people of God of the Old Covenant, never revoked by God,"[28] "the present-day people of the covenant concluded with Moses,"[29] and "partners in a covenant of eternal love which was never revoked."[30]

It should be observed that the draft for the unrealized encyclical *Humani Generis Unitas* could also state that Israel's "election has never been revoked,"[31] but after the Second Vatican Council it was no longer possible to subordinate this notion to an alleged divine curse on Jews for the death of Jesus as the draft had done. Therefore, post–*Nostra Aetate* Catholic teaching has proceeded from a renewed awareness of the perpetuity of the Jewish people's covenant with God to unprecedented expressions of admiration for the post-biblical Jewish religious tradition (see chapter 9).

25. John Paul II, "Address at the Great Synagogue of Rome," April 13, 1986, 4.

26. For example, Pope Benedict XVI, "Address at the Great Synagogue of Rome" (January 17, 2010), and Pope Francis, Apostolic Exhortation *Evangelii Gaudium* (January 24, 2014), §§247-249.

27. Eugene J. Fisher, "Official Roman Catholic Teaching on Jews and Judaism: Commentary and Context," in *In Our Time: The Flowering of Jewish-Catholic Dialogue,* ed. Eugene J. Fisher and Leon Klenicki (New York/Mahwah: Paulist Press, 1990), 6.

28. John Paul II, "Address to the Jewish Community in Mainz, West Germany," November 17, 1980.

29. John Paul II, "Address to the Jewish Community in Mainz, West Germany."

30. John Paul II, "Address to Jewish Leaders in Miami," September 11, 1987.

31. Passelecq and Suchecky, *Hidden Encyclical,* 251.

D. *Nostra Aetate* deplored "all hatreds, persecutions, displays of antisemitism directed against the Jews at any time or from any source." While *Nostra Aetate* did not confess *Christian* antisemitism or discuss the perennial Christian teaching of contempt for Jews, later ecclesial documents acknowledged Christian wrongdoing and labeled antisemitism as a sin against God and humanity. John Paul II, for instance, would insist that a confrontation with the horrors of the Shoah must lead the church to repentance. "For Christians the heavy burden of guilt for the murder of the Jewish people [during the Shoah] must be an enduring call to repentance; thereby we can overcome every form of antisemitism and establish a new relationship with our kindred nation of the Old Covenant."[32] He also related this moral and spiritual challenge to the proper observance of the beginning of the third millennium of Christianity. Thus, on the First Sunday of Lent during the Great Jubilee of 2000, an unprecedented "Mass of Pardon" was offered at St. Peter's Basilica. The highest officials of the Roman Catholic Church joined with the pope in asking God's forgiveness for the sins of Christians during the previous millennium. Among the sins confessed was the teaching of contempt and Christianity's treatment of "the People of Israel." Christian penitence has perhaps been expressed most iconically to date in Pope John Paul II's prayer at the Western Wall on March 26, 2000. Following the Jewish custom of inserting written prayers into the remains of the foundations of the Second Temple, John Paul II placed these words: "God of our fathers, you chose Abraham and his descendants to bring your Name to the Nations: we are deeply saddened by the behavior of those who in the course of history have caused these children of yours to suffer, and asking your forgiveness we wish to commit ourselves to genuine brotherhood with the people of the Covenant."[33] The prayer was signed by the pope personally and stamped with the official papal seal, as if to establish without question the seriousness and permanence of the Catholic Church's ongoing commitment to reform and fellowship with the Jewish people. This is yet another manifestation of *metanoia* since such authoritative public expressions of remorse and solidarity were unheard of before *Nostra Aetate*.

E. *Nostra Aetate* **stressed the need for accurate biblical interpretation**

---

32. John Paul II, "Address to the New Ambassador of the Federal Republic of Germany to the Holy See," November 8, 1990.

33. John Paul II, "Prayer at the Western Wall," March 26, 2000.

and religious education: "all must take care, lest in catechizing or in preaching the word of God, they teach anything which is not in accord with the truth of the Gospel message or the spirit of Christ." This sentence introduced a hermeneutical principle for Catholic biblical interpretation that has been further intensified in later documents.[34]

Of particular note are studies issued by the Pontifical Biblical Commission in 1993 and 2001. Especially significant is the instruction in the 1993 text that:

> Clearly to be rejected also is every attempt . . . [to use] the Bible to justify racial segregation, anti-Semitism, or sexism whether on the part of men or women. Particular attention is necessary, according to the spirit of the Second Vatican Council (*Nostra Aetate,* 4), to avoid absolutely any actualization of certain texts of the New Testament which could provoke or reinforce unfavorable attitudes toward the Jewish people. The tragic events of the past must, on the contrary, impel all to keep unceasing in mind that, according to the New Testament, the Jews remain "beloved" of God, "since the gifts and calling of God are irrevocable" (Rom. 11:28-29).[35]

F. *Nostra Aetate* **called for Catholics and Jews to collaborate in "biblical and theological enquiry and . . . friendly discussions."** This mandate directly contradicted the prior practice of discouraging Catholics from conversing with Jews on religious matters, as expressed by the worry in the draft of *Humani Generis Unitas* about "the spiritual dangers to which contact with the Jews can expose souls."[36] This reversal has contributed to an enormous number of dialogues on all levels around the world, to the establishment in the United States alone of over three dozen academic centers to promote Christian-Jewish studies,[37] and to many joint research initiatives among Jewish and Christian scholars. Such continuing research is bringing to light new evidence of how the Jewish and Christian communities have been interacting — both negatively and positively — for centuries. This ongoing interaction has exerted a major influence on how both traditions live out their covenantal relationship with God.

34. Eugene J. Fisher, "Official Roman Catholic Teaching," 7.
35. PBC, "Interpretation of the Bible in the Church" (1993), IV, A, 3.
36. Passelecq and Suchecky, *Hidden Encyclical,* 252.
37. See the webpages of the Council of Centers for Jewish-Christian Relations (CCJR) at www.ccjr.us.

The past fifty years of dialogue and joint activities that *Nostra Aetate* made possible have also shown that Jews and Christians come together with different interests, concerns, historical knowledge, and (mis)conceptions about each other. Christians tend to want to talk "religion," including why Jews don't "believe in Jesus." Jews, understandably, tend to wonder if the unprecedented Christian overtures to dialogue are only a temporary cessation of the conversionary campaigns of the past, while Christians, usually unfamiliar with the history of Christian oppression of Jews, can be shocked and guilt-ridden when learning of it for the first time. Christians may find it difficult to understand the depth of Jewish anxiety for the survival of the State of Israel or fear over antisemitic incidents, while Jews tend to avoid expressing their general mystification over Christian claims that something called "salvation" is the result of the crucifixion of an individual Jew among the thousands of Jews executed under Roman imperial rule.

Sometimes lurking beneath the surface of interreligious encounters is a fear of what the dialogue will lead to. Co-religionists who have not had much experience of Christian-Jewish dialogue will accuse Christians of "compromising their faith" and will charge Jewish participants with inviting "assimilation."

However, time has shown that authentic interreligious dialogue has nothing to do with syncretism, or some sort of melding of two religious traditions. The boundaries between the two related heritages of Christianity and Judaism must be respected and maintained. However, the dialogue may cause those boundaries to be reconfigured or understood differently.

Fortunately, the past five decades have demonstrated that interreligious dialogue actually leads participants to a deeper understanding of their own tradition as a result of being asked new questions or of viewing their own tradition from the other's perspective. They are not the same Christians or Jews that they were before experiencing dialogue, but they understand themselves to be more committed and discerning Christians or Jews. This transformation in self-understanding can be expected to continue to evolve in the twenty-first century.

G. *Nostra Aetate* **expressed no interest in further efforts to baptize Jews.** "Together with the prophets and that same apostle [Paul], the church awaits the day, known to God alone, when all peoples will call on God with one voice and serve him shoulder to shoulder." This phrase was carefully considered during the Council's deliberations, especially after controversy arose in the public media in the summer and fall of 1964 over whether a leaked draft paragraph would encourage Catholics to try to convert Jews. Famed Rabbi Abraham Joshua Heschel repeatedly and sensationally declared that he was "ready to go to Auschwitz any time, if faced with the alternative of conversion or death."[38]

This was the context for two crucial days of deliberation in the Second Vatican Council on September 28 and 29, 1964.[39] Several cardinals and bishops specifically addressed the topic of conversionary efforts toward Jews. In different ways they urged that the question of a collective Jewish turn to Christianity should be understood as an eschatological matter at the End of Days; in other words, that it was not the task of Catholics in historical time to try to baptize Jews.[40] Thus, the final wording of *Nostra Aetate* — that the church awaits a day known to God alone — was intended to convey, in the words of Cardinal Giacomo Lercaro of Bologna that "only an eschatological turn of events will bring [Jews and Christians] to the common messianic meal of the eternal Pasch."[41]

Today, unlike some other Christian groups, the Catholic Church allocates no financial or personnel resources for the baptism of Jews. Although in the first decades of the twenty-first century there was significant debate in the Catholic world about this question,[42] Popes Benedict XVI and Francis have firmly resolved the matter.[43]

## Conclusion

Hopefully, this chapter has illustrated the process of *metanoia*, of *teshuvah*, begun by *Nostra Aetate*. Its authoritative repudiation of the foundational tenets of the "teaching of contempt" has made possible an ongoing turnaround

38. Beatrice Bruteau, ed., *Merton and Judaism, Holiness in Words: Recognition, Repentance, and Renewal* (Louisville, KY: Fons Vitae, 2003), 223-224.

39. The Council's deliberations are now available in English translation on the website of the Council of Centers on Jewish-Christian Relations. See: http://www.ccjr.us/dialogika-resources/documents-and-statements/roman-catholic/second-vatican-council/na-debate.

40. This, of course, does not exclude individual Jews who might choose to exercise their freedom of religion and seek baptism.

41. Oesterreicher, *New Encounter*, 204-205.

42. See my "Official Ecclesial Documents to Implement the Second Vatican Council on Relations with Jews: Study Them, Become Immersed in Them, and Put Them into Practice," *Studies in Christian-Jewish Relations*, Oct. 2009. http://escholarship.bc.edu/scjr/vol4/iss1/24.

43. See chapter 9 below.

in relations between Catholics and Jews that will continue to unfold into the future. Indeed, as the next chapters will show, it could be said that the ensuing Catholic ecclesial documents have incrementally dismantled all the corollary and consequent anti-Jewish orientations, which could no longer stand without the fundamental presupposition of the teaching of contempt: that Jews were collectively rejected by God because of the crucifixion of Jesus and had been replaced in God's favor by Christians. In my opinion, it is a journey that has gone too far for there to be any possibility of turning back. As Cardinal Edward Idris Cassidy has put it:

> Let us then turn to consider the future. Our first aim must of course be to press forward. To stand still is to risk going backwards — and I feel absolutely confident in stating that there will be no going back on the part of the Catholic Church. At the same time, there can be a lessening of enthusiasm, a growing indifference or even a renewed spirit of suspicion and mistrust among members of the Catholic community should our efforts to keep up the momentum slacken. . . . We remember, but we refuse to be tied down to the past by chains that hold us back from building a new future, a new partnership between Jews and Catholics, a future based on mutual trust and understanding.[44]

44. Cassidy, Edward Idris Cardinal, "Catholic-Jewish Relations: 1990-2001," address delivered at the 17th meeting of the International Catholic-Jewish Liaison Committee, New York, May 1, 2001.

# CHAPTER 9

# Magisterial Contributions toward a "Theology of Shalom"

## Interpreting the Second Vatican Council

In December 2005, Pope Benedict XVI gave an address to the Vatican curia about the proper way of understanding the Second Vatican Council.[1] He described two different approaches to interpreting it. The first, which he named "a hermeneutic of discontinuity and rupture," privileges new or creative aspects of the Council over more traditional formulations. Benedict argued that such an approach misconstrues the nature of an ecumenical council, wrongly suggesting that everything prior to the Council needed correction. He preferred what he called a "hermeneutic of reform." Citing Pope John XXIII, he saw such reform as "faithful and [in] perfect conformity to the authentic [received] doctrine, which, however, should be studied and expounded through the methods of research and through the literary forms of modern thought."[2]

Observing that reform is a "process of innovation in continuity," Bene-

---

1. Benedict XVI, "Address to the Roman Curia" (December 22, 2005).

2. Benedict XVI, "Address to the Roman Curia" (December 22, 2005), §2. Joseph Komonchak has noted that a "hermeneutic of continuity" is the more direct contrast with a "hermeneutic of discontinuity." Presumably, a hermeneutic of continuity in interpreting the Council would value conciliar statements only to the degree that they reiterated pre-conciliar materials. However, Komonchak continued, Benedict spoke of a hermeneutic of reform, "which he describes quite precisely as a combination of continuity and discontinuity on different levels." See Joseph A. Komonchak, "Novelty in Continuity: Pope Benedict's Interpretation of Vatican II," *America* 2003/3 (February 2, 2009): 10-16.

---

Adapted and updated from my "Official Ecclesial Documents."

dict asserted that "It is precisely in this combination of continuity and discontinuity at different levels that the very nature of true reform consists."[3]

However, when it came to *Nostra Aetate,* the Council's Declaration on the Relationship of the Church to Non-Christian Religions, Benedict observed that something discontinuous with the past was needed in regard to Jews and Judaism. "In particular," he said, "[in the face of] the recent crimes of the Nazi regime and, in general, with a retrospective look at a long and difficult history, it was necessary to evaluate and define in a new way the relationship between the Church and the faith of Israel."[4] This "new way" to relate to the Jewish people was *Nostra Aetate*'s repudiation of the long-lived notions that Jews were an accursed people and Judaism an obsolete religion replaced by the church. As Cardinal Walter Kasper has put it: "[T]he old theory of substitution is gone since the Second Vatican Council. For us Christians today the covenant with the Jewish people is a living heritage, a living reality."[5]

Even while acknowledging the break that *Nostra Aetate* made with the past, Benedict took pains to avoid supporting a total disjuncture with preconciliar teachings: "Indeed, a discontinuity had been revealed but in which, after the various distinctions between concrete historical situations and their requirements had been made, the continuity of principles proved not to have been abandoned. It is easy to miss this fact at a first glance."[6] It is not clear to what the "continuity of principles" precisely refers regarding *Nostra Aetate,* but one suspects it is the declaration's reliance on Romans 9-11 to affirm that "Jews remain beloved of God." Of course, in so doing *Nostra Aetate* reached back over centuries of anti-Jewish teachings to the earliest New Testament author to find texts, admittedly of surpassing scriptural authority, to ground its affirmative statements about Jews.

If the "hermeneutic of reform" involves both continuity and discontinuity, it seems undeniable that in terms of the history of Christian deicide teaching, *Nostra Aetate* was far more discontinuous than continuous with the preponderance of the church's past. If Pope Benedict's "continuity of prin-

---

3. Benedict XVI, "Address to the Roman Curia" (December 22, 2005), §3.

4. Benedict XVI, "Address to the Roman Curia" (December 22, 2005), §3. For more on the impact of the Shoah, see Massimo Giuliani, "The Shoah as a Shadow upon and a Stimulus to Jewish-Christian Dialogue," in Philip A. Cunningham, Norbert J. Hofmann, SDB, and Joseph Sievers, eds., *The Catholic Church and the Jewish People: Recent Reflections from Rome* (New York: Fordham University Press, 2007), 54-70.

5. Walter Kasper, *"Dominus Iesus,"* paper delivered at the 17th meeting of the International Catholic-Jewish Liaison Committee (May 1, 2001), 3.

6. Benedict XVI, "Address to the Roman Curia" (December 22, 2005), §3.

ciples" is not a historical category but a theological one, the question then arises as to how transcendent principles could have been disregarded for so much of the church's existence.[7] In any case, Pope Benedict XVI's approach to the Council through a hermeneutic of reform suggests the principle that interpretations of *Nostra Aetate* that do not assert *both* continuity and discontinuity are erroneous.

This chapter charts the unfolding theological trajectory launched by *Nostra Aetate*. There have been serious missteps and controversies along the way.[8] Nevertheless, progress has continued despite these lapses. Therefore, the chapter will focus on the overall forward movement in theological reflection and will take notice of relevant controversies only in passing or in footnotes.

Saint John Paul II clearly believed that a post-conciliar tradition of teachings about Jews was authoritatively established. When he visited the Great Synagogue of Rome in 1986 he reminded everyone that "the guidelines for implementing the Council in this precise field [of Catholic-Jewish relations] are already available to everyone in the two documents published respectively in 1974 and in 1985 by the Holy See's Commission for Religious Relations with the Jews. It is only a question of studying them carefully, of immersing oneself in their teachings and of putting them into practice."[9]

In this book, I have referred to this developing post-conciliar tradition as expressing a "theology of shalom." *Shalom* does not simply mean "peace," but is also "a process of living in wholesome relationship with others, ideally where partners and participants trust each other, act with integrity and are dedicated to the common good rather than threatening each other."[10] As discussed in this book's Introduction, *shalom* thus seems an extremely appropriate term to apply to the Catholic Church's efforts beginning with the Second Vatican Council to develop a theology of "right relationship" with the Jewish people and "wholeness" in terms of Catholic self-understanding.

---

7. N.B. Cardinal Johannes Willebrands's relevant words: "Even though the Jews have never acknowledged Jesus as the holy anointed one and savior of all humanity, 'as regards election they are beloved for the sake of their ancestors, for the gifts and the calling of God are irrevocable' (Rom 11:28-29). *This authentic primitive Christian vision was restored by the council, which, based on the principles of our faith, called upon us to change our attitudes regarding the Jews,* moving toward a full reconciliation as children of the same heavenly Father" (*Church and Jewish People: New Considerations* [New York/Mahwah: Paulist Press, 1992], 3. Italics added).

8. For details see my "Official Ecclesial Documents."

9. John Paul II, "Address at the Great Synagogue of Rome" (April 13, 1986), §5.

10. William Klassen, "Peace," in Edward Kessler and Neil Wenborn, eds., *A Dictionary of Jewish-Christian Relations* (Cambridge: Cambridge University Press, 2005), 338.

## The Second Vatican Council: The Authoritative
## Beginnings of a Theology of Shalom

The documents promulgated by a solemn ecumenical council have enormous authority in the Roman Catholic tradition. The various types of conciliar documents have different weights, with a dogmatic constitution enjoying the greatest authority. Thus, these words of *Lumen Gentium,* the Dogmatic Constitution on the Church (1964), are particularly important:

> Finally, those who have not yet received the Gospel are related to the People of God in various ways. There is, first, that people to whom the covenants and promises were made, and from whom Christ was born according to the flesh (cf. Rom. 9:4-5): in view of the divine choice, they are a people most dear for the sake of the fathers, for the gifts of God are without repentance (cf. Rom. 11:28-29). . . . Those who, through no fault of their own, do not know the Gospel of Christ or his Church, but who nevertheless seek God with a sincere heart, and, moved by grace, try in their actions to do his will as they know it through the dictates of their conscience — those too may attain eternal salvation [§16].

Anticipating *Nostra Aetate*'s stress on chapters 9–11 of Paul's Letter to the Romans, *Lumen Gentium* taught that Jews remain the chosen people, "to whom the covenants and promises were made." Following Paul's use of the plural in "covenants," it is therefore not consistent with *Lumen Gentium* to imagine that Jews today are the living heirs to only *some* of the covenants narrated in the Bible. If Jews are truly "most dear to God," then their covenantal relationship to God — as articulated in the Torah and variously interpreted in rabbinic post-Temple Judaism — must continue to be dynamic and vital, otherwise being "dear to God" makes little difference. Moreover, if any human person can be moved by grace and "may attain eternal salvation," then, in the words of Westminster Archbishop John Heenan to the Council in 1964, "how much more luminous is the Jewish religion which is, at the same time, the root of our faith?"[11] *Lumen Gentium* thus links salvation with God's ongoing grace of election of the Jewish people, as seen in its use of the present tense ("*are* a people"), an interconnection articulated in an authoritative dogmatic constitution.

11. John M. Oesterreicher, *The New Encounter between Christians and Jews* (New York: Philosophical Library, 1986), 211.

*Nostra Aetate,* the Declaration on the Relationship of the Church to Non-Christian Religions, is also a formal statement of an ecumenical council. Although a declaration is not as weighty as a dogmatic constitution, it possesses an authority that few other types of ecclesial documents can match. Its essential features, consistent with *Lumen Gentium,* were described in the previous chapter and need not be repeated here, but one point should be further explained.

There is a decisive but often overlooked sentence in *Nostra Aetate,* §4: "Together with the prophets and that same apostle [Paul], the church awaits the day, known to God alone, when all peoples will call on God with one voice and serve him shoulder to shoulder." This text was meant to convey, as Cardinal Giacomo Lercaro of Bologna put it, that "only an eschatological turn of events will bring [Jews and Christians] to the common messianic meal of the eternal Pasch."[12] In other words, the irreducible differences between Jews and Christians will not be resolved in historic time, but only at the End of Days, at the eschaton, when God's will for all of creation is finally realized in the Age to Come.

As the official Council record explained: "The paragraph concerning the church's eschatological hope is changed. Many fathers asked that in the expression of this hope, since it concerns the mystery [of Israel], any appearance of proselytism be avoided. Other fathers requested that it somehow be expressed that Christian hope also embraces all peoples. By this present [and final] paragraph we wish to satisfy all these desires."[13]

When the Council voted on *Nostra Aetate* on October 14-15, 1965, there were 1,937 votes in favor of the section that included the eschatological phrase about awaiting the day known to God alone, and only 153 votes against it.[14] Given the discussions that had occurred in the Council, and also in the public media, it is reasonable to conclude that the Council Fathers were well aware that this wording postponed any idea of some collective Jewish "turn to Christ" into the indefinite eschatological future. On October 4, 1965, *The New York Times* described the new phraseology as "an expression of the long-term 'eschatological' hope of the Church for the eventual unity of all mankind. . . . But there is no call to active proselytization and no presentation of conversion as the price of brotherhood."

12. Oesterreicher, *New Encounter,* 204-205.

13. *Acta Syn* III.8, 648. My thanks to Thomas F. Stransky, O.S.P., a member of the drafting team for *Nostra Aetate,* for this citation.

14. Oesterreicher, *New Encounter,* 275.

The Council's futurist eschatological approach provides a principal contribution to a "theology of shalom." "Right relationship" with Jews becomes possible when Catholics affirm the mystery that Jews dwell in covenantal relationship with God until the End of Days. *Nostra Aetate*'s futurist eschatology helps explain why in the Catholic Church today "there is no organized Catholic missionary activity towards Jews as is for all other non-Christian religions."[15] In fact, these futurist perspectives were vigorously reiterated in an essay by Cardinal Walter Kasper published in the Vatican newspaper, *L'Osservatore Romano:* "the Church does not take it upon herself to orchestrate the realization of the unfathomable mystery. She cannot do so. Instead, she lays the *when* and the *how* entirely in God's hands. God alone can bring about the Kingdom of God in which the whole of Israel is saved and eschatological peace is bestowed on the world."[16] More recently, Pope Francis responded verbally to a question about whether he wanted to convert the self-described atheist interviewer by replying:

> Convert you? Proselytism is solemn nonsense, it makes no sense. We need to get to know each other, listen to each other and improve our knowledge of the world around us. Sometimes after a meeting I want to arrange another one because new ideas are born and I discover new needs. This is important: to get to know people, listen, expand the circle of ideas. The world is crisscrossed by roads that come closer together and move apart, but the important thing is that they lead towards the Good.[17]

While not having the status of an encyclical or apostolic exhortation, these comments by Pope Francis do reflect a change in Catholic priorities in terms of other religions and non-religion in general. This shift in direction that commenced with *Nostra Aetate* can be expressed as a question: how can people together work toward the Good?[18] Interreligious dialogue and

---

15. Walter Cardinal Kasper, "The Commission for Religious Relations with the Jews," address delivered at Boston College, Nov. 6, 2002, III.

16. Kasper, "Striving for Mutual Respect in Modes of Prayer," IV, *L'Osservatore Romano,* April 16, 2008, 8-9. Emphases in the original.

17. Interview with Eugenio Scalfari, *La Republica,* Oct. 1, 2013. http://www.ccjr.us/dialogika-resources/documents-and-statements/roman-catholic/francis/1265-francis2013oct1.

18. Note also how the beginning of *Nostra Aetate* speaks from the perspective of the whole human family and not, as was previously the norm, from the vantage point of a community possessing revealed truths. See Gregor Maria Hoff, "A Realm of Differences: The Meaning of Jewish Monotheism for Christology and Trinitarian Theology," in Philip A. Cunningham et

collaboration become possible once the other is not seen as a "target," but instead as a potential partner. This principle in terms of interreligious relations in general is exponentially intensified when it comes to relations with Jews with whom Christians are "intrinsically related," in the words of Saint John Paul II mentioned above.

With this beginning of a new openness to Judaism and other religions more generally, the years immediately after the Second Vatican Council were a time of tremendous creativity and excitement.

## The 1974 "Guidelines and Suggestions for Implementing the Conciliar Declaration *Nostra Aetate, 4*"

Soon after the Council, Catholic leaders began to put into action its various decrees and declarations. As Cardinal Jorge Maria Mejía has explained, under the supervision of Cardinal Augustin Bea it was necessary "to institutionalize within the Holy See the absolutely new relationship with Judaism.... [In addition,] guidelines [were needed] so that the Catholic Church and its central governing bodies, as well as the National Episcopal Conferences, could establish these relations, which were equally new, or in fact, totally alien for the great majority of the world's episcopate."[19] Already in 1969, work had begun in the Vatican to compose a document to put into practice the perspectives of *Nostra Aetate*.[20] Thus, soon after October 22, 1974, when Pope Paul VI established the Commission for Religious Relations with the Jews to nurture the embryonic unprecedented relationship with Jews, the new commission finalized drafts that had been composed with the participation "of all the bishops who were members of the Secretariat for Christian Unity."[21] On December 1, 1974, it officially promulgated, "Guidelines and Suggestions for Implementing the Conciliar Declaration *Nostra Aetate, 4*."

As an official Vatican document intended to "help to bring into actual ex-

---

al., eds., *Christ Jesus and the Jewish People Today* (Grand Rapids: Eerdmans, 2011), 202-220, esp. 202-207.

19. Jorge Maria Mejía, "The Creation and Work of the Commission for Religious Relations with the Jews," in Cunningham et al., eds., *Catholic Church and Jewish People,* 153.

20. Raymond Cohen, "The Document that Never Was: People, Land, and State after *Nostra Aetate*" paper presented at the 2014 consultation of the "Promise, Land, and Hope" project of the International Council of Christians and Jews, Hochschule für Jüdische Studien Heidelberg, University of Heidelberg, June 24, 2014.

21. Mejía, "Creation and Work of the CRRJ," 154.

istence in the life of the Church the intentions expressed"[22] by an ecumenical council, the 1974 "Guidelines" is a highly authoritative text whose principles are normative. The following especially should be noted:

## A. Christians Must Respect Jewish Self-Understanding because the Two Traditions Are Linked

[The] links and relationships ["binding the Church to Judaism"] render obligatory a better mutual understanding and renewed mutual esteem. On the practical level in particular, Christians must therefore strive to acquire a better knowledge of the basic components of the religious tradition of Judaism; they must strive to learn by what essential traits Jews define themselves in the light of their own religious experience.[23]

This is an exceedingly important statement. If, because of the spiritual connectedness between Christianity and Judaism, Christians need an awareness of Jewish self-understanding of their lived religious experience, then: (1) Jews must presently enjoy an ongoing and authentic relationship with God; and (2) ignorance of Jewish self-understanding will result in a distorted understanding of Christianity. Or to apply the last point in a particular way, because Judaism and Christianity are organically related, Christian theologians are obliged to reckon with Judaism on its own terms as lived today.

Saint John Paul II, recognizing the significance of this principle, reiterated and expanded upon it on several occasions.[24] His address to Jewish leaders in Mainz, Germany, on Nov. 17, 1980, has major import:

A second dimension of our dialogue — the true and central one — is the meeting between present-day Christian Churches and the present-day people of the Covenant concluded with Moses. It is important here "that

---

22. Vatican, "Guidelines" (1974), Preamble.

23. Vatican, "Guidelines" (1974), Preamble.

24. Thus, as early as March 12, 1979: "The Guidelines . . . whose value I wish to underline and reaffirm . . . stress a point of particular importance: 'Christians must therefore strive to acquire a better knowledge of the basic components of the religious tradition of Judaism; they must strive to learn by what essential traits the Jews define themselves in the light of their own religious experience.'" See also, "Necessary for any sincere dialogue is the intention of each partner to allow others to define themselves 'in the light of their own religious experience' [1974 *Guidelines,* Introduction]" ("Address to Jewish Leaders in Miami," Sept. 11, 1987).

> Christians — so continue the post-conciliar Guidelines — strive to acquire a better knowledge of the basic components of the religious tradition of Judaism; they must strive to learn by what essential traits Jews define themselves in the light of their own religious experience."

As will be discussed in more depth below, here John Paul II connected the imperative for Christians to understand Judaism accurately and on its own terms with "the religious reality lived by . . . the present-day people of the Covenant concluded with Moses." It is the combined recognition of ongoing Jewish covenantal life and the integral relationship between Christianity and Judaism that requires Catholic theology to engage the lived Jewish experience and tradition. And this engagement will deepen and enrich Catholic faith.

In terms of textual weight, it should also be mentioned that the authority already enjoyed by the 1974 "Guidelines," by virtue of implementing the will of an ecumenical council, was intensified by being repeatedly affirmed and utilized by successive popes.[25]

## B. Fulfillment

> When commenting on biblical texts, emphasis will be laid on the continuity of our faith with that of the earlier Covenant, in the perspective of the promises, without minimizing those elements of Christianity which are original. We believe that those promises were fulfilled with the first coming of Christ. But it is nonetheless true that we still await their perfect fulfillment in his glorious return at the end of time.[26]

This paragraph concerning liturgical preaching shows an important consequence of the Council's affirmation in *Nostra Aetate,* 4, that "the church awaits the day, known to God alone, when all peoples will call on God with one voice and serve him shoulder to shoulder." The "fulfillment" language that is used in the Guidelines when speaking of the church's continuity with the "Old Testament" explicitly presents a tension between what has "already"

---

25. For example, Pope Benedict XVI, "Address at the Great Synagogue of Rome" (January 17, 2010), and Pope Francis, Apostolic Exhortation *Evangelii Gaudium* (January 24, 2014), §247-249.

26. Vatican, "Guidelines" (1974), II.

been fulfilled and what has "not yet" been fulfilled with the first coming of Christ. The encounter with the living reality of the Jewish people impacts the Christian understanding of how Christ "fulfills" earlier "promises." In terms of Christian theology, fulfillment is proleptic: it is the present, anticipatory experience of a reality to be fully realized in the future.

## C. Post-New Testament Judaism

> The history of Judaism did not end with the destruction of Jerusalem, but rather went on to develop a religious tradition. And, although we believe that the importance and meaning of that tradition was deeply affected by the coming of Christ, it is still nonetheless rich in religious values. With the prophets and the apostle Paul, "the Church awaits the day, known to God alone, on which all peoples will address the Lord in a single voice and "serve Him with one accord" (Zeph. 3:9) (*Nostra Aetate*, 4).[27]

> . . . An effort will be made to acquire a better understanding of whatever in the Old Testament retains its own perpetual value (cf. *Dei Verbum*, 14-15), since that has not been canceled by the later interpretation of the New Testament. Rather, the New Testament brings out the full meaning of the Old, while both Old and New illumine and explain each other (cf. ibid., 16).[28]

These two statements may be considered together because they both refer to the history of Judaism — both in biblical and post-biblical times — as having perpetual religious values that have not been nullified by the coming of Christ or canceled by the New Testament. It is noteworthy that the explicit recognition of Judaism's post-Temple development into a tradition "rich in religious values" is immediately followed by *Nostra Aetate*'s futurist eschatological formulation.

This leads me to the observation that a thoroughly realized Christian eschatology (one that stresses that Christ has already "fulfilled" the expectations of biblical Israel) tends to overlook post–New Testament Jewish existence, whereas a futurist eschatology (one that underscores what remains unfinished in God's designs) fosters a respect for Judaism's ongoing religious history.

27. Vatican, "Guidelines" (1974), III.
28. Vatican, "Guidelines" (1974), II.

## D. Dialogue

To tell the truth, such relations as there have been between Jew and Christian have scarcely ever risen above the level of monologue. From now on, real dialogue must be established. Dialogue presupposes that each side wishes to know the other, and wishes to increase and deepen its knowledge of the other. It constitutes a particularly suitable means of favoring a better mutual knowledge and, especially in the case of dialogue between Jews and Christians, of probing the riches of one's own tradition. Dialogue demands respect for the other as he is; above all, respect for his faith and his religious convictions.[29]

Continuing in its purpose "to implement . . . the express intentions of the Council,"[30] the 1974 "Guidelines" described the nature of interreligious dialogue between Catholics and Jews that was being established. The defining purpose of such dialogue was to "increase and deepen" knowledge of each other, with a secondary purpose "of probing the riches of one's own tradition" as a result of the interaction with the other. These goals demanded respect for "the other as he is."

Acknowledging that " '[i]n virtue of her divine mission, and her very nature, the Church must preach Jesus Christ to the world' (*Ad Gentes*, 2),"[31] the 1974 "Guidelines" cautioned Catholics to maintain "the strictest respect for religious liberty in line with the teaching of the Second Vatican Council (Declaration *Dignitatis Humanae*)," and to "strive to understand the difficulties which arise for the Jewish soul — rightly imbued with an extremely high, pure notion of the divine transcendence — when faced with the mystery of the Incarnate Word."[32] Since a painful past has caused many Jews to suspect Catholic motives for wanting to discuss religious matters, "it will be vital to guarantee, not only tact, but a great openness of spirit and diffidence with respect to one's own prejudices."[33]

The "Guidelines" for the implementation of *Nostra Aetate*, §4, thus established certain commonsense principles for Catholic-Jewish dialogue that were widely adopted. This dialogue was for the purposes of mutual understanding and self-understanding; it was to be characterized by respect for

29. Vatican, "Guidelines" (1974), I.
30. Vatican, "Guidelines" (1974), Conclusion.
31. Vatican, "Guidelines" (1974), I.
32. Vatican, "Guidelines" (1974), I.
33. Vatican, "Guidelines" (1974), I.

the other's religious convictions; and, while Christians witnessed to their faith in Christ, they had to be open, humble, and alert to their own biases.

It is worth jumping ahead a bit in time and noting that this advocacy of interreligious dialogue between Jews and Christians by the Catholic hierarchy — predicated upon full equality and mutual respect — was to be a formative influence for Jorge Maria Bergogio, the future Pope Francis. As archbishop of Buenos Aires he participated in substantive theological conversation with Jews with whom he became close friends. His experiences led him to describe the nature of such dialogue in ways that surely contribute to a relationship of *shalom:*

> Dialogue is born of an attitude of respect for another person, and a conviction that the other has something good to say; it assumes to make room in our hearts for his point of view, for his opinions and his suggestions. Dialogue involves a warm welcome, not condemnation. To dialogue, one must lower defenses, open doors and provide human warmth.[34]

## The 1985 "Notes on the Correct Way to Present the Jews and Judaism in Preaching and Catechesis in the Roman Catholic Church"

About a decade after issuing the "Guidelines," the Commission for Religious Relations with the Jews promulgated a lengthier and theologically rich document. It was a detailed elaboration on many of the points first made by *Nostra Aetate,* §4, and the 1974 "Guidelines." The "Notes on the Correct Way to Present the Jews and Judaism in Preaching and Catechesis in the Roman Catholic Church" sought not only to continue the implementation of the Council's declaration, but in particular to remedy "a painful ignorance of the history and traditions of Judaism, of which only negative aspects and often caricature seem to form part of the stock ideas of many Christians."[35]

The "Notes" further extended the trajectory of the "theology of shalom," which was launched by *Nostra Aetate* and advanced by the "Guidelines." Two aspects of this trajectory are particularly noteworthy: how the "Notes" understood (1) the vitality of Jewish religious life today; and (2) eschatology and fulfillment.

---

34. Jorge Mario Bergoglio and Abraham Skorka, *On Heaven and Earth,* trans. Alejandro Bermudez and Howard Goodman (New York: Image Books, 2013), xiv.

35. Vatican, "Notes" (1985), Conclusion.

In addition to reiterating the insistence of the 1974 "Guidelines" that Catholics must become familiar with Jewish self-understanding,[36] the "Notes" stressed that its "concern for Judaism in Catholic teaching has not merely a historical or archeological foundation. . . . [It is a concern] for a still living reality closely related to the Church."[37]

The "Notes" described this "still living reality" by quoting from an important address delivered a few years earlier by John Paul II:

> As the Holy Father said in the speech already quoted, after he had again mentioned the "common patrimony" of the Church and Judaism as "considerable:" "To assess it carefully in itself and with due awareness of the faith and religious life of the Jewish people *as they are professed and practiced still today,* can greatly help us to understand better certain aspects of the life of the Church" (italics added). . . . The Holy Father has stated this permanent reality of the Jewish people in a remarkable theological formula, in his allocution to the Jewish community of West Germany at Mainz, on November 17th, 1980: "The people of God of the Old Covenant, which has never been revoked."[38]

The significance of John Paul II's contributions to "unpacking" the meaning of *Nostra Aetate,* §4, will be discussed in the following section. For now, his explicit description of Jewish covenantal life as having "never been revoked" was clearly reflected in the "Notes" in its treatment of post–New Testament Judaism:

> The history of Israel did not end in 70 A.D. (cf. *Guidelines,* II). It continued, especially in a numerous Diaspora which allowed Israel to carry to the whole world a witness — often heroic — of its fidelity to the one God and to "exalt Him in the presence of all the living" (Tobit 13:4), while preserving the memory of the land of their forefathers at the heart of their hope (Passover *Seder*). . . . The permanence of Israel (while so many ancient peoples have disappeared without trace) is a historic fact and a sign to be interpreted within God's design. We must in any case rid ourselves of the traditional idea of a people *punished,* preserved as a *living argument* for Christian apologetic. It remains a chosen people, "the pure olive on

36. Vatican, "Notes" (1985), I, 4.
37. Vatican, "Notes" (1985), I, 3.
38. Vatican, "Notes" (1985), I, 3.

which were grafted the branches of the wild olive which are the gentiles" (John Paul II, 6 March 1982, alluding to Rom. 11:17-24). We must remember how much the balance of relations between Jews and Christians over two thousand years has been negative. We must remind ourselves how the permanence of Israel is accompanied by a continuous spiritual fecundity, in the rabbinical period, in the Middle Ages and in modern times, taking its start from a patrimony which we long shared, so much so that "the faith and religious life of the Jewish people as they are professed and practiced still today, can greatly help us to understand better certain aspects of the life of the Church" (John Paul II, 6 March 1982).[39]

The fact that the "Notes" discussed post–New Testament Judaism in such positive terms is highly significant. If the Jewish people have manifest "a continuous spiritual fecundity" throughout history, such dynamism cannot be unconnected to their covenantal life with God. Their "often heroic" witness of "fidelity to the one God" demonstrates their continuing profound relationship with God, a relationship not delimited by the Christian experience. The repeated invocation of John Paul II by the "Notes" is also striking. Besides continuing the implementation of a conciliar declaration, the commission's "Notes" are rendered additionally authoritative by consistently incorporating relevant papal teachings.

The "Notes" similarly expanded upon the futurist eschatology previously offered by *Nostra Aetate*'s "the church awaits the day" phrase and by the 1974 "Guidelines," III. Like the "Guidelines," the "Notes" linked its discussion of eschatology to the interpretation of Israel's scriptures, in this case regarding Christian typological readings of the "Old Testament." The "Notes" should be quoted at length:

> Typological reading only manifests the unfathomable riches of the Old Testament, its inexhaustible content and the mystery of which it is full, and should not lead us to forget that it retains its own value as Revelation that the New Testament often does no more than resume (Mk. 12:29-31). Moreover, the New Testament itself demands to be read in the light of the Old. Primitive Christian catechesis constantly had recourse to this (e.g., 1 Cor. 5:6-8; 10:1-11).
>
> Typology further signifies reaching towards the accomplishment of the divine plan, when "God will be all in all" (1 Cor. 15:28). This holds true

39. Vatican, "Notes" (1985), VI, 1.

also for the Church which, realized already in Christ, yet awaits its definitive perfecting as the Body of Christ. The fact that the Body of Christ is still tending towards its full stature (Eph. 4:12-19) takes nothing from the value of being a Christian. So also the calling of the patriarchs and Exodus from Egypt do not lose their importance and value in God's design from being at the same time intermediate stages (e.g., *Nostra Aetate,* no. 4).

The Exodus, for example, represents an experience of salvation and liberation that is not complete in itself, but has in it, over and above its own meaning, the capacity to be developed further. Salvation and liberation are already accomplished in Christ and gradually realized by the sacraments in the Church. This makes way for the fulfillment of God's design, which awaits its final consummation with the return of Jesus as Messiah, for which we pray each day. The Kingdom, for the coming of which we also pray each day, will be finally established. With salvation and liberation the elect and the whole of Creation will be transformed in Christ (Rom. 8:19-23).

Furthermore, in underlining the eschatological dimension of Christianity we shall reach a greater awareness that the people of God of the Old and the New Testament are tending towards a like end in the future: the coming or return of the Messiah — even if they start from two different points of view. It is more clearly understood that the person of the Messiah is not only a point of division for the people of God but also a point of convergence (*Sussidi per l'ecumenismo,* Diocese of Rome, no. 140). Thus it can be said that Jews and Christians meet in a comparable hope, grounded on the same promise made to Abraham (Gen. 12:1-3; Heb. 6:13-18).[40]

By its insistence on a futurist eschatology, the "Notes" established a nuanced theological orientation toward "fulfillment" language. Maintaining the "already/not yet" approach of *Nostra Aetate* and the "Guidelines," the "Notes" stated that while salvation has already been "accomplished in Christ" and "gradually realized" by the church's sacraments, these achievements "make way" for the ultimate "fulfillment of God's design" in the future. A set of guidelines for preachers published three years later by the U.S. Bishops' Committee on the Liturgy would complement this nuanced sense of fulfillment by defining "fulfilled" as "irreversibly inaugurated."[41]

An important consequence of this conception of fulfillment is imme-

---

40. Vatican, "Notes" (1985), II, 7-10.
41. BCL, "God's Mercy Endures Forever" (1988), §11.

diately apparent in the references in "Notes" to Jews and Christians being divided but also converging "towards a like end in the future." Christians and Jews, therefore, have a "responsibility to prepare the world for the coming of the Messiah by working together for social justice, respect for the rights of persons and nations and for social and international reconciliation."[42] However, if Christians speak lopsidedly of "fulfillment" as something fully achieved already, then the ongoing witness of Jews to their relationship with God is emptied of much significance.[43] This *Nostra Aetate*–inspired theme of respect for the spiritual vitality of Judaism today has recently been reiterated by Pope Francis: "God continues to work among the people of the Old Covenant and to bring forth treasures of wisdom which flow from their encounter with his word. For this reason, the Church also is enriched when she receives the values of Judaism."[44]

Finally, the "Notes" also offered important insights into the spiritual relationship between Judaism and the church. First, the "Church and Judaism cannot . . . be seen as two parallel ways of salvation and the Church must witness to Christ as the Redeemer for all, 'while maintaining the strictest respect for religious liberty in line with the teaching of the Second Vatican Council declaration, *Dignitatis Humanae*' (*Guidelines and Suggestions*, no. 1)."[45] Because of the close spiritual connections between Jews and Christians, perhaps most fundamentally seen in the inclusion of the "Old Testament" in the Christian Bible, Catholic teaching rejects a total separation between the two traditions.

The constellation of interrelated teachings imparted by the "Notes" is a crucial component of a "theology of shalom." Implementing the conciliar work that Pope Benedict later described as evaluating and defining "in a new way the relationship between the Church and the faith of Israel,"[46] the "Notes" established or reiterated certain parameters: (1) Jewish covenantal

---

42. Vatican, "Notes" (1985), II, 11.

43. N.B. the related later caution of the Pontifical Biblical Commission: "[E]xcessive insistence, characteristic of a certain apologetic, on the probative value attributable to the fulfillment of prophecy must be discarded. This insistence has contributed to harsh judgments by Christians of Jews and their reading of the Old Testament: the more reference to Christ is found in Old Testament texts, the more the incredulity of the Jews is considered inexcusable and obstinate" (PBC, *The Jewish People and Their Sacred Scriptures in the Christian Bible* (2001), II, A, 5).

44. Francis, *Evangelii Gaudium* (2014), 249.

45. Vatican, "Notes" (1985), I, 7.

46. Benedict XVI, "Address to the Roman Curia" (December 22, 2005).

life is permanent and vital; (2) this vitality is evidenced throughout Jewish history; (3) Judaism and Christianity are closely related and are not disconnected "parallel" traditions; (4) Judaism and Christianity are on converging paths toward the eschatological age when all God's plans and promises will achieve their complete fulfillment; and (5) in the present time, both Jews and Christians have the covenantal responsibility to "prepare the world for the coming of the Messiah."

The ecclesial authority of the "Notes" rests on several facts: its promulgation by the competent Vatican dicastery (with the approbation of the Congregation of the Doctrine of the Faith) charged to continue the implementation of a conciliar declaration; together with its quotations of previous authoritative documents (*Nostra Aetate,* the 1974 "Guidelines") and the papal pronouncements of John Paul II.

## The Teachings of Saint John Paul II

As already suggested above, the long papacy of John Paul II was extremely significant for the unfolding post-conciliar new relationship between Catholics and Jews. As a boy growing up in Poland, Karol Wojtyla had many Jewish friends, only a few of whom would survive the Shoah, most famously Jerzy Kluger.[47] When he became Pope John Paul II on October 16, 1978, he had a very personal commitment to *shalom* with the Jewish people at least partly because of these early relationships.

Thus, already on March 12, 1979, he told an international delegation of Jewish leaders that the Second Vatican Council "understood that our two religious communities are connected and closely related at the very level of their respective religious identities. . . . It is on [this] basis . . . that we recognize with utmost clarity that the path along which we should proceed with the Jewish religious community is one of fraternal dialogue and fruitful collaboration."[48] If "fraternal dialogue" is understood as described in the 1974 "Guidelines," which the pope indeed affirmed extensively in this address, then its principal purpose was to increase and deepen knowledge of the other with great respect for the other's faith and religious convictions.

47. See Darcy O'Brien, *The Hidden Pope: The Untold Story of a Lifelong Friendship That Is Changing the Relationship between Catholics and Jews: The Personal Journey of John Paul II and Jerzy Kluger* (New York: Rodale Books, 1998).

48. John Paul II, "Address to Representatives of Jewish Organizations" (March 12, 1979).

While quoting the "Guidelines" that "the Church must preach Jesus Christ to the world," the pope clearly saw interreligious dialogue as the venue for pursuing "that fuller mutual understanding which we are called to achieve."[49]

In fact, John Paul's twenty-six-year-long papacy followed precisely this path. In over fifty addresses and apostolic letters that fill a book-length volume,[50] he gradually constructed a network of theological teachings about the Catholic Church's relationship to the Jewish people that flowed from his understanding of *Nostra Aetate* and his personal experiences with Jewish friends. His contributions to the implementation and development of *Nostra Aetate*'s vision was praised by Jewish commentators during his lifetime and repeated on the occasion of his canonization on April 27, 2014.[51]

Of particular interest is John Paul II's thinking about Jewish covenantal life as reflected in such phrases as "the people of the Covenant" or the covenant "never revoked by God." He first broached this topic during the aforementioned major address delivered in Mainz, Germany, on November 17, 1980.[52] In encouraging the practice of Catholic-Jewish dialogue, he observed:

> The first dimension of this dialogue, that is, the meeting between the people of God of the Old Covenant, never revoked by God [cf. Rom. 11:29], and that of the New Covenant, is at the same time a dialogue within our Church, that is to say, between the first and the second part of her Bible. . . .
>
> A second dimension of our dialogue — the true and central one — is the meeting between present-day Christian Churches and the present-day people of the Covenant concluded with Moses. It is important here "that Christians — so continue the post-conciliar Guidelines — strive to acquire a better knowledge of the basic components of the religious tradition of Judaism; they must strive to learn by what essential traits Jews define themselves in the light of their own religious experience" [Introduction]. The way for this mutual knowledge is dialogue.

At Mainz, John Paul II correlated "the people of God of the [unrevoked] Old Covenant" with the first part of the Christian Bible. "Old Covenant" thus

---

49. John Paul II, "Address to Representatives of Jewish Organizations" (March 12, 1979).

50. Eugene J. Fisher and Leon Klenicki, eds., *The Saint for Shalom: How Pope John Paul II Transformed Catholic-Jewish Relations* (New York: Crossroad, 2011).

51. See the many tributes given by Jewish speakers in Fisher and Klenicki, *The Saint for Shalom.*

52. John Paul II, "Address to the Jewish Community in Mainz" (Nov. 17, 1980).

incorporates the entire corpus of the Christian Old Testament, containing all the distinct "covenants" it narrates, such as the covenants with Abraham, with the entire people at Sinai, with David, etc. Biblically, the covenant at Sinai lies at the heart of Jewish covenantal life, so it was quite appropriate for the pope to also describe the "people of God of the Old Covenant, never revoked by God" as "the present-day people of the Covenant concluded with Moses."

This was not an isolated occurrence. In the years after Mainz he went on to repeat this theme, often explicitly mentioning the centrality of the giving of the Torah at Sinai.[53] In his Apostolic Letter *Tertio Millennio Adveniente,* John Paul again made it clear that for him there was no question that the Second Vatican Council had definitively charted a new course that included a comprehensive understanding of covenant: "No Council had ever spoken so clearly . . . about the specific meaning of the Old Covenant and of Israel. . . ."[54]

Another landmark during John Paul's pontificate was the signing of a Fundamental Agreement between the Holy See and the State of Israel on December 30, 1993, which permitted the establishment of formal diplomatic relations, including the exchange of ambassadors, between the two sovereignties.[55] A legal agreement between a church whose organizational center is a city-state and a nation that self-defines as a Jewish homeland should be expected to have some unusual features. This can be seen, for example, in the statement that "The Holy See takes this occasion to reiterate its condemnation of hatred, persecution and all other manifestations of antisemitism directed against the Jewish people and individual Jews anywhere, at any time and by anyone,"[56] an application of a section of John Paul II's historic address at the Great Synagogue of Rome in April 1986, which in its turn cited *Nostra Aetate.* While sections of the Fundamental Agreement are still awaiting full implementation, the establishment of formal relations also contributed to

53. See his addresses to the Australian Jewish Community, Nov. 26, 1986; American Jewish Leaders, Sept. 11, 1987; the Viennese Jewish Community, June 24, 1988; the New Ambassador of the Federal Republic of Germany to the Holy See, Nov. 8, 1990; his General Audience, April 28, 1999; his Jasna Gora Meditation, Sept. 26, 1990; his Letter concerning Pilgrimage to Places Linked to the History of Salvation, June 29, 1999; and his Homily at Mount Sinai, Feb. 26, 2000.

54. John Paul II, "Apostolic Letter *Tertio Millennio Adveniente* on Preparation for the Jubilee of the Year 2000" (Nov. 10, 1994), III, §19.

55. See: http://www.ccjr.us/dialogika-resources/documents-and-statements/roman -catholic/vatican-curia/292-state-1993.

56. Fundamental Agreement between the Holy See and the State of Israel, Article 2 (2).

the commencement of semi-annual dialogues between representatives of the Holy See and the Chief Rabbinate of Israel.[57]

Given all these developments during his long papacy, which have really only been sketched above, it is fair to describe John Paul II as the definer of the new relationship inaugurated by *Nostra Aetate*. This is not to suggest that there were no moments of great tension between Catholics and Jews while he was pope. Serious controversies erupted over such topics as a papal audience with Austrian President Kurt Waldheim (who had been discovered to have a Nazi past), the establishment of a Carmelite convent on the grounds at Auschwitz, the canonization of Edith Stein/Sr. Teresa Benedicta of the Cross (who was born a Jew and murdered in the Shoah), and the role of Pope Pius XII and indeed of the whole church during the Second World War. Despite these tensions, gradually both formal and informal channels allowed conversation to continue and the new relationship moved forward. In the course of John Paul's pontificate he steadily set forth principles that ensured the continued rapprochement between Jews and Catholics, as has become clear in the reigns of his two successors.

### The Teachings of Pope Benedict XVI

The eight-year papacy of the former Cardinal Joseph Ratzinger was marked by some heated controversies in terms of Catholic-Jewish relations, but also by important further developments in magisterial theological formulations. Throughout his pontificate, Benedict repeatedly stated his *"intention to continue on this path"*[58] of Catholic-Jewish reconciliation pioneered by his predecessor. Indeed, like John Paul, Benedict soon visited a synagogue (followed by several others), and traveled to Israel where he also prayed at Yad Vashem and at the Western Wall. However, as a German national who had been conscripted into Hitler's Youth Corps, he labored under something of a cloud. His addresses were particularly scrutinized for whether they would openly grapple with how Christian antisemitism related to the Shoah, something he seemed reluctant to do.

Most contentious were his efforts to woo back into full communion

---

57. See Norbert J. Hofmann, "A Sign of Great Hope: The Beginning of the Dialogue between the Holy See and the Chief Rabbinate of Israel," in Cunningham, Hofmann, and Sievers, eds., *The Catholic Church and the Jewish People*, 167-175.

58. Benedict XVI, "Address to Delegates of the International Jewish Committee for Interreligious Consultation" (June 9, 2005). Emphasis in the original.

with Rome the schismatic Priestly Society of St. Pius X (SSPX), founded by Archbishop Marcel Lefebvre in rejection of the Second Vatican Council. As an olive branch offered to encourage reconciliation, in January 2009 Benedict lifted the excommunications of four SSPX bishops that had been automatically incurred in 1988 when Lefebvre defied the directive of John Paul not to consecrate them. Unfortunately, it later came to light that one of these bishops was a vocal Holocaust-denier. In the swirl of controversy that followed, Benedict issued a remarkable letter to all the world's Catholic bishops. He wrote: "A gesture of reconciliation with an ecclesial group engaged in a process of separation . . . turned into its very antithesis: an apparent step backwards with regard to all the steps of reconciliation between Christians and Jews taken since the Council — steps which my own work as a theologian had sought from the beginning to take part in and support."[59]

In the end, the effort to bring the SSPX back into full communion with the Catholic Church failed. However, in the process, the authority of *Nostra Aetate's* rapprochement with the Jewish people was intensified when its acceptance became a public *sine qua non* confronting the SSPX. Cardinal Kurt Koch, president of the Commission of the Holy See for Religious Relations with the Jews, publicly insisted that the Catholic Church could not change her position on the Second Vatican Council and the *Nostra Aetate* Declaration: "Absolutely not," he said, "because she cannot question the Council. That is unthinkable. And the Holy Father cannot deny his Magisterium."[60] To be reconciled with the Vatican, the SSPX had to embrace the new relationship with Jews. Their refusal to do so contributed to the breakdown of the negotiations.

As part of his initiative toward the SSPX, Pope Benedict also made it easier for Catholics who no longer felt at home with the Mass offered in the vernacular languages according to the post–Vatican II liturgy to instead pray the older liturgy of the Council of Trent, the Tridentine Rite. Concerned about the insulting language used in the Tridentine Rite's Good Friday intercession for the conversion of the Jews, in February 2008 Benedict composed a new one in Tridentine cadences:

> Let us also pray for the Jews. May the Lord our God illuminate their hearts so that they may recognize Jesus Christ as savior of all men. Let us pray.

59. Benedict XVI, "Letter to Catholic Bishops on the Remission of the Excommunication of SSPX Bishops" (March 10, 2009).

60. *Servizio Informazione Religiosa,* January 15, 2013. http://www.agensir.it/pls/sir/v3_s2doc_a.a_autentication?rifi=&rifp=&tema=Quot_english&oggetto=253607.

Almighty and everlasting God, you who want all men to be saved and to gain knowledge of the Truth, kindly allow that, as the fullness of peoples enter into your Church, all of Israel may be saved. Through Christ our Lord.

This prayer was quite different in tone than the post–Vatican II 1970 Roman Missal prayer in which the Jewish people's covenantal life with God was affirmed:

Let us pray for the Jewish people, the first to hear the Word of God, that they may continue to grow in the love of his name and in faithfulness to his covenant. Almighty and eternal God, long ago you gave your promise to Abraham and his posterity. Listen to your church as we pray that the people you first made your own may arrive at the fullness of redemption.

Even though the new Tridentine prayer would be used by probably less than one percent of the world's Catholic population, the theological dissonance between the two formulations resurfaced questions about Catholic desires to convert Jews that had also roiled the Second Vatican Council (see chapter 8).[61] The consternation abated somewhat when at Pope Benedict's request, Cardinal Kasper published in *L'Osservatore Romano* the article previously cited (see note 16) that cast the new prayer in a futurist eschatological context.[62] Most significantly, Pope Benedict himself explicitly addressed the issue in a book published in 2011:

I should like to recall the advice given by Bernard of Clairvaux to his pupil Pope Eugene III on this matter. He reminds the Pope that his duty

61. In the United States this upheaval was manifest in an ill-considered statement from the Secretariat for Ecumenical and Interreligious Affairs in the summer of 2009, which suggested that, in the context of interreligious dialogue with Jews, Catholics were implicitly (and occasionally explicitly) inviting Jews to baptism. In response to a unanimous letter from Jewish leaders in interreligious activities that had threatened to end further dialogue, officials of the U.S. Bishops Conference took the unprecedented step of striking the problematic sentences from the record. For details on this and related controversies see my "Official Ecclesial Documents."

62. For more on the contributions of Cardinal Kasper to these developments, see my "Celebrating Judaism as a 'Sacrament of Every Otherness'" in Kristen Colberg and Robert Krieg, eds., *The Theology of Cardinal Walter Kasper: Speaking Truth in Love* (Collegeville, MN: Liturgical Press, 2014), 223-240.

of care extends not only to Christians, but: "You also have obligations toward unbelievers, whether Jew, Greek, or Gentile" (*De Consideratione* III/i, 2). Then he immediately corrects himself and observes more accurately: "Granted, with regard to the Jews, time excuses you; for them a determined point in time has been fixed, which cannot be anticipated. The full number of the Gentiles must come in first. But what do you say about these Gentiles? . . ."

Hildegard Brem comments on this passage as follows: "In the light of Romans 11:25, the Church must not concern herself with the conversion of the Jews, since she must wait for the time fixed for this by God, 'until the full number of the Gentiles come in' (Rom 11:25). On the contrary, the Jews themselves are a living homily to which the Church must draw attention, since they call to mind the Lord's suffering (cf. Ep 363) . . ." (quoted in *Sämtliche Werke*, ed. Winkler, I, p. 834). . . .

In the meantime, Israel retains its own mission. Israel is in the hands of God, who will save it "as a whole" at the proper time, when the number of the Gentiles is complete.[63]

More will be said about this eschatological approach in chapter 10 below, but for now it suffices to note two important insights presented here by Pope Benedict. First, conversion of Jews is not on the Catholic agenda; and second, the Jewish people have their own distinctive God-given "mission" in the world.

This relates to a very significant theological contribution by Pope Benedict with regard to Jewish and Christian interpretations of the scriptures of ancient Israel, organized by Jews into the collection known as the Tanakh and by Christians into the collection called the Old Testament. Benedict writes: "After centuries of antagonism, we now see it as our task to bring these two ways of rereading the biblical texts — the Christian way and the Jewish way — into dialogue with one another, if we are to understand God's will and his word aright."[64]

The emphasis here on dialogue, consistent with the church's priorities ever since *Nostra Aetate* and taken up quite vigorously by Pope Francis as we will see, extends to traditions of biblical interpretation.[65] Most provocative

---

63. Benedict XVI, *Jesus of Nazareth*, Part Two, *Holy Week: From the Entrance into Jerusalem to the Resurrection* (San Francisco: Ignatius Press, 2011), 41-45, 46-47.

64. Benedict XVI, *Jesus of Nazareth*, Part Two, *Holy Week*, 35.

65. See also the discussion in chapter 2 of the Pontifical Biblical Commission's 2001 study

is his suggestion that, if Jews and Christians do not bring their distinctive traditions of interpretation into conversation with one another, they run the risk of not understanding "God's will and his word aright." This concept will be developed further in this book's final chapter.

## The Teachings of Pope Francis

Pope Francis is a pope of many firsts: the first Latin American pope, the first modern pope who did not live through the Shoah, the first pope in centuries to choose not to live in the lavish Vatican papal suite, etc. As already mentioned, however, in terms of a theology of *shalom* he is the first pope whose pastoral formation occurred after *Nostra Aetate* and who, as a result, has engaged in theological conversations with Jews who have become close personal friends.

His commitment to this special relationship is evident not only in the published account of his dialogues with Argentinean Rabbi Abraham Skorka,[66] but also in his Apostolic Exhortation, *Evangelii Gaudium*. After summing up many of the church's post–*Nostra Aetate* perspectives, he writes in a personal vein: "Dialogue and friendship with the children of Israel are part of the life of Jesus' disciples. The friendship which has grown between us makes us bitterly and sincerely regret the terrible persecutions which they have endured, and continue to endure, especially those that have involved Christians."[67]

Very significantly, he goes on to emphasize the living covenantal bond between God and the Jewish community that enriches the world today:

> God continues to work among the people of the Old Covenant and to bring forth treasures of wisdom which flow from their encounter with his word. For this reason, the Church also is enriched when she receives the values of Judaism. While it is true that certain Christian beliefs are unacceptable to Judaism, and that the Church cannot refrain from proclaiming Jesus as Lord and Messiah, there exists as well a rich complementarity which allows us to read the texts of the Hebrew Scriptures together and to help one another to mine the riches of God's word. We can also share

---

— issued under the future Pope Benedict's aegis — *The Jewish People and Their Sacred Scripture in the Christian Bible.*

66. Bergoglio and Skorka, *On Heaven and Earth.*

67. Francis, *Evangelii Gaudium* (Jan. 24, 2014), §248.

many ethical convictions and a common concern for justice and the development of peoples.[68]

Here we can see Francis tying together several themes from his two predecessors and the post–*Nostra Aetate* documentary tradition: Judaism's covenantal life is alive and dynamic, Jews and Christians, despite their differences, can enhance each other's understandings of their respective and related experiences of God, and both have responsibilities to the wider world.

However, Francis expresses these theological convictions in a very personal way, as when he responded to a written question as follows:

> You also asked me . . . what should be said to the Jewish brethren concerning the promise that God made to them: is that an empty promise? This question, believe me, is a radical one for us Christians because with the help of God, especially in the light of the Second Vatican Council, we have rediscovered that the Jewish people remain for us the holy root from which Jesus was born. I too have cultivated many friendships through the years with my Jewish brothers in Argentina and often while in prayer, as my mind turned to the terrible experience of the *Shoah,* I looked to God. What I can tell you, with Saint Paul, is that God has never neglected his faithfulness to the covenant with Israel, and that, through the awful trials of these last centuries, the Jews have preserved their faith in God. And for this, we, the Church and the whole human family, can never be sufficiently grateful to them.[69]

There is a deep irony here of which the pope must surely be aware: Christianity can never thank Jews enough for remaining faithful to their covenantal life with God despite the strenuous efforts of many — particularly in Europe of Christians — over the centuries to induce or coerce them to forsake it! These few sentences convey the remarkable developments of the past fifty years of Catholic magisterial thinking: from the early 1960s, when bishops and theologians debated whether and how to say anything positive about Jews and Judaism, to today when a pope casually praises Jews for remaining steadfast to their covenanting with God in the face of persistent Christian hostility.

---

68. Francis, *Evangelii Gaudium,* §249.

69. Francis, "Letter to a Non-Believer" (Sept. 4, 2013). http://w2.vatican.va/content/francesco/en/letters/2013/documents/papa-francesco_20130911_eugenio-scalfari.html.

## Conclusion

As the drafters of *Nostra Aetate* worked their way through its successive drafts, they realized that unlike most Catholic ecclesiastical documents this one could not cite past councils, theologians, or popes. First, there had never before been a defining ecclesiastical statement about the church's relationship with Judaism. Second, in a sense there had never been a need to compose one because the patterns of anti-Judaism were too pervasive and enduring.

Therefore, the drafters' efforts to speak of Jews and Judaism positively would have to rely on the earliest (and most normative) Christian texts: the sacred scriptures. Fortunately, as seen in Part One, new, critical methods for actualizing the Bible in a post-Shoah world were now available. However, the question with which we began this chapter remains an important one. Are the radical transformations initiated by *Nostra Aetate* continuous with the Catholic tradition, or are they so discontinuous with the centuries of prior anti-Jewish teaching as to question their legitimacy, as the members of the Priestly Society of St. Pius X insist?

Pope Benedict's response would be that *Nostra Aetate* represents a hermeneutic of reform. It is both in continuity with the core tradition — especially in the New Testament texts actualized anew — and seeks to correct errors and abuses that have accreted over time. The words of the Vatican II declaration *Unitatis Redintegratio* apply here:

> Christ summons the Church to continual reformation as she sojourns here on earth. The Church is always in need of this, in so far as she is an institution of people here on earth. Thus if, in various times and circumstances, there have been deficiencies in moral conduct or in church discipline, or even in the way that church teaching has been formulated — to be carefully distinguished from the deposit of faith itself — these can and should be set right at the opportune moment.[70]

Thus, the Catholic Church's rapprochement with the Jewish people is an act of reform, of *teshuva,* of *metanoia.* It is the result, as the Mass of Pardon on the First Sunday of Lent in 2000 suggests, of a communal examination of conscience in the wake of the Shoah that has prompted the church community to rediscover aspects of its own roots and identity that were

---

70. Second Vatican Council, *Unitatis Redintegratio,* The Decree on Ecumenism (1964), §6.

for too long hidden or even repressed. But the primary reason for the new relationship from a Christian point of view is out of fidelity to the Gospel, the Good News itself.

Today, unlike fifty years ago when the drafters of *Nostra Aetate* had few positive precedents to draw upon, Catholics today have an unparalleled and multi-dimensional ecclesial tradition to draw upon. It may be brief in comparison with the church's long history, but in terms of Catholic polity it is highy authoritative: a global council, all post-conciliar popes, several Vatican dicasteries, and numerous national conferences of bishops have declared that God cannot be unfaithful, either to the church or to the people of Israel. We are both covenanting with the Holy One. Now we must discover together what this new context of friendship between Jews and Catholics means for us all.

# CHAPTER 10

# Retelling the Christian Story in a Post-*Nostra Aetate* Church

## Erasing Supersessionism from the Christian Story

Part One of this book presented the development of a dialectical approach to interpreting the Christian Bible within the Catholic community, and then utilized that approach in terms of particular biblical writers and texts that shape Christian attitudes and theologies toward Jews. In parallel fashion, this second part began by charting the incremental advance of magisterial reflection on the church's relationship to Jews and Judaism, beginning with *Nostra Aetate*. The remaining chapters will apply the principles and parameters that have emerged over the past decades to specific theological topics relating to this new relationship. One of the most important considerations when engaging these topics is how to tell the "Christian story" in ways that affirm a positive understanding of ongoing Jewish covenantal life, which, as we have seen, is a hallmark of the new relationship.

What is "the Christian story"? It is a master narrative that expresses what Christianity is all about. It tells about God, Jesus Christ, and salvation. It shows the origins of the church, its purposes, its history, and its mission for the future. Most Christians have some such sweeping tale either consciously or unconsciously embedded in their religious imaginations. The Christian story conveys core theological convictions and orientations in narrative form. It helps Christians interpret new experiences that the church and its members encounter. These experiences, in turn, can revise or refine aspects of the Christian story.

---

This chapter adapts portions of my *A Story of Shalom: The Calling of Christians and Jews by a Covenanting God.*

A certain "classic" telling of the foundational Christian story has prevailed for almost twenty centuries. It could be outlined as follows.[1]

### The Classic Foundational Christian Story

1. God created the world and created humanity in the divine image.
2. God wanted humanity to live in happiness with God.
3. Humanity sinned through disobedience. They were driven from God's presence into a world of toil, disease, and death.
4. God promised to send a Savior. The People of Israel prepared for his coming.
5. Eventually, the Son of God was incarnated as a human, and died for the sins of humanity.
6. Through baptism into Christ, people can now become united with God. If they live Christian lives, they will spend eternity with God in heaven.
7. One day this world will end and God's Kingdom will prevail.

This classic Christian story line needs major revision in a post–*Nostra Aetate* church. The following orientations or principles can help shape its contours in productive ways:

## Today's Christian Story Must Affirm
## Jewish Covenantal Life[2] with God

In the second through fourth centuries of the Common Era, two forces motivated Christian apologists to develop an anti-Jewish theology: (1) pa-

---

1. Mary C. Boys has also developed a synthesis of what she calls the "conventional account" of Christian origins. Although her synthesis contains some different elements than my own, she, too, has concluded that it is supersessionist. See her *Jewish-Christian Dialogue: One Woman's Experience — The 1997 Madeleva Lecture in Spirituality* (New York/Mahwah: Paulist Press, 1997), 81-85. Similarly, R. Kendall Soulen has noted that the overarching Christian master reading of the Bible has been "a drama in four acts: creation, fall, redemption in Christ Jesus, and final consummation." He likewise deems this construal to be supersessionist. See his "Removing Anti-Judaism" in Howard Clark Kee and Irvin J. Borowsky, eds., *Removing Anti-Judaism from the New Testament* (Philadelphia: American Interfaith Institute/World Alliance, 1998), 151, and also his *The God of Israel and Christian Theology* (Minneapolis: Fortress Press, 1996).

2. To reiterate a point made previously in chapter 8, the phrases "[the People] Israel's covenantal life" or "Jewish covenantal life" or "Israel's covenanting" intend to assert both that the covenantal bond between God and the Jewish people has never been revoked *and* that this bond is organically united to the church's covenanting in Christ.

gan criticisms of the church as a heretical deviation from Judaism; and (2) the immense attractiveness of Judaism for both Christians and non-Christians in the Roman Empire[3] (see chapter 3). Following the rhetorical customs of the time, church leaders in this patristic era drew upon polemical passages in the New Testament to enhance Christianity's status by denigrating its Jewish rival. In a body of literature known as the *adversus Judaeos* tradition, but also in commentaries, sermons, and Christian instructions, originally disparate claims were organized into an anti-Jewish theological superstructure. It was premised upon the conviction that the church had superseded Judaism as God's Chosen People because of the alleged "Jewish" rejection and killing of Christ. "The Fathers of the church of the first centuries, as much in the East as in the West, were in agreement in showing the Jewish people as 'repudiated' definitively by God, and the church as the selected people in 'substitution' to bring salvation to everyone."[4]

This supersessionist understanding dominated Christian thinking for over a millennium. It contributed to what the U.S. Catholic Bishops have called "a de-Judaizing process" in Christianity. It led "not only [to] social friction with the Jews, but often to their oppression."[5] In the words of Cardinal Edward Idris Cassidy, second President of the Vatican Commission for Religious Relations with the Jews, the "anti-Jewish tradition stamped its mark in different ways on Christian doctrine and teaching."[6]

To put it another way, supersessionism stamped its mark on how the Christian story has been told. In the "classic" narrative outlined above, the community of Israel existed only to prepare for the redemptive act of Christ. Once that was accomplished, Israel really had little reason to continue to exist. It had been rendered obsolete. The classic account is premised on supersessionism.

3. For more on this social situation, see these works by Robert L. Wilken, *The Christians as the Romans Saw Them* (New Haven: Yale University Press, 1984); *John Chrysostom and the Jews: Rhetoric and Reality in the Fourth Century* (Berkeley: University of California Press, 1983); and *Judaism and the Early Christian Mind: A Study of Cyril of Alexandria's Exegesis and Theology* (New Haven: Yale University Press, 1971). See also David P. Efroymson, "The Patristic Connection," in Alan T. Davies, ed., *Antisemitism and the Foundations of Christianity* (New York/Ramsey/Toronto: Paulist, 1979).

4. Pier Francesco Fumagalli, "*Nostra Aetate:* A Milestone," address delivered at the Vatican Symposium on *The Roots of Anti-Judaism in the Christian Environment* (October 31, 1997).

5. NCCB, "Statement on Catholic-Jewish Relations" (1975).

6. Cassidy, Edward Idris Cardinal, "Reflections: The Vatican Statement on the Shoah," *Origins* 28/2 (May 28, 1998): 31.

The classic story cannot be told today in a church that has renounced supersessionism. This is a new moment in Christian history. In the decades since the Shoah, church instructions across a wide range of denominations have officially repudiated the two cornerstones of supersessionism. These documents declare that the Jewish People remain in a perpetual covenantal relationship with God and condemn any blaming of "the Jews" for the crucifixion of Jesus.[7] As Saint John Paul II stated on numerous occasions, Jews are "the people of God of the Old Covenant, never revoked by God;"[8] "the present-day people of the Covenant concluded with Moses;"[9] and partners "in a covenant of eternal love which was never revoked."[10] Many of these ecclesial documents also understand that Judaism has an ongoing vocation in the world that Christians must learn to accept in terms of Jewish self-understanding.[11] Today's church is post-supersessionist. It seeks to overcome past supersessionist habits.

However, if only because of its historic origins, the Christian story cannot be told without reference to Judaism. As the Catholic bishops of West Germany expressed it, "He who encounters Jesus Christ encounters Judaism."[12] Thus whenever today's post-supersessionist church tells its story anew, it inevitably must affirm the validity of Jewish self-understandings of Israel's covenantal life with God.

Moreover, as the Commission on Faith and Order of the World Council of Churches noted, "there is no doctrine of Christian theology which is not influenced in some way by the confrontation with the Jewish people."[13]

7. See the two volumes edited by Franklin Sherman, *Bridges: Documents of the Christian-Jewish Dialogue* (2011 and 2014).

8. John Paul II, "Address to the Jewish Community in Mainz, West Germany" (Nov. 17, 1980).

9. John Paul II, "Address to the Jewish Community in Mainz."

10. John Paul II, "Address to Jewish Leaders in Miami" (Sept. 11, 1987).

11. E.g., "[Christians must] strive to learn by what essential traits the Jews *define themselves in the light of their own religious experience*" (Vatican, "Guidelines" [1974], Preamble); "There is special urgency for Christians to listen . . . to ways in which Jews understand their history and their traditions, their faith and their obedience 'in their own terms'" (World Council of Churches, "Ecumenical Considerations" [1982], 1.7); "I think that in this sense you [the Jewish people] continue your particular vocation, showing yourselves to be still the heirs of that election to which God is faithful. This is your mission in the contemporary world before the peoples, the nations, all of humanity, the church" (John Paul II, "Address to Jewish Leaders in Warsaw" [June 14, 1987]).

12. [West] German Bishops' Conference, "The Church and the Jews" (1980), I.

13. World Council of Churches, Faith and Order Commission, "The Church and the Jewish People" (1967), V, in World Council of Churches, *The Theology of the Churches and the Jewish*

Therefore, an acknowledgement of Israel's ongoing covenanting will automatically impact many theological fields, including Christology, ecclesiology, and soteriology. Today's post-supersessionist Christian story will necessarily have to speak differently about Jesus, the church, and salvation than did the supersessionist classic rendition because "the entire self-understanding of the church is at stake."[14]

## Today's Christian Story Must Actualize the Bible Critically

In the twentieth century, critical methods of reading the Bible have been officially embraced by the Catholic Church (see chapters 1 and 2). Such approaches recognize that the cultures, traditions, literary conventions, and circumstances of the writers of the Bible have shaped the compositions of their texts. Therefore, these influences must be assessed when interpreting the meaning of biblical texts. In my own Roman Catholic community with regard to one form of biblical criticism:

> The historical-critical method is the indispensable method for the scientific study of the meaning of ancient texts. Holy Scripture, inasmuch as it is the "word of God in human language," has been composed by human authors in all its various parts and in all the sources that lie behind them. Because of this, its proper understanding not only admits the use of this method but actually requires it.... [O]ne must reject as unauthentic every interpretation alien to the meaning expressed by the human authors in their written text.[15]

The last sentence also means that the intentions of the biblical text now serve as a template for judging the appropriateness of later applications of them in Christian history. This is particularly significant for the texts of the Old Testament, which have traditionally been read in the church only as foreshadowing Christianity.

The principles of biblical criticism and concern for Jewish-Christian relations have combined in an instruction to Catholic preachers to "avoid ap-

---

People: Statement by the World Council of Churches and Its Member Churches (Geneva: WCC Publications, 1988), 24.

14. World Council of Churches, "The Church and the Jewish People," III.

15. PBC, "The Interpretation of the Bible in the Church" (1993), I, A; II, B, 1.

proaches that reduce [the Old Testament] to a propaedeutic or background for the New Testament."[16] This, of course, is precisely what was done when supersessionism prevailed and molded the classic telling of the Christian story.

This point can be illustrated by considering God's words to the serpent in Genesis 3:15, "I will put enmity between you and the woman, and between your offspring and hers; he will strike your head, and you will strike his heel." Some versions of the supersessionist classic Christian story claimed that those words constituted a divine promise "to send into the world a Savior to free man from his sins and to reopen to him the gates of heaven."[17] Thus, Israel was introduced as merely a temporary stage in preparation for the church at the very beginning of the Christian retelling of Israel's scriptures.

Critical exegeses of this Genesis passage typically see no such idea in the mind of its Yahwistic author. "Christian tradition has sometimes referred to [the offspring] as Christ, but the literal reference is to the human descendants of Eve, who will regard snakes as enemies."[18] If Catholics today "must reject as unauthentic every interpretation alien to the meaning expressed by the human authors in their written text,"[19] then Christian stories based on what are now identified as eisegetical readings of biblical texts cannot be told without significant qualification. The text's own outlook would need to be honored first before noting subsequent interpretations in the church's history.

Biblical criticism also diminishes the authority and influence of polemical scriptural passages. For example, statements about Jews, such as John 8:44, "you are from your father the devil," or Matthew 27:25, "His blood

16. NCCB, "God's Mercy Endures Forever" (1988), 31c. Note also, "Typological reading only manifests the unfathomable riches of the Old Testament, its inexhaustible content and the mystery of which it is full, and should not lead us to forget that it retains its own value as revelation that the New Testament often does no more than resume" [Vatican, "Notes" (1985), II, 7].

17. *New St. Joseph Edition of the Baltimore Catechism, No. 2* (New York: Catholic Book Publ., 1962), 36, 46.

18. Richard J. Clifford and Roland E. Murphy, "Genesis," in Raymond E. Brown, Joseph A. Fitzmyer, and Roland E. Murphy, eds., *The New Jerome Biblical Commentary* (Englewood Cliffs, NJ: Prentice Hall, 1990), 12. This volume is a compendium of centrist biblical scholarship. As further examples, see also Walter Brueggemann, *Genesis*, Interpretation Bible Commentary (Atlanta: John Knox Press, 1982), 46; Robert B. Coote and David Robert Ord, *The Bible's First History* (Philadelphia: Fortress, 1989), 63; and E. A. Speiser, *Genesis*, Anchor Bible Commentary (New York: Doubleday, 1964), 24.

19. PBC, "Interpretation" (1993), II, B, 1.

be on us and our children!" are critically understood as products of their authors' specific contentious situations (see chapter 5).[20]

Not only are Catholics instructed to read the Bible critically, they are also admonished not to actualize or apply in their contemporary context any understandings of scripture that demean Jews and Judaism. In the words of the Pontifical Biblical Commission:

> Particular attention is necessary, according to the spirit of the Second Vatican Council (*Nostra Aetate*, 4), to avoid absolutely any actualization of certain texts of the New Testament which could provoke or reinforce unfavorable attitudes toward the Jewish people. The tragic events of the past must, on the contrary, impel all to keep unceasing in mind that, according to the New Testament, the Jews remain "beloved" of God, "since the gifts and calling of God are irrevocable" (Rom. 11:28-29).[21]

Present-day retellings of the Christian story, since they must be significantly based on the biblical witness, in fact are ways of actualizing the scriptures for our times. Again, the story cannot be told in ways that promote "unfavorable attitudes toward the Jewish people."

## Today's Christian Story Can Be Told to Emphasize Relationality

A historical consciousness pervades Western society in our post-Freudian, post-Darwinian era. This is an awareness that people's experiences, cultures, and histories mold their subjective consciousness and perceptions. It grounds biblical criticism. This mindfulness of cultural conditioning also relates to our current societal preferences for an experience-based approach to reality and for empirically demonstrable truth claims.

However, the classic Christian story is significantly based on certain Greek philosophies that were the prevalent mode of thought in the patristic

---

20. See David P. Efroymson, Eugene J. Fisher, and Leon Klenicki, eds. *Within Context: Essays on Jews and Judaism in the New Testament* (Collegeville, MN: Liturgical Press, 1993).

21. PBC, "Interpretation" (1993), IV, A, 3. It seems logically inescapable that this principle must also relate to the texts of the Old Testament. So to apply it to the example of Genesis 3:15, a construal of that passage in an exclusively christological fashion would not only maintain a now-rejected supersessionist version of the Christian story, it would also disrespect the inherent revelatory value of the inspired texts of ancient Israel on their own terms. Unfavorable attitudes to Judaism would thereby be promoted.

era when many Christian doctrines were formulated. Major concepts underlying the Christian story were established in an intellectual environment that
was concerned with rationally defining the inherent *ontos* or "being" of God
and reality. These were philosophies based on an ontological metaphysics
that sought to deduce rationally the essential being of transcendent realities.

"Metaphysical theology," explains Joseph Stephen O'Leary, "wants to
construct an account of Christ independent of faith and of historical context,
an account which can be indifferently repeated in any historical context."[22]
It supposes that people can step outside history by means of reason. This
notion conflicts with current Western culture's acute awareness of the historical and cultural conditioning of personal perceptions,[23] and is one reason
why certain elements of the classic rendition of the Christian story require
intense explanation for believers today. As O'Leary notes:

> Within the horizons of [ontology, the Councils of] Nicea and Chalcedon
> said all that could be said, and needed to be said, about Christ. Yet for us
> the question about Christ and its answer can no longer be formulated in
> that particular way. The question, "Who do you say that I am?" (Mark
> 8:29) continues to sound in a pre-metaphysical way, but the metaphysical
> tradition is of only indirect assistance to us in our search for a contem-
> porary answer.[24]

This leads to a pastoral and educational conclusion: the Christian story
today should not be articulated according to currently unfamiliar philosophical presuppositions, but rather should utilize the prevalent historical
consciousness.[25] It must be stressed that an avoidance of ontological meta-

22. Joseph Stephen O'Leary, *Questioning Back: The Overcoming of Metaphysics in Christian Tradition* (Minneapolis/Chicago/New York: Winston Press, 1985), 73.

23. Note, for example: "Timebound humanity must recognize that no interpretation from one time, place, and language is ever translatable without remainder into another time, place, and language. . . . We can never escape our particularity in our interpretation. However, to-day as we try to respond to the rise of historical consciousness, we bear the burden of many centuries in which faith has sought understanding in the categories of timeless metaphysics." Bernard J. Lee, *Conversation on the Road Not Taken*, vol. 2, *Jesus and the Metaphors of God: The Christs of the New Testament* (New York/Mahwah: Paulist Press/Stimulus Books, 1993), 19.

24. O'Leary, *Questioning Back*, 76.

25. See Vatican Council II, *Gaudium et Spes*, 4: "In language *intelligible to every generation*, [the church] should be able to answer the ever recurring questions which people ask about the meaning of this present life and of the life to come, and how one is related to the other." Emphasis added.

physics and an employment of historically conscious ideas do not equal a denial of the existence of the Transcendent. It simply means that people in many parts of today's world are convinced that the Transcendent can only be discerned and rationally considered by mortals as it is mediated in the created world through history. As Saint John Paul II put it, "History . . . becomes the arena where we see what God does for humanity. God comes to us in the things we know best and can verify most easily, the things of our everyday life, apart from which we cannot understand ourselves."[26]

Likewise this move is not a rejection of the spiritual wealth of patristic philosophical theologizing. The labors of the church fathers produced a rich apprehension of the divine realities that should be honored and preserved in the Christian tradition. But people possessing a historical consciousness must necessarily discern and articulate these realities in historically conscious ways.[27]

This leads to another reason to avoid patristic-era metaphysical approaches in relating post-supersessionist versions of the Christian story. Jewish understandings of God often conflict with rational, ontological outlooks. As Bernard J. Lee explains:

> We exist in the world in our bodies. We exist in the world in time. We can only know what is related to us in the world and is together with us in time. To claim to experience God is also, therefore, to claim that God is in the world with us, and that God, therefore, is truly historical. In classical theism, the religious object (God) is not historical. God is interpreted as essentially non-temporal. The biblical experience witnesses to the contrary: God is an essential component of the evolving history of the Jewish people. But equally, Jewish history is a real component of the experience of God, which is to say, of the concrete reality of God.[28]

The historically conditioned patristic engagement with a particular type of metaphysical theologizing was thus also a move away from the re-

---

26. John Paul II, *Fides et Ratio*, 12, in *Origins* 28/19 (October 22, 1998): 321-322.

27. N.B. this comment in PBC, "Interpretation" (1993), III, B, 2: "The allegorical interpretation of Scripture so characteristic of patristic exegesis runs the risk of being something of an embarrassment to people today. But the experience of the church expressed in this exegesis makes a contribution that is always useful. . . ."

28. Bernard J. Lee, *Conversation on the Road Not Taken*, vol. 1, *The Galilean Jewishness of Jesus: Retrieving the Jewish Origins of Christianity* (New York/Mahwah: Paulist Press/Stimulus Books, 1988), 25.

lational view of life characteristic of the Hebrew/Jewish biblical tradition. This philosophical step occurred in the same era when socio-religious rivalry was spurring the creation of the *adversus Judaeos* theology. The patristic philosophical milieu and its competitive social setting thus concurrently reinforced the gradual process of de-Judaizing Christianity that was mentioned by the U.S. Catholic Bishops.[29]

Conversely, an effort to tell the Christian story non-ontologically could contribute to a renewed appreciation of the church's Jewish roots and of its kinship with Judaism today. As O'Leary observes, "The step back out of [ontological] metaphysical theology is a step towards the Jewish matrix of all our theology. . . . It is thus perhaps in the renewal of Jewish-Christian dialogue that the counter-metaphysical protest of the last four or five centuries is carried forward most radically today."[30]

Since we are human beings immersed in and restricted by time and space, our knowledge of God, the Transcendent Holy One beyond time or space, is limited to how we sensibly experience God in our lives, histories, rituals, and traditions. Even though God may be powerfully encountered, our knowledge of God is invariably partial and always mediated.[31] Faith communities' knowledge of God grows and becomes normative as their traditions unfold, but such knowledge is always open to further growth and to being experienced anew.

Thus, a retelling of the Christian story today should describe the distinctive and characteristic Christian teaching that God is Triune by portraying the Triune One as relationally experienced: constantly and simultaneously creating and sustaining, inviting into relationship, and empowering that invitation's acceptance. Likewise, Catholics are not limited to describing Jesus Christ ontologically in terms of a hypostatic union of two natures. He can also be understood as mediating covenantal relationship between humans and God within his own being. Again, such a move does not reject "meta-

---

29. NCCB, "Statement on Catholic-Jewish Relations" (1975). An illustration of "de-Judaizing" may be seen in the Nicene Creed. It asserted both the humanity and divinity of Christ using ontological terminology, but never mentions Israel or that Jesus was a Jew.

30. O'Leary, *Questioning Back,* 128-129.

31. Note the words of John Paul II, who in discussing the incarnational nature of divine revelations observes, "[O]ur vision of the face of God is always fragmentary and impaired by the limits of our understanding. Faith alone makes it possible to penetrate the mystery in a way that allows us to understand it coherently" (*Fides et Ratio,* 13). Biblically, faith is being in relationship with God, so it is relationship with God that allows a congruent understanding of God's self-disclosures.

physics," in the sense of denying transhistorical reality. Rather, a "metaphysics of relationship" should ground new renderings of the Christian story.[32] This might also be expressed as a "relational ontology."[33]

## Today's Christian Story Can Present Divine Revelation as Occurring through Our Relationships with God in Time

Based on the biblical witness and on a historically conscious approach to reality, a retelling of the Christian story today would helpfully be premised on the conviction that all human encounters with God are mediated through life's experiences in the created world and are also essentially relational.

To say that human encounters with God are relational means that humans must respond to the myriad historical mediations of God's presence and actions in order for revelations to occur. A subjective, human decision to interpret particular, concrete experiences as disclosive of the divine is required.[34] Different people can witness or experience the same events or

---

32. See Paul M. van Buren, *A Theology of the Jewish-Christian Reality,* Part 3, *Christ in Context* (San Francisco: Harper and Row, 1988), 257-258, who in a discussion of the unity between the Father and the Son observes that: "If it is predetermined that reality is to be analyzed in term of *hypostasis* (substance or subsistence) and *physis* (nature), then the hypostatic union will be judged ontological and the unity of the covenant [or relationship] only volitional. If, on the other hand, reality is analyzed in personal terms with the relationship of love between human beings taken as the highest visible form, if reality consists primarily of relationships of love and trust and forgiveness, and then, only secondarily, of material relationships, then it could be said that the covenantal model of unity is indeed ontological by its own metaphysical presuppositions." Note also John Paul II in *Fides et Ratio,* 32: "[B]elief is often humanly richer than mere evidence because it involves *an interpersonal relationship* and brings into play not only a person's capacity to know, but also the deeper capacity to entrust oneself to others, to enter into a relationship with them which is intimate and enduring." Emphasis added.

33. This term is used in Catherine Mowry LaCugna, *God for Us: The Trinity and Christian Life* (New York: HarperCollins, 1991). E.g., "A relational ontology establishes that no person can be thought of by himself or herself, apart from other persons. Even less can we reify the person of the Spirit, trying to point out what the Spirit is in and by himself or herself. . . . God's immutability is God's fidelity, both to be God and to be God-for-us. God remains eternally faithful to the Covenant made with Israel. God's self-given name, YHWH, speaks of God's promise always to be with Israel. For Christians, Jesus Christ is the definitive and fully personal sign of God's everlasting fidelity to-be-with-us. The Spirit is divine fidelity in action, as the Spirit leads all creatures into an ever-deeper communion with each other and with God" (298, 301-302).

34. Note these pertinent comments of John Paul II: "By the authority of his absolute transcendence, God who makes himself known is also the source of the credibility of what he reveals. By faith, men and women give their assent to this divine testimony. This means that

series of occurrences, but only some of them might conclude that God's activity has been revealed. Not everyone who participated in or witnessed the escape of some forced laborers from Egypt would conclude that God had chosen these people for special purposes; nor would everyone who observed an empty tomb automatically conclude that a corpse had been transformed to the life of the Age to Come.[35] Sometimes a revelation occurs only with hindsight, when sufficient time has passed for the true nature of certain experiences to be discerned and acknowledged.

These dynamics probably reflect God's profound respect for the divine gift of free will to humanity. Dramatic displays of divine power would be coercive. They would overwhelm human capacities to choose freely. Both Israel and the church experience God as one who does not use force or might to subjugate human beings. Instead, God subtly and ambiguously calls out to people. In this way they must freely choose whether to respond.[36]

Recognition of the relational nature of revelation raises the possibility that such disclosures are divinely aimed or addressed. Not only must divine self-disclosure be mediated through the created world — because of the limitations of time-bound mortals — but it is conceivable that God selects the recipients and form of particular disclosures.

The resurrection appearance narratives in the Christian Gospels illustrate this. With one famous exception, the Crucified and Raised One is only manifested to people who already were his disciples. Persons such as Pontius Pilate or Caiaphas, for instance, do not encounter the exalted Jesus. Rather, prior relationship with the Crucified One seems to have facilitated the revelation of him as raised. On the other hand, New Testament texts are also com-

---

they acknowledge fully and integrally the truth of what is revealed because it is God himself who is the guarantor of that truth. They can make no claim upon this truth, which comes to them as a gift and which, set within the context of interpersonal communication, urges reason to be open to it and embrace its profound meaning" (*Fides et Ratio*, 13).

35. PBC, "Instruction on the Bible and Christology," 1.2.6.2: "This ["decision of faith"] must be applied in a special way to the resurrection of Christ, which by its very nature cannot be proved in an empirical way. . . . [O]ne may not simplify this question excessively, as if any historian, making use only of scientific investigation, could prove it with certainty as a fact accessible to any observer whatsoever. In this matter there is also needed 'the decision of faith' or better 'an open heart,' so that the mind may be moved to assent."

36. For more on the subtlety of divine self-disclosure, see Samuel Therrien, *The Elusive Presence: Toward a New Biblical Theology* (New York/Hagerstown/San Francisco, London: Harper and Row, 1978). For an interreligious, philosophical-theological approach to the human knowing of God see David B. Burrell, *Knowing the Unknowable God: Ibn-Sina, Maimonides, Aquinas* (Notre Dame, IN: University of Notre Dame Press, 1986).

fortable depicting God as selecting for a particular revelation people without such prior relationships, Paul of Tarsus being the noteworthy example.

Thus, a relational understanding of revelation offers a further explanation of why a certain specific event makes God known to some people and not to others. Not only must the human participants choose to respond to God's invitation, but God must also have extended the particular self-disclosure in that specific setting in the first place. Given our limited perceptions, it is impossible for human beings to judge what combination of divine and human intentions prevented a revelation from occurring to specific people through a certain event or particular situation. However, understanding revelation as relational explains why some of his contemporaries would have become convinced that the Crucified One had been raised, while others would not. To use Pauline language, "God would be pleased to reveal his Son" (Gal. 1:15-16) to certain people and apparently not to reveal him to others.

For the Christian tradition, the Triune God is always at work in any relational self-disclosure of the divine. The One who sustains creation delicately invites people to relationship, while at the same time enabling them to choose to perceive and to accept the invitation. These continuous and simultaneous divine movements permeate processes of revelation. All created reality may serve as instruments of God's activity. This includes natural beauty, seasonal changes, living things, and perhaps most especially, human interactions — the camaraderie of friends, the touch of a spouse, the smile of a son or daughter. For Christians, God's invitation to relationship was revealed most powerfully in the life and death of the Galilean Jew, Jesus, and continues to be dynamically extended today in the church, the locus of the enduring activity of that Crucified and Raised One.

The human partners to a revelatory process are driven to communicate their experience to others. Again, the first preachers of Jesus as raised illustrate this. Through their agency, relationship to God through Christ was spread to others who had never had direct personal contact with Jesus the Galilean. However, due to the subjective quality of human encounters with divine self-disclosure, such transcendent experiences are invariably difficult to convey to other people. Metaphors and symbols are by nature capable of sustaining both the multi-dimensionality and ambiguity of divine self-disclosure, and so are very frequently used to attempt to impart revelatory experiences. They may indeed be the most powerful human means to describe human meetings with the divine in human history.

Once more, the Gospel resurrection accounts illustrate this very well, though many other biblical examples could be adduced. When the evangelists described the earliest perceptions that the crucified Jesus was transcendently alive, they used "appearance" narratives. Confusion and lack of recognition by Jesus' friends and a lack of consistency in terms of settings, timings, and characters typify these narratives.[37] The power of this relational revelatory event was such that efforts to conceptualize it and express it in human speech were inevitably difficult. The same holds true in varying degrees for other human interactions with the divine. Nonetheless, the creative energy unleashed by such revelatory encounters with God has generated texts of transcendent power that invite readers into encounters with God through the mediation of the written word.

## Today's Christian Story Can Understand Christ as Embodying Covenanting Life

In line with all of the above, a retelling of the Christian story today can introduce Christ as historically experienced by his Jewish contemporaries, by his Jewish disciples, and, after his death by the Jewish apostles.

Beginning a Christology with the life and death of the Galilean Jew, Jesus of Nazareth, one typically encounters the problem of how to introduce his divine status as the incarnate *Logos* or Word of God. On the other hand, starting a Christology with the pre-existent *Logos* often leads to difficulty in honoring Jesus' authentic humanity. It seems likely that the dichotomous categories utilized in conventional ontological Christologies lie at the root of these difficulties.

An approach grounded on the historical mediation of the divine and on a relational metaphysic can help avoid such problems by shifting the thought categories that are being utilized. Since, the church, as John Paul II has observed, does not "canonize any one particular philosophy in preference to others,"[38] there is no reason in principle why this should not be tried.

Thus, one can tell the Christian story by introducing Jesus historically as a Galilean Jew who undertook a mission of preparing his People Israel for the imminent commencement of the Reign of God. His contemporary impact would be described in the Jewish theological categories of his time:

---

37. See Raymond E. Brown, *The Virginal Conception and Bodily Resurrection of Jesus* (New York: Paulist, 1973), 69-129; and Pheme Perkins, *Resurrection: New Testament Witness and Contemporary Reflection* (Garden City, NY: Doubleday, 1984), esp. 71-330.

38. John Paul II, *Fides et Ratio,* 49.

thus, some people who encountered him tangibly felt the life of the Age to Come mediated through his ministry. After his death at the hands of the Roman occupiers and their pawns, his followers experienced a revelation. From a Christian perspective, they were enabled by God to perceive that the Crucified One had been raised to transcendent new life. He was living and manifesting the new life of the Age to Come. This conviction was not something that could be demonstrated empirically, because the concrete evidence of the empty tomb could be variously interpreted. However, once having affirmed this revelation his apostles were enabled to comprehend that they were experiencing God's continuous invitation to relationship through the Crucified and Raised One.

A post-supersessionist retelling of the Christian story, therefore, can understand Jesus, the faithful son of Israel, as embodying Israel's covenanting life with God. He epitomized what life in covenant was and is all about and continues to do so. One consequence of this perspective is that Israel's covenanting life with God must be permanent and vital in order for the church's covenanting with God through Christ also to be permanent and vital. If Israel's covenanting is deemed to be obsolete or inert, then Jesus would be mediating and inviting the church to a relationship with God that is also possibly temporary, obsolete, or inert. This is unthinkable. It would be contrary to character of the God of Israel and the character of Jesus to establish a covenantal bonding that was not founded upon divine fidelity and empowerment.[39] A Christology that understands Jesus as epitomizing and mediating Israel's covenanting life, then, must inevitably affirm the "covenant of eternal love which was never revoked"[40] between God and the Jewish people.[41]

Jesus walked God's Way with perfect fidelity and, like the People Israel in history, he suffered for his faithfulness to God.[42] Just as the People Israel have experienced restoration after terrible disasters, so, too, Jesus experienced a unique divine covenantal restoration after his suffering, a raising up

---

39. N.B. NCCB, *God's Mercy Endures Forever* (1988), 8: "[F]alse or demeaning portraits of a repudiated Israel may undermine Christianity as well. How can one confidently affirm the truth of God's covenant with all humanity and creation in Christ (see Rom 8:21) without at the same time affirming God's faithfulness to the Covenant with Israel that also lies at the heart of the biblical testimony?"

40. John Paul II, "Address to Jewish Leaders in Miami" (Sept. 11, 1987), 105.

41. See chapters 5 and 7 above for how the Gospel of Matthew conceives of Jesus as the embodiment of Israel's covenant and history.

42. See chapter 9 above for the remarkable comment by Pope Francis about Christians and the world not being able to thank Jews enough for their fidelity to God.

to transcendent life that showed that death itself would be defeated in the inevitable Reign of God.

As the personification of divine outreach, and the epitome of perfect human covenanting partnership with God, Jesus Christ, the Crucified and Raised One, opens up the possibility of covenanting life with God to all the nations. The Christian experience of relationship with God is christomorphic. It is shaped by the mediation of Christ.

The christological approach could loosely be called a "covenantal Christology" because it apprehends the significance of Jesus Christ through a relational metaphysic. It might be noted, using ontological language for a moment, that this covenantal Christology distinguishes between the divine *Logos* and the historical experience of that *Logos* as present in the crucified and resurrected Christ. *Logos* and Christ are not co-extensive terms. While Christ (since the incarnation) is the historical activity of the incarnate *Logos* in time — in the life, death, and resurrection of Jesus of Nazareth — Christ is not the only experience by which human beings can detect the historical activity of the *Logos*. God's constant divine invitation to relationship, the *Logos,* must be operative throughout the created universe, or God is not God of all existence. However, since the incarnation of the *Logos* in the Jew Jesus, all divine activity of the *Logos* occurs in union with the exalted Crucified One (see chapter 11).

A detailed retelling of the Christian story should incorporate recent understandings of the diversity of Jewish messianic expectations in the late Second Temple period. There did not exist one universally acknowledged messianic template with which Jesus of Nazareth could simply be compared. After experiencing him as transcendently raised, the apostles indeed understood him as Israel's messiah, but in ways that no Jew had previously imagined. The radical novelty of Christian post-resurrectional messianic understandings can be conveyed by using the Greek term "Christ" to refer to the church's experience of God in the Crucified and Raised One. The fact that this term quickly became a name rather than a title for the Raised Jesus shows how inadequately the term "messiah" (which had diverse meanings in late Second Temple Judaism in any case) expressed the apostles' experiences of their glorified master.

A post-supersessionist Christology can also have a certain eschatological focus. While recognizing that "salvation and liberation are already accomplished in Christ,"[43] it highlights the reality that Christians still await the

---

43. Vatican, "Notes" (1985), II, 9.

final establishment of that Kingdom of God for which Jesus lived, died, and was raised. In some ways both Israel's exodus and the birth of the church are "intermediate stages" in the ultimate fulfillment of God's designs.[44]

This christological perspective lends itself to the post-supersessionist goal of Jewish and Christian collaboration, as the 1985 Vatican "Notes" observed:

> [I]n underlining the [futurist] eschatological dimension of Christianity we shall reach a greater awareness that the people of God of the Old and New Testament are tending towards a like end in the future: the coming or the return of the Messiah — even if they start from two different points of view. . . . Attentive to the same God who has spoken, hanging on the same word, we have to witness to one same memory and one common hope in [the One] who is the master of history. We must also accept our responsibility to prepare the world for the coming of the Messiah by working together for social justice, respect for the rights of persons and nations, and for social and international reconciliation. To this we are driven, Jews and Christians, by the command to love our neighbor, by a common hope for the Kingdom of God, and by the great heritage of the Prophets.[45]

## Today's Christian Story Can See Salvation as Participation in God's Unfolding Plans for Creation

One of the issues that has arisen in post-supersessionist theological reflection is whether to conceive of the covenantal character of Christianity and Judaism in terms of a single covenant with different modalities or as two distinct, parallel covenants.[46] The tensions between the two approaches are partially based on concerns that, on the one hand, a single covenant model runs the constant risk of sliding into Christian supersessionism. On the other hand, a dual covenant model seems to dilute the universal salvific significance of Jesus Christ.

In retelling the Christian story, care should be taken not to discuss "cov-

44. Vatican, "Notes" (1985), II, 8.

45. Vatican, "Notes" (1985), II, 10-11.

46. See the helpful summary in John T. Pawlikowski, *Jesus and the Theology of Israel* (Wilmington, DE.: Michael Glazier, Inc., 1989), 15-47. N.B. the Vatican "Notes" (1985), I, 7: "Church and Judaism cannot be seen as two parallel ways of salvation. . . ."

enant" simplistically as a contract, an agreement, or an object. Covenant is better comprehended as a continuing action, as "covenanting." Covenanting is an ongoing sharing-in-life between God and human partners. It is not a thing that can simply be bestowed or transferred. Rather, covenanting is a relationship into which people enter and which constantly grows and deepens, unless specific individuals choose subsequently to deny the relationship's existence.

Applying this awareness to the single/dual-model debate, it seems reasonable to conclude that both Jews and Christians are sharing in a similar covenanting life with the One God. They have entered into this way of walking through life through different means — Jews through their historical encounters with God now mediated through the Torah, and Christians by encountering in Christ the embodiment of Israel's covenanting life and of God's divine invitation to relationship — but both are engaged with God in preparing for the Age to Come. Their participation in this divine endeavor saves them from falling victim to the corrosive effects of their own sin, egocentrism, and destructiveness.

This approach, therefore, has affinities with the one-covenant model. However, because of the relational and active understanding of "covenant," both Jews and Christians are seen to be fully involved in the divine instruction to complete the world. Both are covenanting with God because of the divine outreach for relationship, an invitation sustained and empowered by God, but each covenanting community has its own unique and distinctive traditions and way-of-walking with God. Supersessionism is disallowed in this approach, because it requires the ongoing dynamism of Israel's covenanting in order for Christian covenanting to be similarly vital.

Conversely, Christians might wonder if this formulation does not suffer from a critique often leveled at the two-covenant model. Namely, how is the universal salvific significance of Jesus Christ to be maintained in the case of Israel? This crucial question will be examined in detail in the following chapter. Here it may simply be observed that the historical reality of Christian oppression of Jews renders discussion of the potential theological significance of Jesus for Jews delicate and perilous for Jewish and Christian commentators alike.

In this regard, Peter von der Osten-Sacken points out the importance for current Jewish-Christian relations of Zechariah's Canticle in Luke 1:68-75. In this passage, Zechariah is portrayed as singing about his newborn son, John the Baptist, and the soon-to-be-born Jesus. He declares, "[The Lord] has raised up for us a horn for our salvation within the house of David his servant, even as he promised through the mouth of his holy prophets from of old: salvation from our enemies and from the hand of all who hate us . . . and to grant us that, rescued from the hand of our enemies, without fear we might worship him, in holiness and righteousness before him all our days" (Luke 1:69-71, 73).

Osten-Sacken points out that since Israel's enemies were Gentiles, Luke seems to hope that in the church Gentiles will become the friends of the Jewish people and so enable Jews to worship God in their way without fear. Of course, this is not what happened historically.[47]

## Today's Christian Story Can Move
## Beyond Binary Thinking into Mutuality

I think most Christians and Jews unthinkingly assume that "something went wrong" with the parting of the ways — the origins of Christianity and rabbinic Judaism as separate communities (see chapter 3). This separation is thought to have been contrary to God's will. Christians can consciously or unconsciously imagine that most Jews did not accept the Good News about Jesus because God "blinded" them (following Paul in Romans 11:25),[48] or because Jews were innocently mistaken due to a misplaced myopic focus on the Torah, or less benignly, because of their obstinacy. Jews may consciously or unconsciously assume that if not Jesus, then Paul distorted the essence of Judaism and so created the fundamentally misguided Gentile church.

Related to the feeling that something went wrong during the formative decades of Christianity and rabbinic Judaism are zero-sum speculations about what will happen at the End of Days. There exists a tendency for Jews and Christians to imagine that at the dawning of the messianic age one tradition will finally learn that it was wrong and that the other was right. Some Christians envision that Jews will finally recognize their error in failing to acknowledge Jesus Christ as the Messiah and Son of God. On the other hand, some Jews "believe that the worship of Jesus as God is a serious religious

---

47. See Peter von der Osten-Sacken, *Christian-Jewish Dialogue,* 80-81, quoted in chapter 4 above.

48. For an analysis of Pauline eschatology that concludes it is a misreading Paul to see him as arguing for a "zero sum eschatology," see Philip A. Cunningham and Mark D. Nanos, "Implications of Paul's Hopes for the End of Days for Jews and Christians Today," in *Studies in Christian-Jewish Relations* 9/1 (2014): 1-45.

error displeasing to God even if the worshipper is a non-Jew, and that at the end of days Christians will come to recognize this."[49]

Such binary thinking, which basically casts Jews and Christians in the role of either winners or losers, seems increasingly self-serving as the new relationship between Jews and Christians deepens and both come to appreciate the reflection of the Holy One in each other. As friendship between Christians and Jews grows, this tendentiousness seems more and more incompatible with the gracious, covenanting God of Israel and the church. Surely Christian theologians who are committed to overcoming supersessionism toward the Jewish people and tradition can be more creative than simply postponing the hour (even into the unknowable future) when Jews will supposedly acknowledge the error of their ways. Such assumptions must surely impair the ability of Christians to be fully open to learning from Jews' experiences of God.

I suggest an alternative presupposition to "something went wrong" in retelling the Christian story today. Why can we not suppose that the origins of our two traditions unfolded *according* to God's will? Is it not possible that God would desire two related covenanting communities in the world, perhaps to serve as enablers and correctors of one another? This alternative makes greater sense if divine revelation, God's self-disclosure, is understood as described above as essentially relational in nature. God obviously must be perfectly free to reveal different (though not contradictory) things selectively to different people. This has implications for how we imagine the dawning of the Age to Come. Note this paragraph in the 2001 study of the Pontifical Biblical Commission:

> What has already been accomplished in Christ must yet be accomplished in us and in the world. The definitive fulfillment will be at the end with the resurrection of the dead, a new heaven and a new earth. Jewish messianic expectation is not in vain. It can become for us Christians a powerful stimulant to keep alive the eschatological dimension of our faith. Like them, we too live in expectation. The difference is that for us the One who is to come will have the traits of the Jesus who has already come and is already present and active among us.[50]

49. David Berger, "On *Dominus Iesus* and the Jews," paper delivered at the 17th meeting of the International Catholic-Jewish Liaison Committee, New York, May 1, 2001.

50. Pontifical Biblical Commission, *The Jewish People and Their Sacred Scriptures in the Christian Bible* (2001), II, A, 5.

The use of such expressions as "we, too, live in expectation" and "the eschatological dimension of our faith" remind readers that both Judaism *and* Christianity will, in a sense, be superseded in the Reign of God. The practices of both traditions will be altered in the Age to Come, e.g., Catholic sacramental life would be rendered obsolete by life in God's direct presence and there would be little need for Jews to study Torah in the divine presence.

In particular the formulation that the eschatological messiah will have "the *traits* of Jesus," which would be recognized as such by Christians, is very notable. Crucially, Jewish recognition of the eschatological "One who is to come," since their "messianic expectation is not in vain," must logically depend on Jews perceiving some identifiable messianic "traits" conveyed through the Jewish tradition. One way of conceiving of these messianic matters, although there are diverse ideas both among and between Jews and Christians, is that the eschatological messiah will therefore be recognizable by both Jews and Christians on the basis of different legitimate but converging "traits." This is the "both/and" option.

It follows that each community, by seeing the other's recognition, would fully understand for the first time the "rightness" of not only its own point of view, but of the other's as well. What had been opaque about the other in historic time would become transparent in eschatological "time."

This all means that eschatological scenarios need to have much greater sophistication than simplistic zero-sum phrases like "a Jewish turn to Christ" or "Christians will see their error." The God of Israel and of Christ Jesus deserves better theologizing than that. If Christians and Jews are to live in *shalom,* in right relationship with each other, then theologies that promote mutuality are required.

## Teaching a Retold Christian Story

It seems appropriate at this point to sketch a few educational dimensions of retelling the Christian story in a post-*Nostra Aetate* church. Obviously, volumes could be written about each of them, but these brief statements may be helpful launching points for educators and homilists in their ministries.[51]

First, preachers and teachers might exhibit a certain humility in presenting the Christian faith. Although we Christians are covenanting with

---

51. For detailed recommendations for Christians about teaching and preaching on Jews and Judaism, see my *Education for Shalom* (Collegeville: The Liturgical Press, 1995), 121-135.

God through Christ, the One with whom we are in relationship is far beyond our full comprehension or experience. We must always be mindful of our dependence on our Creator and Sustainer. Humility also arises when one considers our small place in the vast universe or our brief existence as a species on the scale of cosmic time. While the psalmist perceived that humans are little less than divine (Ps. 8:6), he was also awestruck by God's concern for such seemingly insignificant creatures.

Second, because God so transcends us, we must not present our faith tradition as if we are in possession of all the answers to every conceivable question. Even if it were possible to reveal the totality of God to human mortals, our minds would be unable to cope with such revelation. Such a scenario would also overwhelm our freedom of choice and is something that a covenanting God just does not and will not do. Indeed, part of covenanting is that *we* must constantly decide how to promote the Age to Come in our particular and ever-changing circumstances. Therefore, our Christian tradition should be presented as a journey with God on which we stumble and grow in response to our call.

Third, emphasize that God has intentions for our still incomplete world and that these intentions include human participation in building the world according to God's will. No doubt it is impossible in the present to foresee all of the ways that human beings can advance God's Reign in the future. We must consciously and conscientiously pursue our covenanting responsibilities for all the future opportunities to become clear.

Fourth, when referring to the Jewish people, always note that their relationship with God is ongoing and perpetual. It is a relationship which bestows on Jews certain covenantal obligations that only they can define for themselves. However, since Jews and Christians covenant with the same One God, some of those obligations surely converge, particularly with regard to the world at large.

Fifth, stress Christian baptismal responsibilities. Through baptism, Christians have undertaken to continue the mission of Jesus Christ. This commitment and duty is renewed each time one shares in the Eucharist. Participation in and dedication to the mission of Christ sweeps one into God's salvific plans for Creation.

Sixth, observe whenever appropriate that Jews, Jesus Christ, and Christians each are living in the service of the coming Reign of God. Consequently, Christians and Jews are divinely intended to be partners and collaborators in preparing the world for the Age to Come. Despite their violent history, the formation of wholeness and right relationship, of true *shalom,* between Jews and Christians will be a powerful sign to a world in need of reconciliation and healing.

Finally, it should be noted that although tremendous progress has been made in recent decades in removing the negative Christian teaching of contempt for Jews and Judaism from official statements and textbooks,[52] there has not yet been sufficient time to reshape similarly the popular Christian religious imagination. Pope Francis's words in Israel in 2014 are relevant here:

> We need to do more than simply establish reciprocal and respectful relations on a human level: we are also called, as Christians and Jews, to reflect deeply on the spiritual significance of the bond existing between us. It is a bond whose origins are from on high, one which transcends our own plans and projects, and one which remains intact despite all the difficulties which, sadly, have marked our relationship in the past.[53]

---

52. Cunningham, *Education for Shalom.*
53. Francis, "Address to the Chief Rabbis of Israel" (May 26, 2014).

# CHAPTER 11

# Jews as Covenanting with a Triune God?

## A Question that Touches on Christianity's Central Nervous System

An enormous and inescapable theological topic confronting Christians arising from the recent rapprochement with Jews and Judaism is how to understand the relationship between the universal saving significance of Christ and the post–*Nostra Aetate* church's appreciation of the Jewish people's ongoing covenantal life with God. Cardinal Walter Kasper has framed the question this way: "How can the thesis of the continuing covenant be reconciled with the uniqueness and universality of Christ Jesus, which are constitutive for the Christian understanding of the new covenant?"[1] Or to put it another way: how should Catholics and other Christians understand the links between Christ and Israel's covenanting?

### A. The Utter Uniqueness of Christ (and of the Church)

As expressed by the 2000 declaration *Dominus Iesus,* Catholic teaching rejects a religious relativism in which "one religion is as good as the other"

---

1. "The Relationship of the Old and the New Covenant as One of the Central Issues in Jewish-Christian Dialogue," address delivered at the Centre for the Study of Jewish-Christian Relations, Cambridge, England, Dec. 6, 2004, §5.

---

This chapter adapts and expands "A Covenantal Christology," *Studies in Christian-Jewish Relations* 1 (2005-2006): 41-52. Available at http://escholarship.bc.edu/scjr/vol1/iss1/art6. It also draws upon the essay co-written with Didier Pollefeyt of the Universiteit Katholieke Leuven, "The Triune One, the Incarnate *Logos,* and Israel's Covenantal Life" in Cunningham, et al., eds., *Christ Jesus and the Jewish People Today,* 183-201.

because "Jesus Christ has a significance and a value for the human race and its history, which are unique and singular, proper to him alone, exclusive, universal, and absolute."[2] Therefore, "the Church, a pilgrim now on earth, is necessary for salvation: the one Christ is the mediator and the way of salvation; he is present to us in his body which is the Church."[3]

This does not mean, as some claim, that the Catholic Church holds that personal, individual baptism is necessary for salvation.[4] To continue with the words of *Dominus Iesus:*

> For those who are not formally and visibly members of the Church, "salvation in Christ is accessible by virtue of a grace which, while having a mysterious relationship to the Church, does not make them formally part of the Church, but enlightens them in a way which is accommodated to their spiritual and material situation. This grace comes from Christ; it is the result of his sacrifice and is communicated by the Holy Spirit;" it has a relationship with the Church, which "according to the plan of the Father, has her origin in the mission of the Son and the Holy Spirit." With respect to the *way* in which the salvific grace of God — which is always given by means of Christ in the Spirit and has a mysterious relationship to the Church — comes to individual non-Christians, the Second Vatican Council limited itself to the statement that God bestows it "in ways known to himself." Theologians are seeking to understand this question more fully.[5]

It must be noted that *Dominus Iesus* did not address the reality of the unique relationship between Judaism and Christianity,[6] a uniqueness ac-

---

2. Congregation for the Doctrine of the Faith, "*Dominus Iesus,* Declaration on the Unicity and Salvific Universality of Jesus Christ and the Church" (2000), III, 15.

3. *Dominus Iesus,* VI, 20, citing Second Vatican Council, *Lumen Gentium,* 14.

4. N.B. *Dominus Iesus,* note 82: "The famous formula *extra Ecclesiam nullus omnino salvatur* is to be interpreted in this sense (cf. Fourth Lateran Council, Cap. 1. *D Fide Catholica: DS* 802). Cf. also the *Letter of the Holy Office to the Archbishop of Boston: DS* 3866-3872."

5. *Dominus Iesus,* VI, 20-21, citing John Paul II, *Redemptoris missio,* 10; Second Vatican Council, *Ad Gentes,* 2, 7.

6. See Cardinal Joseph Ratzinger, "The Heritage of Abraham: The Gift of Christmas," *L'Osservatore Romano* (Dec. 29, 2000): "It is evident that, as Christians, our dialogue with the Jews is situated on a different level than that in which we engage with other religions." Cardinal Walter Kasper, "*Dominus Iesus,*" address delivered at the 17th meeting of the International Catholic Jewish Liaison Committee, New York, May 1, 2001, §2: "Because of its purpose, [*Dominus Iesus*] does not deal with the question of the theology of Catholic-Jewish relations, proclaimed by *Nostra Aetate,* and of subsequent Church teaching. What the document tries

knowledged by Saint John Paul II and his papal successors: "The Jewish religion is not 'extrinsic' to us, but in a certain way is 'intrinsic' to our own religion. With Judaism therefore we have a relationship which we do not have with any other religion."[7] However, the insistence of *Dominus Iesus* that Christ may not be theologically separated from the salvation of all human beings, including Jews, recalls an earlier statement from the Pontifical Commission for Religious Relations with the Jews:

> Jesus affirms that there shall be "one flock and one shepherd" (Jn. 10:16). The Church and Judaism cannot, then, be seen as two parallel ways of salvation and the Church must witness to Christ as the Redeemer for all, "while maintaining the strictest respect for religious liberty in line with the teaching of the Second Vatican Council declaration, *Dignitatis Humanae.*"[8]

This rejection of comprehending Judaism and Christianity as "two parallel ways of salvation" stems from the Christian conviction that the salvific effect of the "Christ event" is definitive for all, and so any understanding of Israel's covenanting that is totally disconnected from Christ would be untenable. Indeed, it could be argued that such would be a form of Marcionism since it risks disengaging Jesus and the church from their roots in biblical Israel.

## B. Israel's Covenanting as Saving

Beginning with *Nostra Aetate*'s present-tense citation of Romans 9:4 — "to them belong the glory, the covenants, the giving of the law" — and of Romans 11:28-29 that Jews are beloved of God and have received an irrevocable calling, Catholic teaching has increasingly valued the covenantal relationship between God and the People Israel. In addition to John Paul II's frequent references to that relationship, as, for example, one of "partners in a covenant of eternal love which was never revoked,"[9] there have been other ecclesial recognitions of its ongoing vitality.

---

to 'correct' is another category, namely the attempts by some Christian theologians to find a kind of 'universal theology' of interreligious relations, which, in some cases, has led to indifferentism, relativism and syncretism."

7. "Address at the Great Synagogue of Rome" (April 13, 1986), §4.

8. "Notes on the Correct Way to Present the Jews and Judaism in Preaching and Catechesis in the Roman Catholic Church" (1985), I.7.

9. "Address to Jewish Leaders in Miami" (Sept. 11, 1987). See also his addresses to "Rep-

The Pontifical Commission for Religious Relations with the Jews has extolled post-biblical Judaism for bringing "to the whole world a witness — often heroic — of its fidelity to the one God and to 'exalt Him in the presence of all the living' (Tobit 13:4)"[10] and called upon Christians to "strive to learn by what essential traits Jews define themselves in the light of their own religious experience."[11] It has also reminded Christians "how the permanence of Israel is accompanied by a continuous spiritual fecundity, in the rabbinical period, in the Middle Ages and in modern times . . . so much so that 'the faith and religious life of the Jewish people as they are professed and practiced still today, can greatly help us to understand better certain aspects of the life of the Church' ( John Paul II, 6 March 1982)."[12]

The Pontifical Biblical Commission has made an important hermeneutical affirmation concerning the vitality of Judaism's ongoing covenantal life with God:

> Christians can and ought to admit that the Jewish reading of the Bible is a possible one, in continuity with the Jewish Sacred Scriptures from the Second Temple period, a reading analogous to the Christian reading which developed in parallel fashion. Each of these two readings is part of the vision of each respective faith of which it is a product and an expression. Consequently, they cannot be reduced one into the other.[13]

This "irreducible" quality of the two traditions relates to the commission's earlier observation that "Jewish messianic expectation is not in vain. It can become for us Christians a powerful stimulant to keep alive the eschatological dimension of our faith. Like them, we too live in expectation. The difference is that for us the One who is to come will have the traits of the Jesus who has

---

resentatives of Jewish Organizations" (March 12, 1979); "The Jewish Community in Mainz, West Germany" (Nov. 17, 1980); "Experts Gathered by the Pontifical Commission for Religious Relations with the Jews" (March 6, 1982); "Jewish Leaders in Warsaw" ( June 14, 1987); "At Mount Sinai" (Feb. 26, 2000). See also his "Prayer at the Western Wall" (March 26, 2000) and *Ecclesia in Europa* ( June 28, 2003), II, 56.

10. "Notes" (1985), VI, 1.

11. Pontifical Commission for Religious Relations with the Jews, "Guidelines and Suggestions for Implementing the Conciliar Declaration, *Nostra Aetate* No. 4" (1974), Prologue.

12. "Notes" (1985), VI, 1.

13. *The Jewish People and Their Sacred Scriptures in the Christian Bible* (2001), II, A, 7. See: http://www.vatican.va/roman_curia/congregations/cfaith/pcb_documents/rc_con_cfaith _doc_20020212_popolo-ebraico_fr.html.

already come and is already present and active among us."[14] This acknowledgement that the covenantal life of Israel will endure throughout until the eschatological end of human history, distinct from, but related to the church's covenantal life,[15] is a further example of the Catholic respect that has been unfolding since *Nostra Aetate* for the living, post-biblical Jewish religious tradition.[16]

The recognition that Israel's covenanting with God will develop until the End of Time, combined with an awareness that a covenantal relationship is an intimate interaction of mutuality, also has implications for how Christians understand the "salvation" of Israel. Cardinal Walter Kasper has considered this topic in two addresses during his tenure as president of the Commission of the Holy See for Religious Relations with the Jews, which deserve to be quoted in full:

> [T]he Document *Dominus Iesus* does not state that everybody needs to become a Catholic in order to be saved by God. On the contrary, it declares that God's grace, which is the grace of Jesus Christ according to our faith, is available to all. Therefore, the Church believes that Judaism, i.e. the faithful response of the Jewish people to God's irrevocable covenant, is salvific for them, because God is faithful to his promises.[17]

14. *The Jewish People and Their Sacred Scripture,* II, A, 5.

15. In regard to the related but distinct covenantal lives of Jews and Christians, Gregor Maria Hoff has made the fascinating suggestion that Christians might think of their relationship along the lines of the classic christological formulation of the Council of Chalcedon. He notes: "From a Christian point of view Judaism and Christianity are both inter-dependent — and as expressed in the language of the Council of Chalcedon — *inseparable and distinct,* linked together. God's self-revelation in history desires the salvation of all humanity. This disallows any notion that Israel is to be excluded from salvation for failing to recognize Jesus of Nazareth as the messiah" ("A Realm of Differences: The Meaning of Jewish Monotheism for Christology and Trinitarian Theology," in Cunningham et al., eds., *Christ Jesus and the Jewish People Today* [Grand Rapids: Eerdmans, 2011], 218).

16. This respect has recently been powerfully articulated in Pope Francis's 2014 Apostolic Exhortation *Evangelii Gaudium:* "God continues to work among the people of the Old Covenant and to bring forth treasures of wisdom which flow from their encounter with his word. For this reason, the Church also is enriched when she receives the values of Judaism. While it is true that certain Christian beliefs are unacceptable to Judaism, and that the Church cannot refrain from proclaiming Jesus as Lord and Messiah, there exists as well a rich complementarity which allows us to read the texts of the Hebrew Scriptures together and to help one another to mine the riches of God's word. We can also share many ethical convictions and a common concern for justice and the development of peoples" (§249).

17. *"Dominus Iesus,"* paper delivered at the 17th meeting of the International Catholic-Jewish Liaison Committee, May 1, 2001, §3.

But whilst Jews expect the coming of the Messiah, who is still un-known, Christians believe that he has already shown his face in Jesus of Nazareth whom we as Christians therefore confess as the Christ, he who at the end of time will be revealed as the Messiah for Jews and for all na-tions. The universality of Christ's redemption for Jews and for Gentiles is so fundamental throughout the entire New Testament (Eph 2:14-18; Col 1:15-18; 1 Tim 2:5-7 and many others) and even in the same Letter to the Romans (Rom 3:24; 8:32) that it cannot be ignored or passed over in silence. So from the Christian perspective the covenant with the Jewish people is unbroken (Rom 11:29), for we as Christians believe that these promises find in Jesus their definitive and irrevocable Amen (2 Cor 1:20) and at the same time that in him, who is the end of the law (Rom 10:4), the law is not nullified but upheld (Rom 3:31).

This does not mean that Jews in order to be saved have to become Christians; if they follow their own conscience and believe in God's prom-ises as they understand them in their religious tradition they are in line with God's plan, which for us comes to its historical completion in Jesus Christ.[18]

It is noteworthy that in both these formulations, "salvation" is seen as a characteristic quality of Israel's covenantal life with God, though not unrelated to the redemptive work of Christ. We have thus come full cir-cle to the question with which this chapter began: how are Catholics to understand the relationship between the universal "saving" significance of Christ with the post–*Nostra Aetate* church's appreciation of the Jewish people's ongoing covenantal life with God. Or to put it crudely, "How are Jews 'saved'?"

## C. Summary

The chapter thus far has set forth some significant guiding parameters. A Catholic theology of Israel's covenanting must affirm that:

1. Israel's distinctive covenantal life with God will continue until the Eschaton;

18. "The Commission for Religious Relations with the Jews: A Crucial Endeavour of the Catholic Church," address delivered at Boston College, Nov. 6, 2002, §III.

2. Jesus Christ has a unique, universal significance for the "salvation" of all humankind; and

3. An "intrinsic" bond exists between the covenanting peoples of Israel and the church.

## Defining Our Concepts

In order to pursue the question of how Christians should understand Israel's covenanting in relation to Jesus Christ, one must grapple with the definitions of some key Christian concepts:

### A. "Salvation"

There are many ways that "salvation" is understood in Christian tradition. How one thinks about "salvation" will shape how the soteriological status of Jews is comprehended.

In an essay entitled "What Does It Mean to Be Saved?" Clark Williamson has helpfully sketched out a variety of traditional approaches.[19] He posits that all approaches to salvation involve being brought by God *from* a dire situation *to* a new and transformed situation. How these two situations are understood informs the definition of salvation. Thus, he sets forth the following Christian approaches to salvation:

*Salvation as redemption:* rooted biblically in the notion of "buying back," this approach understands salvation as a rescue: the Israelites being saved from slavery to freedom or Gentiles being freed from bondage to idols to freedom in Christ. "We are liberated from sin and evil and liberated to love the neighbor."[20]

*Salvation as reconciliation:* this approach stresses that being "saved" is principally being justified: brought or restored to full relationship with God and others. It is a transition from estrangement and hostility to intimacy and affection.

*Salvation as sanctification:* this approach stresses the entering into a life of holiness, a life grounded in ethics and a Christian character that is lived

---

19. In Philip A. Cunningham, ed., *Pondering the Passion: What's at Stake for Christians and Jews?* (Franklin, WI, and Chicago: Sheed & Ward, 2004), 119-128.

20. Williamson, "What Does It Mean to Be Saved?" 121.

out with gratitude to God. "Salvation as sanctification means that the God who calls us forward into the future that God has in mind for us . . . is a God who is never finished with us. Nor are we ever finished with God who is the ground of all possibilities and ever calls us forward into a future of blessing and well-being."[21]

*Salvation as everlasting life:* grounded in the Christian experience of Christ's resurrection, this approach thinks in terms of "salvation from death, from being utterly forgotten, from final meaninglessness and salvation to life everlasting with God."[22] It points beyond the world as we know it to the ultimacy of God's steadfast live.

These four approaches that Christians have used over time make it clear that "salvation" is a wonderfully multi-faceted concept. It ought not to be collapsed into a single, one-dimensional formula. Any working definition of salvation should be expansive enough to incorporate the rich diversity conveyed by Williamson's schema.

For the purposes of this discussion, then, salvation will be defined as being in a relationship with God that involves the ongoing acceptance, as individuals and communities, of God's invitation to participate in God's unfolding plans for the world, plans that will lead to the Reign of God, the Age to Come. Relationships with God that generate this participation are "salvific." People are "saved" from sin, meaninglessness, and death by this sharing-in-life with God, and are set on a path of reconciliation, holiness, and steadfast love. For Christians, as will be seen below, all divine invitations that bring salvation are bound up with the life, death, and resurrection of Jesus Christ.

## B. God as "Triune"

A factor that likely impedes the development of a theology of Israel's covenanting in relationship to Christ is a tendency in the West toward Christomonism, by which I mean an inclination to consider the significance of Christ's work without keeping a Trinitarian perspective in the forefront of the Christian theological imagination.

The God with whom the church covenants is a Triune God. The God of Israel is known by Christians as constantly and simultaneously creating and

21. Williamson, "What Does It Mean to Be Saved?" 125.
22. Williamson, "What Does It Mean to Be Saved?" 125.

sustaining existence, revealing and inviting people into relationship, and enabling people to perceive that continuous invitation and empowering them to accept it. These three "ways of interrelated being" or *hypostases,* known in Christian tradition as Father, Son or Word, and Spirit, are concurrently participating in a resonating dynamism in all of God's deeds in historic time. Therefore, from a Christian perspective, all human interactions with God always involve interacting with all three of the divine *hypostases* because of "their" eternal interrelationship.

As Anthony Saldarini has explained,

> The triune Christian God is one reality with inner relations among three subsistents, the begetter, the begotten and the spirated one. [. . .] In all else, in all activity, in all relationships with humans, God is, acts, loves and saves as one, indivisibly. To say that God saves humans means that the Father saves as do the Son and the Spirit. To say that Jesus the Son of God saves is to say that God saves. When God saves Israel, in the Christian understanding of God, the Spirit of God and the Son of God as well as God the Father save Israel. God has acted and acts today in and for Israel and the church. [. . .] At the most fundamental level of theology Christians need to emphasize God more than they have and Jesus Christ as savior within the context of God's relationship to humanity. Christians too frequently center everything on Jesus to the detriment of the God who sent him, guided him and sustained him.[23]

Thus, the incarnation, life, death, and resurrection of Jesus — the Jew in whom the divine *Logos* is incarnated — all occurred in "cooperation," with the dynamic involvement of the Father and the Spirit. Trinitarian thinking requires this or God is no longer One, but three. Likewise, humans experiencing a divine self-disclosure — even though revelation is fittingly attributed to the distinctive activity of the *Logos,* the Word — are always engaging all three *hypostases* inasmuch as their mortal existence is sustained by God the Father, their mortal existence is being addressed by God the Son, and their mortal existence is being empowered by God the Spirit to discern God.

---

23. Anthony J. Saldarini, "Christian Anti-Judaism: The First Century Speaks to the Twenty-first Century," Joseph Cardinal Bernardin Jerusalem Lecture, April 14, 1999.

## C. Jesus as "Christ"

Although the term *Christ* comes from the Greek word meaning "anointed one," it means much more than that in the life of the church. "Christ" is above all the term that expresses the church's experience of God's *Logos* incarnated in the human life, death, and resurrection of the first-century Jew, Jesus of Nazareth.[24] The *Logos,* the "Word" of God, is that subsistent of the Triune God that the church knows as constantly revealing God and inviting people into relationship with that One. After the experience of the resurrection, the embryonic church began to understand that the *Logos* had taken on flesh in Jesus. As the Pontifical Biblical Commission has put it, "This [Christian] faith has its origins and progressive growth in Jesus' resurrection; it was an event of salvation introduced among people who already shared the religious experience of diverse Jewish communities."[25] Ongoing reflection on the meaning of this recognition of Jesus as "Christ" and how he relates to the Father and the Spirit also led to the eventual development of Trinitarian thought. Thus, all distinctively Christian understandings of God are "christomorphic"; they are shaped by the church's experience of God as mediated through Christ.

Sometimes Christians think of "Christ" and the *"Logos"* as co-extensive terms, but this is imprecise. *Dominus Iesus* emphasized that "With the incarnation, all the salvific actions of the Word of God are always done in unity with the human nature that he has assumed for the salvation of all people. . . . Therefore, the theory which would attribute, after the incarnation as well, a salvific activity to the *Logos* as such in his divinity, exercised 'in addition to' or 'beyond' the humanity of Christ, is not compatible with the Catholic faith."[26] This means that from within the human perspective of linear time, ever since the incarnation everything that the divine *Logos* does is done in unity with the humanity of Jesus, which, since the resurrection, is a glorified humanity. What this does *not* mean is that anyone who glimpses the continuous activity of God in their lives, even if it includes a specific perception of the divine *Logos* at work, will therefore be able to glean the involvement of the transcendent Jesus, since the experience of Jesus as Christ — as the *Logos* incarnated, ministering, dying, and being raised — is a precondition for such an identification. Christians experience the *Logos* as Christ, but others may

---

24. Since the revelation of the *Logos'* incarnation in Jesus is a post-resurrectional development, the name "Jesus" herein refers to the human nature, human self-awareness, and human life and activities of that Nazorean Jew.

25. "Instruction on the Bible and Christology" (1984), 1.2.3.

26. *Dominus Iesus,* II, 10.

experience the *Logos* in non-christomorphic ways even though the church understands that Christ is always involved.

## D. The "Christ-event" as Universally Saving

With these perspectives, then, how are the incarnation, life, death, and resurrection of Jesus, sometimes collectively referred to as "the Christ-event," to be understood as universally and uniquely important for all humanity?

Again, as with other foundational questions, there are a variety of approaches that have been utilized in Christian history. Eastern Christianity, for instance, has tended to focus on the incarnation, while Western Christianity has tended to stress Jesus' death and resurrection. Even with an emphasis on the death of Jesus, there are numerous understandings of its meaning and significance just within the pages of the New Testament itself.[27]

Without attempting to delineate all the richness of the Christian tradition in this regard, and with a view to the discussion of salvation above, I propose that the salvific importance of Christ be understood as springing from the totality of the "Christ-event," (i.e., not concentrating on the incarnation or the ministry or the crucifixion or the resurrection to the exclusion of the other aspects of Jesus' life) and that the biblical model of "covenant" provides a very useful approach to understanding Christ's universal significance.

The biblical writers adapted the language of "covenant" *(b'rit)* from the various types of legal relationships in ancient societies and applied it to different moments of interaction between God and humans (e.g., with Noah, Abraham, at Sinai, etc.). Indeed, it could be argued that "covenant" is the Bible's favorite term for describing divine-human interrelationships. Thus, "covenant" can be understood in a theological sense as God and humans walking through life together in a relationship of mutual responsibilities. This concept of covenant as an ongoing, active sharing-in-life offers a primary biblical metaphor for Christians to understand the unity of the divine *Logos* with the Jew Jesus: a covenantal Christology.

Thus, it is the church's experience that Jesus Christ incarnates both the

---

27. For instance, in the New Testament one can find that Jesus' death is understood as the vindication of the righteous sufferer (Luke 24:47), the death of the ultimate martyred prophet (Luke 13:33), the justification of humanity (Rom. 4:25), the hour of Jesus' glorification (John 17:1), the supreme sacrifice (Heb. 10:12), and the revelation of Jesus as God's Son (Mark 15:39).

People Israel's covenantal relationship with God and God's constant divine self-revealing *Logos* that brings people into relationship with the Triune God.

*By embodying Israel's covenantal life with God,* Jesus, the faithful Son of Israel, epitomized what life in covenant was and is all about. Israel's experience of being in covenant with God and of trying to walk in God's Way has included times of disaster and suffering that were brought about by a combination of internal failings and external Gentile hostility. However, the People of Israel have also experienced restorations and revivals after these calamities.

For Christians, Jesus walked God's Way with perfect fidelity and epitomized the perfect Jewish covenantal partner. Like Israel, he suffered for his faithfulness to God. He also experienced a divine covenantal restoration after his suffering that was uniquely eschatological in nature, a raising up to transcendent life that showed that death itself would be defeated in the inevitable Age to Come.

The revelation of this exaltation discloses to the church the identity of Jesus as the Triune God's Word that invites people into relationship. Through Christ, through the Crucified and Raised Jew, the church continuously encounters God's sustaining invitation to and empowerment of covenantal life. Jesus Christ brings the church into ongoing covenantal life with Israel's God. God's will for the church, now become a Gentile assembly rooted in Israel's story, is made known through its Christ-shaped encounter with God.

If Jesus Christ is understood as personifying Israel's covenanting with God, and thereby making possible a similar if distinctive life for the church, then Israel's covenanting with God in biblical times and down to the present must be permanent and vital. This would explain why the church knows its own covenanting with God through Christ to also be permanent and vital. If Israel's covenanting could be obsolete or inert, then as Jesus the Jew, Christ would be mediating and inviting the church to a relationship with God that is also susceptible to being rendered outmoded by God. This is unimaginable. It would be contrary to the character of the God of Israel and the character of Jesus to establish a covenantal bonding that was not founded upon divine fidelity and empowerment.[28]

28. N.B. Bishops' Committee on the Liturgy, National Conference of Catholic Bishops, "God's Mercy Endures Forever: Guidelines on the Presentation of Jews and Judaism in Catholic Preaching" (Washington, D.C.: United States Catholic Conference, 1988), 8: "[F]alse or demeaning portraits of a repudiated Israel may undermine Christianity as well. How can one confidently affirm the truth of God's covenant with all humanity and creation in Christ (see Rom 8:21) without at the same time affirming God's faithfulness to the Covenant with Israel that also lies at the heart of the biblical testimony?"

There is a further dimension to this realization. If salvation is being in a relationship with God that involves the ongoing acceptance, as individuals and communities, of God's invitation to participate in God's unfolding plans for the created world, then Israel's covenanting life with God has always been "salvific." Although as fallible humans, the People of Israel have not always been faithful to their covenantal duties, nonetheless their covenantal life with God has endured and has contributed — and continues to contribute — to God's plans for the world. Despite failures, Israel prays for God's mercy and recommits itself to doing God's will. Christ's embodiment of Israel's covenantal life, now mediated to the church in its covenanting, is saving despite its failures as well. One might say that Christ epitomizes "saved existence." Both the People Israel and the Christian people fail in their covenantal duties, both pray for God's mercy, and both recommit themselves to doing God's will. The salvation brought through the Christ-event by the church into the whole world is an invitation to enter into covenanting life with God in service to God's Reign, and thus Israel's saving work in the world is enhanced.

The eschatological perspective introduced by reference to the Reign of God is important in this christological approach. The "exodus-event" (i.e., the escape from slavery, the giving of the Torah) can be understood as a point on the journey of humanity through history toward the Age to Come. Israel enters into covenanting life to participate in the unfolding of God's plans. The "Christ-event" (i.e., the incarnation, life, death, and resurrection of Jesus) is an essential additional point on that journey, one that both intensifies Israel's covenanting with God and universalizes it in the distinctive covenanting of the church.

*By incarnating God's self-revealing Logos,* Jesus unites in himself the covenanting life of Israel with the inner relationality of the Triune God. Through the covenanting life of the post-resurrectional church, humans are invited into a sharing-in-life with God that mirrors God's own Triune being on a mortal scale. Christians might say that the divine invitation that the church finds embodied in Jesus Christ draws people into the very way of life of the Triune God. This concept is essentially the mutual indwelling *(perichoresis)* formulation of the Gospel of John. That text portrays the Father, Son, and Spirit as "abiding in" one another. In Johannine terms eternal life is a sharing in the love-relationship between the Father and the Son in the Spirit. It is a love-life that transcends human death, as shown by the resurrection of Jesus.

Indeed, it is the love-life of the Trinity that transforms the rather routine Roman execution of what had appeared to just be one more Jew judged to be seditious into an event of universal significance. The utter self-giving of

God in the incarnation in the Jew Jesus, itself a deepening of divine intimacy with Israel for the benefit of humanity, is reflected in the self-giving of Jesus to Israel and all humanity through his death in service to God's Reign. As Louis Roy expresses it:

> More than [only] a human being, it is the Son equal to the Father who undergoes the passion. In this way, Jesus' movement of love is identical to the movement of the eternal Son. He constantly gives back to the Father everything he receives from him. This offering is not only that of the man Jesus, but inseparably that of the eternal Son. . . . The Father is the source. He gives himself entirely to his Son and he gives us the incarnate Son as well as their mutual Spirit. The Son returns this gift without reserve. . . . [W]hat salvation makes accessible is participation in the Trinitarian life.[29]

The resurrection of Jesus, which "introduced [him] into 'the world to come,' "[30] is therefore both a foretaste of the fullness of life of God's Reign and an essential step in making it inevitable. Indeed, both the incarnation and resurrection can be understood as "proleptic" (early intrusions or preliminary eruptions into historic time) manifestations of the Age to Come when God will be "all in all" (1 Cor. 15:28).

All of this should make it clear that the "Christ-event" is "unique and singular, proper to him alone, exclusive, universal, and absolute."[31] By it, the transcendent life of God that will pervade existence at the Eschaton entered into human history proleptically, thereby making the full realization of God's intentions inevitable. What a covenantal approach ensures is that this "event" is related to Israel's covenanting in ways that affirm and complexify Israel's ongoing covenantal life.

## Propositions toward a Christology in Relation to Israel's Covenanting

So how, then, are Catholics to understand the relationship between the universal "saving" significance of Christ with the post–*Nostra Aetate* church's appreciation of the Jewish people's ongoing covenantal life with God? It

29. Louis Roy, "Why Is the Death of Jesus Redemptive?" in Cunningham, *Pondering the Passion,* 137-138.
30. Pontifical Biblical Commission, "Scripture and Christology" (1984), 1.2.6.2.
31. *Dominus Iesus,* III, 15.

might be most useful to set this forth by means of a series of Christian theological propositions:

1. The One God is Triune. The inner relationality among the Three in the One God is operative in all divine-human interactions.

2. God desires and invites human beings to participate in God's unfolding plans for the establishment of God's Reign throughout all existence. This continuous work of God redeems, reconciles, sanctifies, and shares divine life with the human participants.

3. God's invitation to the People of Israel has produced a covenantal sharing-in-life between God and the Jewish people that will endure until the Age to Come.

4. As part of God's unfolding plans, God's revealing and inviting *Logos* was incarnated in a son of Israel, Jesus of Nazareth.

   A. As son of Israel, Jesus embodied Israel's covenanting life with God.

      i. Therefore, from a Christian point of view it could be said that the Holy One's intimacy with Israel attained an even greater degree of intensity in the circumcised flesh of Jesus.

      ii. Therefore, Israel's covenanting life with God must be ongoing and vital if Jesus Christ is to mediate such a covenanting life to the church.

   B. As divine *Logos,* Jesus embodied the relationality of the Triune God.

      i. Therefore, the relationality of God entered into human history in a unique way through the ultimate union of the divine with humanity.

5. The "Christ-event" — Jesus' birth, life, death, and resurrection — was a proleptic manifestation of the life of the Age to Come into human history and had these effects:

   A. The church was called into being and began a covenanting sharing-in-life with God in service to the Age to Come. The church's covenanting is "christomorphic." It is mediated and sustained through Christ, the church's experience of the divine *Logos* in his life, death, resurrection, and ongoing transcendent life.

   B. Christ personifies Israel's covenanting life for the church. He is the exemplar of human life in covenant with God.

   C. All humanity is invited to enter into the salvific participation in the unfolding of God's plans for creation.

   D. The "Christ-event" both anticipates and was necessary to make inevitable the ultimate establishment of God's Reign.

6. Since Israel covenants with God until the Age to Come, then Israel dwells in intimate relationship with the Holy One whom Christians know as Triune.
   A. Therefore, from a Christian point of view, Israel knows God's revealing and inviting *Logos,* not christomorphically, but in Jewish grapplings with the Torah, both written and oral.
7. Therefore, Jews are "saved" by their ongoing covenantal participation in God's unfolding plans for the created world, a covenanting that from a Christian point of view involves an intimate relationship — since the Holy One is Triune — with the eternal *Logos* unified with the son of Israel, Jesus.
   A. Therefore, it could be said from a Christian point of view that Jesus Christ "saves" Israel by virtue of his epitomizing and deepening of Israel's life with God, although, since Israel does not covenant with God christomorphically, the Jewish people are correct not to perceive their covenanting in this Christian way.
   B. Jewish covenanting with God involves interacting with the Torah, God's word to Israel.
   C. Jewish covenanting with God is intended by God to render a non-christomorphic service on behalf of the Age to Come.

Therefore, to paraphrase John Paul II, the Catholic people have a relationship with the Jewish people which we do not have with any other religion. Judaism is not extrinsic to us, but intrinsic.[32] Perhaps Christians might say something similar concerning Israel's relationship to the divine *Logos,* and so to Jesus, son of Israel and *Logos* incarnate. He is not extrinsic to Israel's covenanting, but intrinsic to it.

32. "Address at the Great Synagogue of Rome" (April 13, 1986), §4.

# CHAPTER 12

# Biblical Land Promises and the State of Israel:
# A Challenge for Catholic (and Jewish) Theology

## The Significance of *Eretz Yisrael*

One of the most fundamental building blocks of the new relationship between Catholics and Jews — one that still presents challenges to our inherited reflexes as Christians — was articulated in the 1974 "Guidelines and
Suggestions for Implementing the Conciliar Declaration *Nostra Aetate*, No.
4." Its preamble states, "Christians must . . . strive to acquire a better knowledge of the basic components of the religious tradition of Judaism; they must
strive to learn by what essential traits Jews define themselves in the light of
their own religious experience."

However, for Christians it is especially difficult to appreciate one particular aspect of Jewish self-understanding: the centrality for Jews of the
Land of Israel *(Eretz Yisrael)*. This is because there is no analogous dynamic
in Christianity. The Land of Israel is not inextricably connected to Christian
theology, it has no central place in the Christian effort to live as Christ, and
Christians around the world have no deeply-felt liturgical yearning for the
Land or for Jerusalem, except perhaps in the sense of the heavenly or eschatological Jerusalem.

It is true that for Christians, the region has a historical or even a sacramental aspect[1] as the place where Jesus lived and died, and so there is also
a history of pilgrimages there. It is also true that Palestinian Christians have

---

1. See Richard C. Lux, *The Jewish People, the Holy Land, and the State of Israel: A Catholic
View* (New York/Mahwah: Paulist, 2010).

This chapter updates and enlarges my "A Catholic Theology of the Land?: The State of the
Question," *Studies in Christian-Jewish Relations* 8/1 (2013).

a distinctive self-understanding as being the "living stones" whose church communities have continuously witnessed to the events of Jesus' life in the places where they physically occurred. In general, though, Christianity strongly emphasizes that God can be encountered anywhere, that holiness may be found in any land or place.

Indeed, far from resonating with the centrality of *Eretz Yisrael* for Judaism, there is what might be called "a counter-history" of Christian denial of a Jewish covenantal bond with the Land. Supersessionist Christianity claimed that Jews had forfeited any religious tie to the Land because of their alleged collective guilt for the crucifixion of Jesus. Those who polemicized against Judaism argued that God had cursed all Jews, as evidenced by the destruction of the Temple and the supposed condition of Jews as homeless wanderers.[2] As is well known, this outlook was expressed by Pope Pius X to Theodor Herzl in 1904. According to Herzl, who was seeking papal approval for his Zionist project, Pius said, "The Jews have not recognized our Lord, therefore we cannot recognize the Jewish people. . . . The Jewish faith was the foundation of our own, but it has been superseded by the teachings of Christ, and we cannot admit that it still enjoys any validity."[3]

All of these factors make it very difficult for most Christians to resonate with the spiritual significance of the Land of Israel for Jews. We have no cognate covenantal connection, we stress the universality of the Christian Gospel, and we have long precedents of rejecting any ongoing Jewish spiritual ties to the Land. For today's post-supersessionist Catholics, it is additionally challenging to develop a theology of the Land that respects its significance for our Jewish brothers and sisters who covenant with God. This chapter surveys the state of the question in post–*Nostra*

---

2. To just cite two examples spanning a millennium: Origen (ca. 248): "And that same Providence which of old gave the law, and has now given the Gospel of Jesus Christ, not wishing the Jewish state to continue longer, has destroyed their city and their temple: it has abolished the worship which was offered to God in that temple by the sacrifice of victims, and other ceremonies which He had prescribed. And as it has destroyed these things, not wishing that they should longer continue . . . (*Contra Celsum*, 7:26); Pope Innocent III (1209): "The Lord made Cain a wanderer and a fugitive over the earth, but set a mark upon him, making his head to shake, lest any finding him should slay him. Thus the Jews, against whom the blood of Jesus Christ calls out, although they ought not be killed, . . . yet as wanderers ought they to remain upon the earth, until their countenance be filled with shame and they seek the name of Jesus Christ, the Lord" (Solomon Grayzel, *The Church and the Jews in the XIIIth Century — A Study of Their Relations during the Years 1198-1254* [New York: Hermon Press, 1966], 95).

3. Raphael Patai, *The Complete Diaries of Theodor Herzl*, translated by Harry Zohn (New York/London: Herzl Press, Thomas Yoseloff, 1960), 1603.

*Aetate* Catholicism; prior to the Second Vatican Council, magisterial or papal documents would have posited that Jewish covenantal life had been either divinely revoked or cursed, as in the case of Pius X. Nonetheless, it is possible to delineate the current parameters of the question of a theology of *Eretz Yisrael* in the Catholic community today and to sketch avenues for future thought.

## "Notes on the Correct Way to Present Jews and Judaism in Preaching and Catechesis in the Roman Catholic Church"

The Vatican II declaration *Nostra Aetate* made no reference to *Eretz Yisrael,* except perhaps indirectly when it stated: ". . . in her rejection of every persecution against any person, the Church, mindful of the patrimony she shares with the Jews and moved *not by political reasons* but by the Gospel's spiritual love, decries hatred, persecutions, displays of anti-Semitism, directed against Jews at any time and by anyone."[4] The phrase "not by political reasons" was included because of opposition to the declaration stemming from the Arab-Israeli conflict, as it was then called. Some Council fathers argued that any positive statement about Judaism would be seen as favoring the State of Israel and might bring retaliation upon the Christian minorities living in predominantly Muslim countries.[5] Thus, *Nostra Aetate* sought to separate its theological inspiration from any political considerations. This motivation, incidentally, may have contributed to Pope Paul VI's careful avoidance of the word "Israel" in his historic visit to the "Holy Land" in January 1964. An ill-chosen sentence uttered during his closely scrutinized pilgrimage could have scuttled *Nostra Aetate*'s chances in the Council.

The first post-conciliar Vatican text to fully engage the existence of the modern State of Israel came from the Pontifical Commission for Religious Relations with Jews (and note, again, the adjective "religious" — in contrast to "political" — in the commission's title). In its 1985 "Notes on the Correct Way to Present Jews and Judaism in Preaching and Catechesis in the Roman Catholic Church," it stated the following:

4. Second Vatican Council, *Nostra Aetate,* §4 (1965). Emphasis added.

5. See, e.g., the interventions of Cardinal Ignatius Gabriel Tappouni and Archbishop Joseph Tawil during the Second Vatican Council's "Great Debate" on what would become *Nostra Aetate,* respectively on Sept. 28 and 29, 1964; available at: http://www.ccjr.us/dialogika -resources/documents-and-statements/roman-catholic/second-vatican-council/na-debate.

The history of [the people of] Israel did not end in 70 A.D. It continued, especially in a numerous Diaspora which allowed Israel to carry to the whole world a witness — often heroic — of its fidelity to the one God and to "exalt Him in the presence of all the living" (Tobit 13:4), while preserving the memory of the land of their forefathers at the heart of their hope (Passover Seder). Christians are invited to understand this religious attachment which finds its roots in Biblical tradition, without however making their own any particular religious interpretation of this relationship. The existence of the State of Israel and its political options should be envisaged not in a perspective which is in itself religious, but in their reference to the common principles of international law. The permanence of Israel (while so many ancient peoples have disappeared without trace) is a historic fact and a sign to be interpreted within God's design. We must in any case rid ourselves of the traditional idea of a people *punished,* preserved as a *living argument* for Christian apologetic. It remains a chosen people. . . .[6]

This paragraph sets forth the Vatican's highly nuanced distinction between the theological and politico-historical aspects of Christian attitudes toward the State of Israel. It could be summed up in these three points:

1. Catholics cannot think of Jews as punished and so divinely detached from *Eretz Yisrael.*
2. The continued existence of the Jewish people, *B'nai Yisrael* or *'Am Yisrael,* is God's will.
3. Catholics should respect and seek to understand Jewish attachment to *Eretz Yisrael,* but the existence of the modern State of Israel *(Medinat Yisrael)* should not be interpreted by Catholics primarily in religious or biblical categories, but according to international legal principles.

To elaborate on this third point: the State of Israel is a nation-state that is not co-extensive with the covenanting community of *b'nai Yisrael* (i.e., the Jewish people) even though *Eretz Yisrael* is a defining reality for the Jewish people as a whole. The 1985 "Notes" thus expressed a certain unresolved tension: methodologically, how do Catholics go about respecting the religious centrality of the Land of Israel for Jews while considering the modern State of Israel only in terms of distinct, non-religious international legal norms?

The Catholic magisterium acknowledges that religious activity (includ-

6. Vatican, "Notes" (1985), VI, 1.

ing the composition of the Bible itself) is historically conditioned.[7] Although making distinctions is possible, a recognition of historical conditioning would seem to lead to the conclusion that the religious and secular realms cannot be fully separated.[8] This misgiving grows when one realizes that to suddenly claim that a renewed Jewish presence in the Land is devoid of religious meaning after alleging for centuries that Jewish exile from the Land was theologically significant seems capriciously inconsistent.

Even more troubling, since both Judaism and Christianity are premised on the idea that God is involved in human history, a radical disjuncture between the "secular" and "religious" realms cannot be absolutely maintained in either tradition without undermining their respective truth claims.

This tension between religious convictions and modern geopolitics can also be found among Jewish thinkers. For example, Rabbi Henry Siegman made a presentation to the 1976 Jerusalem meeting of the International Catholic-Jewish Liaison Committee,[9] in which he observed, on the one hand, that "The State of Israel is the result not only of modern forces of nationalism, or even of the persecution of the Jew. . . . The Jew is driven by a force as old as the Bible to reunite with the Land. The importance of this 'internal' significance of Israel is one which Christians (and Jews) often fail to grasp." On the other hand, he cautioned that

> [T]he recognition that Judaism — unlike Christianity — is a faith uniquely dependent on the national existence of a particular people does not translate itself automatically into an argument for Jewish political rights in Palestine. We have been less than meticulous in making those necessary distinctions that need to be made when invoking religious tradition and Biblical texts. . . . To raise this concern is not to bring into question the fundamental Jewish unity of faith, land and people. This unity remains at the core of our identity and existence. What it does emphasize is the dan-

---

7. Congregation for the Doctrine of the Faith, *Mysterium Ecclesiae* (1973).

8. This point is also relevant to another element in Catholic-Jewish relations; namely, the way in which Rabbi Joseph Soloveitchik's 1964 essay "Confrontation" is used by some Orthodox Jews to seek to restrict conversation between Jews and Catholics to only secular or civil topics. See Joseph B. Soloveitchik, "Confrontation," *Tradition: A Journal of Orthodox Thought* 6/2 (1964): 5-29.

9. Henry Siegman, "Ten Years of Catholic-Jewish Relations: A Reassessment," in International Catholic-Jewish Liaison Committee, *Fifteen Years of Catholic-Jewish Dialogue, 1970-1985: Selected Papers* (Libreria Editrice Vaticana, 1988), 26-45. See especially the section on "The State of Israel," 33-37.

ger of blurring the crucial distinction between the religious meaning that Jews appropriate . . . from political events (a Biblically-conditioned Jewish reflex), and imbuing these events with an absolute sacredness that removes them from the realm of history. The latter is Jewishly uncharacteristic, and can lead to a chauvinism that is oblivious to the rights and aspirations of others. In theological terms, it risks becoming *avodah zarah* — idolatry.

## The Catholic Biblical Renaissance

For Catholics, this need to discern the intertwined political and religious realms is augmented by the renaissance in Catholic biblical studies that began in 1943 with an encyclical letter by Pope Pius XII, *Divino Afflante Spiritu* (see chapters 1 and 2). In brief, Catholic teaching today insists that "For the correct understanding of what the sacred author wanted to assert, due attention must be paid to the customary and characteristic styles of perceiving, speaking, and narrating which prevailed at the time of the sacred writer. . . ."[10] This is because "Holy Scripture, inasmuch as it is the 'word of God in human language,' has been composed by human authors in all its various parts and in all the sources that lie behind them."[11]

How does this relate to the subject of a Christian theology of the Land? Since the scriptures of ancient Israel are part of the Christian Bible, traditionally called the "Old Testament," then passages concerning the promise or leasing or bequest of *Eretz Yisrael* to the Hebrew peoples must be interpreted by Christians today in the light of the existence of the modern State of Israel. What, if any, is the relationship between those texts from over two thousand years ago and the foundation of a self-defined Jewish nation-state in the twentieth century? To give one specific example, can the Bible be expected, for instance, to specify the boundaries of the present-day State of Israel?

If so, how do today's readers decide among the various contradictory delineations found even in a single biblical book, the Book of Joshua? As Cornelis de Vos has explained, Joshua 1:1-4 describes an expansive "Euphratic Israel," which never belonged to the Israelites, but instead reflects the promise to Abraham in Genesis 15:18. Most of Joshua outlines a smaller territory (from Dan to Beer Sheva), which was probably the greatest extent

10. Second Vatican Council, *Dei Verbum* (1965), §12.
11. PBC, "The Interpretation of the Bible in the Church" (1993), I, A.

of land under the Davidic/Solomonic united kingdom. In Joshua, the ideal geography is to portray the division of the territory of Canaan. However, Joshua 13 describes remaining non-captured land, including the Philistine area (roughly today's "Gaza Strip"), so there is a clash between the "ideal" territory (Josh. 11:21-23) and the "real" situation (13:1-7).[12]

Given such dilemmas, the Catholic approach to biblical interpretation insists that the very different social, historical, and perspectival contexts of the ancient world must be dialectically related to the social, historical, and perspectival contexts of the world of today through a dialogue across the millennia. It objects to simply uprooting scriptural passages from their cultures and transplanting them into our own times.[13]

This defining Catholic scriptural orientation rules out the facile application of biblical land promises to the modern world. From a Catholic perspective, some Christians (and Jews) attempt this kind of simplistic temporal transplantation when they argue that "God gave the Land of Israel to the Jews" as if this should settle all contemporary geopolitical disputes. Rather, biblical texts, in the Catholic understanding, have to be "reread in the light of new circumstances and applied to the contemporary situation of the people of God."[14]

Thus, the Catholic community today finds itself in the unprecedented situation of grappling with the centrality of *Eretz Yisrael* for Jews while renouncing its supersessionist past, and in the context of the existence of a modern Jewish nation-state. Clearly, one pathway that is closed to us is a simplistic "fundamentalist" implementation of biblical land promises.

## Jews as the "Chosen People"

On the other hand, another pathway closed to Catholics is to backslide into a supersessionist "default position" that denies or minimizes the vitality of

---

12. Cornelis de Vos, "The Book of Joshua on the Land," paper presented at the Promise, Land, and Hope research project of the International Council of Christians and Jews, Catholic Theological Union, Chicago, August 14, 2013.

13. See PBC, "Interpretation" (1993), I, F: "It is a question of overcoming the distance between the time of the authors and first addressees of the biblical texts, and our own contemporary age, and of doing so in a way that permits a correct actualization of the Scriptural message so that the Christian life of faith may find nourishment."

14. PBC, "Interpretation," IV, A. How these Catholic hermeneutical principles relate to Jewish interpretative practices would be a worthwhile subject for interreligious discussion.

Jewish covenantal life. This was vividly illustrated when after a 2010 special bishops' Synod on the Middle East in the Vatican, Melkite Archbishop Cyril Bustros said in a news conference conducted in French:

> [W]e say that we cannot resort to theological and Biblical assumptions as a tool to justify injustice. We want to say that the promise of God in the Old Testament, relating to the "promised land" . . . as Christians, we're saying that this promise was essentially nullified [in French, "abolished"] by the presence of Jesus Christ, who then brought about the Kingdom of God. As Christians, we cannot talk about a "promised land" for the Jews. We talk about a "promised land" which is the Kingdom of God. That's the promised land, which encompasses the entire earth with a message of peace and justice and equality for all the children of God. There is no preferred or privileged people. All men and women from every country have become the "chosen people." This is clear for us. We cannot just refer to the "promised land" to justify the return of the Jews in Israel, and [ignore] the Palestinians who were kicked out of their land. Five million Jews kicked out three or four million Palestinians from their land, and this is not justifiable. There's no "chosen people" any longer for Christians. Everybody is the "chosen people." What we say is something political. Sacred scripture should not be used to justify the occupation of Palestinian land on the part of the Israelis.[15]

From the perspective of the principles of Catholic biblical interpretation, Archbishop Bustros was quite correct in saying that Old Testament Land promises cannot be simply transposed into the twentieth or twenty-first centuries. However, in rightly rejecting this crude procedure, he drew upon supersessionist argumentation from the patristic period; namely, that Christian universalism has supplanted Jewish particularism.

In his later Apostolic Letter in response to the Synod on the Middle East, Pope Benedict XVI seemed to be responding to Archbishop Bustros when he wrote:

> The bonds uniting Christians and Jews are many and they run deep. They are anchored in a precious common spiritual heritage. There is of course our faith in one God, the Creator, who reveals himself, offers his unending

---

15. John L. Allen, Jr., "Thinking Straight about Israel, the Jews, and the Archbishop," *NCR Online* (Oct. 27, 2010).

friendship to mankind and out of love desires to redeem us. There is also the Bible, much of which is common to both Jews and Christians. For both, it is the word of God. Our common recourse to sacred Scripture draws us closer to one another. Moreover, Jesus, a son of the *Chosen People,* was born, lived and died a Jew (cf. Rom. 9:4-5). Mary, his Mother, likewise invites us to rediscover the Jewish roots of Christianity. These close bonds are a unique treasure of which Christians are proud and for which they are indebted to the *Chosen People.* The Jewishness of the Nazarene allows Christians to taste joyfully the world of the Promise and resolutely introduces them into the faith of the *Chosen People,* making them a part of that People. Yet the person and the deepest identity of Jesus also divide them, for in him Christians recognize the Messiah, the Son of God.[16]

The affirmative use of the phrase "Chosen People" three times in one paragraph is certainly noteworthy in this context. The pope is implicitly correcting Archbishop Bustros's universalization of the concept of chosenness when that denies the ongoing covenantal status of the Jewish people.

It thus seems clear that Catholic theological engagement with the centrality of *Eretz Yisrael* for Jews can endorse neither a fundamentalist extreme that blithely asserts, "The Bible says that God gave the Land to the Jews," nor a supersessionist universalization that dismisses the particularity of the Jewish covenantal experience. The task awaiting us is how to positively articulate a centrist hermeneutic.

## Some Particular Challenges

It seems to me that Archbishop Bustros was caught in a still unresolved theological challenge that takes a particularly acute form for Middle East Christians: How should post–*Nostra Aetate* Catholics critically actualize biblical land passages in the twenty-first century?[17] Given their experience of statelessness and Israeli governance, it is plainly and understandably difficult for Christians in the Middle East, including Palestinian Catholics, to

16. Benedict XVI, *Ecclesia in Medio Oriente* (2012), §20. Emphases added.

17. As described in chapter 1, "actualization" is the companion activity with "Explanation" in the dialectical process of biblical interpretation. The interpreter exegetes the biblical text to "explain" it in its own frames of reference but also actualizes the text to understand its significance for today's world by putting ancient witnesses to faith into dialogue with today's faith community. See PBC, "Interpretation" (1993), IV.

embrace the post–Vatican II renunciation of classic supersessionism because they perceive this renunciation as legitimating claims that the Bible demands their own physical supersession by Israelis.

There is an additional spiritual problem for Middle-Eastern Catholics that has been raised in dialogues between the International Council of Christians and Jews (ICCJ) and some signatories of the December 2009 statement, "Kairos Palestine: A Moment of Truth: A word of faith, hope, and love from the heart of Palestinian suffering." Palestinian Christians find it difficult to draw spiritual sustenance from the Old Testament.[18] Understandably, they tend to react negatively to biblical references to "Israel" because they relate them to their experiences of the modern Israeli state. To quote from a recent ICCJ text, "Those scriptures — which because they emerged from situations of oppression (e.g., Exodus), despair (e.g., Lamentations) and suffering (e.g., Job), and have over the centuries brought hope to countless distressed people — are tragically unhelpful to many Palestinian Christians. We admire and encourage those Christian pastors who are struggling valiantly against circumstances that promote a kind of modern neo-Marcionism, a very early distortion of Christianity that discarded the Hebrew scriptures."[19]

The work of relating Jewish covenantal life, including its Land dimensions, to Christian theology will continue in various parts of the world, but the uniquely challenging pastoral situation confronting Palestinian Christians should not be overlooked. In addition, to paraphrase the late Rabbi Leon Klenicki, everyone should make conscious efforts to "have mercy upon their words."[20]

It might also be kept in mind that Catholic grappling with these questions occurs on a different footing than it does in other churches. The Holy See maintains a diplomatic corps and has formal ambassadorial-level relations with many nations, including the State of Israel.[21] This means that the

18. See the relevant comments in Patriarch Michel Sabbah, "Reading the Bible in the Land of the Bible" (November 1, 1993).

19. ICCJ, "'As Long as You Believe in a Living God, You Must Have Hope': Reflections on the Role of Religious and Interreligious Groups in Promoting Reconciliation about and in the Troubled Middle East" (May 13, 2013), §5.

20. See ICCJ, "'Let Us Have Mercy Upon Words': A Plea from the International Council of Christians and Jews to All Who Seek Interreligious Understanding" (July 26, 2010).

21. The 1993 "Fundamental Agreement" between the Holy See and the State of Israel does not contain any elements useful in developing a Catholic "Land theology" and so has not been quoted here. Some legal aspects of that agreement still have not been fully implemented despite years of negotiations.

Catholic hierarchy relates both to the Jewish people around the world in more explicitly religious ways through dialogues and collaborative action, and also to the citizens of Israel (Jews, Christians, and Muslims) diplomatically and politically through the Holy See's Secretariat of State. The diplomatic connection with the State of Israel and with neighboring countries gives the Vatican unique perspectives and access to important leaders in times of increased tension and violence.[22]

The challenging question, "How should Catholics critically actualize biblical Land passages today?" is further complicated by an observation made by the U.S. Catholic Bishops in 1975: "In dialogue with Christians, Jews have explained that they do not consider themselves as a church, a sect, or a denomination, as is the case among Christian communities, but rather as a peoplehood that is not solely racial, ethnic or religious, but in a sense a composite of all these."[23] This understanding of Jewish identity as a "peoplehood" means that Christian theologies must distinguish among the various ways — religious, spiritual, ethnic, political, historical, etc. — in which the Land is central to Jews. But how and by what criteria?

## Catholics and a Theology of the Land: Next Steps

In this concluding section, we will consider how Catholics might move forward in critically actualizing biblical Land texts today. Our concern is not to analyze or adjudicate the multiple conflicted geo-political and legal issues that afflict the Middle East today. It is, rather, to focus rather narrowly on the religious meaning of the existence of a self-defined Jewish nation-state.

Still, it must be admitted that there is something ultimately unsatisfying with positing a categorical separation between the religious and geo-political realms.[24] This is perhaps particularly true for Christians who believe

22. This was perhaps most dramatically evident in recent years by the invitation of Pope Freancis to the Presidents of Israel and the Palestinian Authority to join him and Ecumenical Patriarch Bartholomew to pray for peace in the Vatican gardens on June 8, 2014.

23. NCCB, "Statement on Catholic-Jewish Relations" (1975).

24. See Ruth Langer, "Theologies of the Land and State of Israel: The Role of the Secular in Christian and Jewish Understandings," *Studies in Christian-Jewish Relations* 3 (2008): http://escholarship@bc.edu/scjr/vol3. Also of interest in terms of Christian churches' statements about the Middle East is Adam Gregerman, "Sacred Past, Secular Present?: Contemporary Church Statements on the State of Israel," paper presented at the 2014 consultation of the

that God's divine Word entered into human history and was enfleshed in the Jew Jesus. It seems more faithful to the incarnational nature of Christianity to seek to discern God's activity in human events rather than unconditionally ruling God out of the historical picture. Maybe this is why Christians find it difficult to avoid invoking biblical themes when commenting on current geopolitics in the region.

Discerning God's role in history was a pressing topic for some Catholic leaders after the 1967 Six-Day War when the State of Israel emerged victorious from a multi-national conflict that left it in possession of the Sinai Peninsula and all territory west of the Jordan River, including the entire city of Jerusalem. Some Christians (and Jews) asked themselves if they had witnessed a miracle unfolding before their eyes. One cardinal, perhaps operating with a theology that sees revelation as unfolding over time (see chapter 10) cautiously opined, "After the Six Day War, in Rome, we contemplated this phenomenon and we came to the conclusion that it is a mystery beyond our immediate capacity to grasp, to plumb its depths, and we decided to wait to see how this will unfold."[25] Without banishing God from any role in history, this conclusion respects the limits of what human beings can know and perhaps informs the perspective of the 1985 Vatican "Notes" cited above.

David Hartman has helpfully turned away from the question as to whether or not the establishment of the State of Israel was God's will. After all, if one is appropriately modest about the extent to which mortal humans can grasp the mind of God, it becomes clear that this is an irresolvable and futile debate. Hartman writes:

> I do not interpret current events in nature and history as direct expressions of God's will or design. I look exclusively to the Torah and *mitzvot* [commandments] as mediators of the personal God of the covenant. That, however, does not mean that I must . . . ascribe no religious significance to the rebirth of Israel. From my perspective, the religious meaning one gives to events relates not to their divine origin but to their possible influence on the life of Torah. If an event in history can be a catalyst for a new perception of the scope of Torah, if it widens the range of halakhic [commandment-centered] action and responsibility, if it provides greater

"Promise, Land, and Hope" project of the International Council of Christians and Jews, Hochschule für Jüdische Studien Heidelberg, University of Heidelberg, June 24, 2014.

25. Raymond Cohen, "The Document that Never Was: People, Land, and State after *Nostra Aetate*," paper presented at the 2014 consultation of the "Promise, Land, and Hope" project of the International Council of Christians and Jews, June 24, 2014, 2.

opportunities for hearing God's *mitzvot,* then this already suffices to endow the event with religious significance, for it intensifies and widens the way God can be present in the daily life of the individual and the community. One can religiously embrace modern Israel not through a judgment about God's actions in history but through an understanding of the centrality of Israel for the fullest actualization of the world of *mitzvot.*[26]

In line with Hartman's perspective here, Christians who are trying to understand their Jewish neighbors better might productively ask what religious significance the establishment of the State of Israel has had for Jews. For Catholics, this question flows from the effort "to learn by what essential traits Jews define themselves in the light of their own religious experience."[27]

In exploring what the existence of a Jewish nation-state might mean for Jews, Christians should be aware that Jews themselves — whether living in Israel or the United States or elsewhere in the world — are also struggling to come to grips with the new reality of the State of Israel. Clearly, being a majority in a particular country presents unmatched opportunities for Jews to live out their covenantal lives in new ways. Tragically, the peace over time that is necessary to comprehend more fully what this means has been elusive. There are diverse Jewish religious understandings of the existence of the State of Israel and their ongoing process of reflection has implications for how Christians consider these matters, too. But it is an internal Jewish process.

Therefore, if Christians truly respect the integrity of the Jewish relationship with God, then they cannot presume to instruct Jews about the particularities of their own covenantal life, especially by using traditional (usually anti-Jewish) Christian approaches to do so. Humility is perhaps especially called for with regard to the complex relationship between the Land of Israel, *Eretz Yisrael,* and the State of Israel, *Medinat Yisrael.* We Christians have inherited long-standing reflexes of invidiously contrasting in dichotomous and anti-Jewish ways a supposed Christian universality with an alleged Jewish particularity (as was seen in the comments of Archbishop Bustros above).

Because Christian theologians lack any positive theological traditions about Jewish attachment to *Eretz Yisrael* of their own, perhaps the most im-

26. David Hartman, *A Living Covenant: The Innovative Spirit in Traditional Judaism* (Woodstock, VT: Jewish Lights, 1997), 281.

27. Vatican, "Guidelines" (1974), Preamble.

portant thing that they can do is to stand ready to support Jewish colleagues in grappling with the deeply challenging questions that the creation of the State of Israel poses for Jewish covenantal identity. Such Christian support would not take the form of invoking perspectives reminiscent of the church's supersessionist legacy. Rather, it would emerge from the sharing of experiences of walking with God together in our different ways. In other words, I am suggesting that Christians cannot develop their own theology of the Land in isolation from Jews who are wrestling today with similar questions. After all, today's Jews and Christians are both challenged to actualize the Land dimensions of Judaism's covenantal life — couched in ancient political systems and worldviews — in our very different twenty-first-century social, historical, and religiously plural contexts.

Is it not conceivable that we could collaborate in bringing our different traditions of interpretation to bear on these complex issues? Since we both find the pertinent questions perplexing within our respective frames of reference, perhaps we could creatively open up new approaches if we intensified our dialogue in a sustained and focused way. Perhaps we could each make progress, not despite our different traditions and perspectives, but actually *because* of them. Our blessed, if still youthful, "new relationship" gives us opportunities for a mutually enriching interreligious synergy that our ancestors could not have imagined. This tantalizing prospect presents itself as the fiftieth anniversary of *Nostra Aetate* is celebrated.

# CHAPTER 13

# Reflections on the Dynamics of Catholic-Jewish Rapprochement

## Taking Stock

This book is devoted to the development of a "Theology of Shalom," a theology of right relationship between Christians and Jews. As has been repeated continuously, this endeavor only became possible with the issuance in 1965 of *Nostra Aetate* by Pope Paul VI and the Second Vatican Council. After fifty years of unprecedented and intensifying conversations, it seems an appropriate moment to take stock of what we've learned about the nature of our dialogue and the dynamics of our interaction. Obviously, I will regard the Catholic-Jewish interrelationship from a Catholic perspective, though I'll engage with some Jewish voices as well.

It makes sense to begin with an axiom that has been expressed in the Catholic community. Difficult to maintain in practice, it has been cited many times in this book because of its crucial importance: "Christians must . . . strive to learn by what essential traits Jews define themselves in the light of their own religious experience."[1] Logically, the same should hold true in reverse; namely, that Jewish theological thinking about Christianity needs to reckon with Christian self-understandings. It is there that a Christian theologian can make some contribution, just as Jews have offered invaluable assistance to Christians as we reformulate our teachings

---

1. Vatican, "Guidelines" (1974), Preamble.

This chapter draws upon but significantly reworks my "Reflections from a Roman Catholic on a Reform Theology of Christianity," *CCAR Journal: A Reform Jewish Quarterly* 52 (Spring 2005): 61-73.

about Judaism.[2] Indeed, one conclusion is that Jews and Christians must collaborate closely in sustained study if they are to develop enduring theologies of each other that are authentic to their respective traditions. Such partnership is necessary to contribute to *shalom* or right relationship between them.

## Inhibiting Factors

In response to the *Shoah,* many Christian communities have embarked on a process of reforming inherited negative theological attitudes toward Jews and Judaism. Given the longevity and pervasiveness of supersessionism in Christian teaching, this is an unparalleled and difficult process. It touches on all aspects of Christian faith including Christology, ecclesiology, soteriology, ethics, and liturgy.

However, because of our history and our majority status everywhere in the western world we Christians pursue such work in a different context than Jews engaged in similar reappraisals about Christianity. In addition, for most of Christian European history Jews were a tolerated and marginalized minority. Our different historical memories and demographic realities combine to produce several consequences when today we seek a new relationship. Not least among them are the different effects they have on the theological self-understandings of Jews and Christians.

It is only natural for Christians working for friendly relations between our faith communities to look for signs of acknowledgement, affirmation, and perhaps even reciprocity from Jews. However, I believe that the perennial Christian "teaching of contempt" for Jews precludes Christians from expecting Jews to respond on any kind of predetermined path or timetable. It is perfectly reasonable for Jews to be skeptical of Christian overtures, waiting to see if relatively recent reforms are sincere and long lasting.

Additionally, the different demands placed on Jews and Christians by their new, positive relationship should be respected. For one thing, the relative sizes of the two communities are highly significant, with Jews being a

---

2. For example, the multi-year research project presented in Cunningham et al., eds., *Christ Jesus and the Jewish People Today* (Grand Rapids: Eerdmans, 2011), focused on an inner-Christian theological question: How to relate Christ as universal savior to Jewish covenantal life with a saving God? However, the research team also included Jewish consultants, "whose role was to ensure the accuracy of any references to Jewish concepts and teachings. They also offered very helpful insights from within their own tradition" (xxi).

tiny minority everywhere in the world except the State of Israel, and there the Jewish majority faces the unfamiliar challenge of how to relate to religious minorities.

In my view, our own religious values demand that we Christians vigorously pursue our theological reform about Jews. This duty is not contingent upon Jewish approbation. We need to demonstrate by our behavior over time that true *teshuvah,* a genuine change of heart, is occurring.[3]

Moreover, both of our communities are habituated to the centuries-old practice of defining our own identities in zero-sum opposition to one another. This "oppositional self-definition" is a cause of stereotyping. It promotes the reflexive impulse that if Christians believe such-and-such then Jews must not, and vice-versa. Therefore, until fairly recently it has been difficult for both Christians and Jews to engage the core religious truth claims of the other with anything other than rejection because their respective self-understandings are implicated. The borders between our communities that for centuries helped define our respective identities could become uncomfortably fuzzy and altered as we learn we've misconstrued the other's positions. Catholics who affirm Jewish perspectives can be accused of "watering down the faith" or even of "apostasy." Jews who affirm Christian perspectives can be accused of abandoning their Jewish heritage and assimilating into the wider culture.

## Some Factors in Developing Theologies of Each Other

It seems to me that an interest in minimally making some sort of theological space for each other requires that Christians and Jews presuppose that the other tradition has some sort of religious legitimacy. It must be granted that in some way each is "of God." After all, why try to develop a positive theological stance toward a religion if it presumably exists contrary to God's will?

This presupposition is perhaps easier for Christians to make because early in its formative centuries the emerging mainstream church rejected the ideas of Marcion. It judged the scriptures of ancient Israel to be canonical for Christians. Although until the last century Christians understood the

---

3. Cf. Cardinal Edward Idris Cassidy: "That anti-Semitism has found a place in Christian thought and practice calls for an act of *teshuvah* (repentance) and of reconciliation on our part. . . ." Cited in International Catholic-Jewish Liaison Committee, "A Common Declaration on Anti-Semitism" (Sept. 6, 1990), Prague, Czechoslovakia.

"Old Testament" to have religious validity only in reference to Christ and the church, it was and remains heretical to hold that ancient Israel was not in covenant with the One God. Supersessionist Christians wanted to argue that the Jewish covenant was moribund after Christ, and the Roman destruction of the Second Temple provided them with powerful argumentation. Nonetheless, the biblical conviction that God chose the People Israel — at least in the past, as traditionally believed — is normative for Christianity. The change in recent decades is the growing realization among Christians that covenantal relationship with God must by definition be eternal because the Holy One is ever-faithful.

However, for Jews today to hold that Christianity owes its existence to God requires both an engagement with Christian truth-claims on their own terms and a relating of these claims to Jewish understandings. The biblical and later Jewish tradition's tendency to view the non-Jewish world as an undifferentiated, generic religious other is an important factor here. Moreover, given the adversarial relationship between Christians and Jews in European history, the vast majority of Jews over the centuries had little incentive to view Christianity positively, let alone to agree with (or not dispute) Christian truth-claims. It was safer to avoid religious conversations with Christians, who, after all, were consistently seeking to convert Jews.

Already in the first few centuries of the Common Era, rabbis had developed a remarkably inclusive approach to the question of whether any Gentiles could be admitted into the Age to Come. The mainstream position was that non-Jews who observed seven injunctions understood to have been given by God to all humanity through Noah would be judged righteous by God. The Noahide laws prohibited idolatry, murder, robbery, sexual immorality, blasphemy, and the eating of flesh from a living animal, and they required a legal system to promote justice.[4] This system gave Jews over the centuries a way of affirming the righteousness of Gentiles with whom they interacted, without needing to delve very much into specific Christian beliefs.

However, this approach is inadequate to the task of a Jew engaging Christianity in its own particularity, as distinct from other non-Jewish traditions such as Islam or Hinduism. A solely Noahide perspective implicitly delegitimizes Christian self-claims by ignoring them. Christians are reduced to the status of the generic Gentile. Despite laudable inclusivity (a char-

---

4. See Ruth Langer, "Jewish Understandings of the Religious Other," *Theological Studies* 64 (2003): 255-77.

acteristic that has hardly been prominent in Christian thought), Noahide theologies are theologies about Gentiles, not about Christians.[5]

In the Middle Ages, driven primarily by the unavoidable need to engage in business transactions with Christians, some Jewish thinkers tackled the question of whether Christians were idolaters (which would have made contractual relations with Christians impossible for Jews). Menachem Meiri (1249-1310) is often cited today because he argued that Christians were not idolaters merely because they had religious ideas that were forbidden to Jews.[6] Likewise Rabbi Isaac Dampierre reasoned that Christians pray "to the Maker of Heaven and Earth too; and despite the fact that they associate the name of Heaven with an alien deity [Christ], we do not find that it is forbidden [for] Gentiles to make such an association *(shituf)*."[7] Thus, Christians should not be considered idolaters.

While this is a more direct encounter with Christianity, it does sidestep some troublesome questions that cannot be avoided today. It addresses the other only up to a certain point. If Christianity is not idolatrous, then it must be in some relationship with the Holy One of Israel, even if imperfectly by Jewish standards. But eventually one must ask: How did this come about? How could some relationship with Israel's God come about through the agency of an "alien deity"? If Jesus is not really a deity then how and why did Jews and then non-Jews come to so distort a genuine encounter with God? Although the discussion about *shituf* stemmed from the limited question of whether Jews could enter into business arrangements with Christians, today a thoroughgoing Jewish theology about the Christian other would have to deal with these sorts of questions. As Rabbi Leon Klenicki has commented, the Christian other cannot simply be objectively observed; there must be a meeting between human subjects who sojourn with each other's perspectives.[8]

Of course, such a project was impossible when Christianity was actively supersessionist and aggressively trying to baptize Jews. It is to the credit of

5. See the discussion in Eugene Korn, "Covenantal Possibilities in a Post-Polemical Age: A Jewish View," *Studies in Christian-Jewish Relations* 6 (2011): 3-4; and Michael S. Kogan, *Opening the Covenant: A Jewish Theology of Christianity* (Oxford/New York: Oxford University Press, 2008), 238.

6. For a detailed analysis of Meiri's thought, see Moshe Halbertal, "'Ones Possessed of Religion': Religious Tolerance in the Teachings of the Me'iri," *Edah Journal* 1 (2000): 1-24.

7. Cited in Jan Katzew, "From Other to Brother," *CCAR Journal: A Reform Jewish Quarterly* 52 (Spring 2005): 32.

8. Leon Klenicki, "*Ecclesia et Synagoga:* Judaism and Christianity, A Reflection toward the Future," *CCAR Journal: A Reform Jewish Quarterly* 52 (Spring 2005): 22-25.

such nineteenth and early twentieth-century Jewish thinkers as Abraham Geiger, Franz Rosenzweig, Martin Buber, and Leo Baeck that they even considered the subject in times when Christian supersessionism, and anti-semitism, were rampant. But what about today?

## Can We Really Talk to One Another?

In the 1960s, change was clearly in the air. In the United States there had been decades of ecumenical and interreligious collaboration on such issues as labor rights and child labor laws. Christians and Jews were talking to each other more and more, and becoming curious about each other's religious ideas. Will Herberg's book, *Protestant, Catholic, Jew: An Essay in American Religious Sociology* (Anchor, 1960) was a popular exploration of religious pluralism in the United States. Public media reported that the Second Vatican Council, meeting in Rome, was "opening the windows" to the world, including the world's many religious traditions.

American Jews were in varying degrees caught up with their fellow citizens in this "ecumenical" movement. Orthodox Jewish leaders, however, feared the assimilation of the tiny Jewish minority into the predominantly Christian American ethos. In 1967, Rabbi Moshe Feinstein, an influential leader of very traditional Orthodox Jews who tended to shy away from much contact with the wider culture, invoked earlier, negative Jewish judgments about Christianity when he responded to a question about Orthodox involvement in an upcoming interfaith meeting:

> Even though what you will discuss there will be nontheological in nature, it is clear and simple that such participation constitutes a grave violation of the prohibition against appurtenances to idolatry. For a plague has now broken out in many locales on the initiative of the new pope, whose only interest is to cause all the Jews to abandon their pure and holy faith so that they will accept Christianity. . . . Consequently, all contact and discussion with them, even on worldly matters, is forbidden, for the act of "drawing near" is in and of itself forbidden, as it falls under the category of the grave prohibition against "rapprochement with idolatry — hitkarvut 'im 'avodah zarah."[9]

9. Quoted in David Ellenson, "A Jewish Legal Authority Addresses Jewish-Christian Dialogue: Two Responsa of Rabbi Moshe Feinstein," *American Jewish Archives Journal* 52 (2000): 122.

In marked contrast to Moshe Feinstein, Rabbi Joseph Soloveitchik, a leading voice among those "modern Orthodox" who were open to interactions with the wider culture, believed it was appropriate for Jews to converse with non-Jews about non-religious matters. Common social concerns such as poverty, race relations, and nuclear warfare were certainly concerns that affected Jews as much as anyone else, and Jews ought to participate in civic discourse about them. Religious topics, however, were another matter. In an influential 1964 article entitled "Confrontation," he declared that Jews should avoid theological discussions with Christians. His arguments are conveniently summarized in the following quotation:

> [W]e could readily speak of a Judeo-Hellenistic-Christian tradition within the framework of our Western civilization. However, when we shift the focus from the dimension of culture to that of faith — where total unconditional commitment and involvement are necessary — the whole idea of a tradition of faiths and the continuum of revealed doctrines which are by their very nature incommensurate and related to different frames of reference is utterly absurd, unless one is ready to acquiesce in the Christian theological claim that Christianity has superseded Judaism. . . .
>
> Therefore, any intimation, overt or covert, on the part of the community of the many [Christians] that it is expected of the community of the few [Jews] that it shed its uniqueness and cease existing because it has fulfilled its mission by paving the way for the community of the many, must be rejected. . . .[10]

Soloveitchik's reasoning could be summarized in three points: (1) Religious experiences are so individual and personal that they cannot be adequately communicated between people. This incommensurability is even more acute between the religious communities of Jews and Christians. (2) The "community of the many" (Christians) is by its nature determined to absorb the "community of the few" (Jews). Christianity's supersessionist character and numerical superiority means that there will never exist the "level playing field" that would be an absolute precondition for theological dialogue. (3) Normal human social interaction would exert an overwhelming desire to exchange "theological favors" with one another in a reciprocal fashion, which would result in a dangerous loss of identity, especially for the minority group.

10. Joseph B. Soloveitchik, "Confrontation," *Tradition* 6/2 (1964): 22-23.

Rabbi Soloveitchik was quite correct in claiming that a level dialogical playing field did not exist in 1964. However, are the circumstances as imbalanced today, particularly in the case of Jewish-Catholic relations? After a number of missteps and tentative initiatives, dialogue with Jews is understood today as devoid of conversionary intent. In the words of Cardinal Walter Kasper, past president of the Pontifical Commission for Religious Relations with the Jews: "Dialogue implies personal commitments and witness of one's own conviction and faith. Dialogue communicates one's faith and, at the same time, requires profound respect for the conviction and faith of the partner. It respects the difference of the other and brings mutual enrichment."[11]

Setting aside the question of conversionary motives, Rabbi Soloveitchik seems to have argued that interreligious dialogue was impossible even theoretically. "The great encounter between God and man is a wholly personal private affair incomprehensible to the outsider — even to a brother of the same faith community. The divine message is incommunicable since it defies all standardized media of information and all objective categories." In his 1964 context, he went on to say that if the community of the few and the community of the many sought to discuss such things, one of them would "be impelled to avail himself of the language of the opponent. This in itself would mean surrender of individuality and distinctiveness."[12]

While respecting the historical context out of which Rabbi Soloveitchik wrote, as well as the profoundly unique experiences of each "lonely man of faith" (the title of one of his important books), it seems to me that the intervening fifty years have demonstrated not only that deep dialogue is possible between Jews and Catholics, but also that it is beneficial to both.

Is it really true that a person's "encounter" with God, what I would call a religious or transcendent experience, is incomprehensible to co-religionists, let alone outsiders? How could a religious thinker such as Rabbi Soloveitchik become rightly revered as a significant leader — one who dedicated his life

---

11. Walter Kasper, *"Dominus Iesus"* (2001). See also the more recent words of Pope Francis: "Dialogue is born from a respectful attitude toward the other person, from a conviction that the other person has something good to say. It supposes that we can make room in our heart for their point of view, their opinion and their proposals. Dialogue entails a warm reception and not a preemptive condemnation. To dialogue, one must know how to lower the defenses, to open the doors of one's home and to offer warmth" (Jose Mario Bergoglio and Abraham Skorka, *On Heaven and Earth: Pope Francis on Faith, Family, and the Church in the Twenty-First Century,* trans. Alejandro Bermudez and Howard Goodman [New York: Image Books, 2013], xiv).

12. Soloveitchik, "Confrontation," 24.

to sharing his religious convictions — if this were true? And even if there is a unique relationship between each person and God, and even if experiences of the transcendent are ultimately ineffable, cannot people understand their common inability to express these encounters fully, particularly if they both were socialized into a shared traditional grammar of faith experiences? Can they not comprehend to some degree the partial articulations of each other's religious experiences? How could communities of faith even exist, let alone develop communal liturgical traditions, if this were not so? It seems to me to be a fundamental Jewish concept that God enters into relationship with communities of people as well as with individuals, which presupposes some sort of inner-community comprehensibility of transcendent experiences.

In addition, as explored in chapter 3, today's Christians and Jews also have common origins in late Second Temple Judaism. We have been interacting for millennia and, therefore, it is fallacious to imagine "Judaism" and "Christianity" as pure, unalloyed categories that are not influenced by each other.

While we have taken different paths and often use the same words with different meanings (increasing the likelihood of conflict based on misunderstandings of the other), there are nonetheless foundational religious concepts that we share. This makes it far easier for Christians and Jews to comprehend one another than for either to engage deeply in the thought-worlds of other religions. Had Christians and Jews really been so utterly "incomprehensible" to one another, the centuries of conflict between us would have unfolded quite differently. Our relatedness unites and divides us in unique ways.

Moreover, although it is true that in interfaith dialogue it is necessary to some extent to adopt the language (i.e., enter into the thought-world) of the religious other (Soloveitchik's "opponent"), does that inevitably lead to a "surrender of individuality and distinctiveness"? Again respecting the legacy of oppositional self-definition that is at work here, the experience of the last fifty years of Catholic-Jewish dialogue almost invariably results in a deepening of one's religious identity precisely because of the engagement with the religious other. I am not the same Catholic I was before engaging in dialogue with Jews, but I understand and am committed to my enriched Catholicity more profoundly than before. Jewish dialogue partners regularly express the same sentiment.

While it is surely true that one's innermost selfhood and its relationship to God cannot be communicated to another, it seems to me equally certain that the *reality* of another's relationship to God *can* be divined. Perhaps this reality could be articulated by the word "holiness." Even though I would not imagine that I could ever enter into Jews' own experience of faith, I know holiness when I experience it in Jewish friends or in the Jewish tradition. Nor does this perception automatically lead me to desire to absorb or appropriate the holiness of the Jewish other. Krister Stendahl's evocative phrase "holy envy" comes to mind.[13] I glimpse holiness, for example, when I discern the profundity of rabbinic debate on this or that subject or when I see a friend don *tefillin* (phylacteries) for prayer. I also realize that these engagements with the divine presence are not mine. They belong to Jews. But I have learned from them.

So the question "Can we talk meaningfully across religious lines?" has already been answered in the affirmative.

## Coming to an Understanding of the Catholic-Jewish Relationship

A constant thread running through the entire post–*Nostra Aetate* ecclesial document tradition is the Catholic claim that Jews and Christians "are connected and closely related at the very level of their respective religious identities,"[14] as John Paul II expressed it. The strongest articulation of this idea is probably his later and oft-quoted statement at the Great Synagogue of Rome:

> [T]he Church of Christ discovers her "bond" with Judaism by "searching into her own mystery" (cf. *Nostra Aetate*) The Jewish religion is not "extrinsic" to us, but in a certain way is "intrinsic" to our own religion. With Judaism therefore we have a relationship which we do not have with any other religion. You are our dearly beloved brothers and, in a certain way, it could be said that you are our elder brothers.[15]

It is probably understandable that Christians cannot think of themselves as disconnected from Judaism because of the defining decision made in the second century to include the scriptures of ancient Israel as the "Old Testament" of the church's biblical canon. To posit a radical spiritual disjuncture between Christianity and Judaism (it seems to me in whatever era) at least flirts with the heresy of Marcionism (see chapter 2).

13. See Yehezkel Landau, "An Interview with Krister Stendahl," *Harvard Divinity Bulletin* 35/1 (2007): 29-31.
14. John Paul II, "Address to Representatives of Jewish Organizations," March 12, 1979.
15. John Paul II, "Address at the Great Synagogue of Rome," April 13, 1986, §4.

A question, of course, is how Jews today should respond to Christian claims of an intimate, intrinsic relationship. Statements such as those of John Paul II could come across as Christians once again telling Jews how they should understand their own identity. This is not only a matter of Christians making assertions to which Jews have not agreed, but also a question about the actual content being claimed. Are Jews and Christians intrinsically linked?[16]

If Christians are driven to answer this question in the affirmative because of their own anti-Marcionite self-understanding, it could be argued that Jews are inclined to answer in the negative if only to preserve their own identities in the face of the numerically astronomically larger Christian community, to say nothing of the history of Christian contempt for Jews.

At several points in this book, it has been noted that Jews and Christians have been interacting for nearly two thousand years, for good and for ill. Clearly, the two communities have been related historically. But Catholic references to "the links between the Church and the Jewish people [as] founded on the design of the God of the Covenant"[17] are making a *theological* claim, not merely a historical one.

However, if history and theology are symbiotically related, then it would appear unavoidable that the long history between Christians and Jews, not to mention their common origins in late Second Temple Judaism, has also produced theological interconnections. Jews, of course, must grapple with what this might mean for them in the years ahead, especially if the ongoing reform of Christian attitudes toward Jews continues to deepen and become internalized. I realize that for me as a Christian it is something of a starting point that Judaism and Christianity are theologically interrelated, which probably explains why to me the more captivating question is whether in the future that relationship will continue to be oppositional.

## Can We Appreciate Divine Revelations We Do Not Share?

At the absolute heart of Christian faith is the conviction that a crucified first-century Jew was divinely raised to the transcendent life of the Age to Come.

16. The preceding paragraphs are particularly indebted to conversations with my colleague Adam Gregerman.

17. John Paul II, "Address to Episcopal Conference Delegates and Consultors of the Pontifical Commission for Religious Relations with the Jews," March 6, 1982.

All of the defining and distinctive Christian incarnational and Trinitarian theologies spring from this primordial numinous experience. Over the centuries Jews have wondered, "How can Christians believe such a thing?" while Christians have puzzled, "How can Jews not perceive this epochal event?"

Thus, a central question that a Jewish engagement with the particularity of Christianity must eventually confront is: "Has the Christian experience of the life, death, and exaltation of Jesus somehow established a covenantal relationship between Christians and the God of Israel? Are Christians, therefore, participants in preparing for the eschatological events of the last days?"

I have framed the first question in terms of "the Christian experience" because it is not an experience shared by the Jewish community (nor does the church any longer condemn Jews for not sharing Christian viewpoints). However, being in covenantal relationship with the Holy One is something that the People Israel knows well, thereby opening up the possibility of recognizing something similar, if also quite different, in the other religious community. Even if the Christian story of the origins of its relationship with God sounds inconceivable to Jewish ears, is it possible that when Christians live covenantally so as to disclose holiness, Jews can discern some echoes of their own relationship with God?[18] Unless Christians are thought to be in relationship with no deity at all or with a non-existent "other" deity, then relationship with the same Holy One of Israel ought to be expected to produce some similarities in living a covenanted life.[19]

A certain theology of revelation is at work here. As an eschatological intervention into actual human history, the resurrection of Jesus is understood in Christianity as a transcendent, trans-historical event. "By it Jesus was introduced into the 'world to come,'" as the Pontifical Biblical Commission has put it.[20] As a revelatory experience, it is not something that can be proven or empirically verified. (Hence, it would be fruitless to ask, "Did the resurrection of Jesus happen?") Divine activity is not simply a phenomenon that a security camera would record or that can be proven "with certainty as a fact accessible to any observer whatsoever. . . . [T]here is also needed

18. This was Paul's hopeful speculation even in the first century. See Rom. 11:11-14.

19. I might note in passing that while there is little rabbinic engagement with the question of whether Christians *qua* Christians are in covenant with God, the Noahide laws are based on the idea that God had entered into a covenant with all of humanity. This provides a precedent for thinking about God entering into covenants outside of Israel. (My thanks to Ruth Langer for this insight.)

20. Pontifical Biblical Commission, "Instruction on the Bible and Christology" (1984), 1.2.6.

'the decision of faith,' or better 'an open heart,' so that the mind may be moved to assent."[21] Revelation is relational. It occurs as part of an interaction between human beings and the Holy One to which the human participants must consent.

Israel's primordial religious experiences, the exodus and giving of the Torah, are likewise not susceptible to historical verification. The sudden and utter destruction of one of the Mediterranean world's superpowers would have to leave historical evidence, if only in the records of imperial rivals who would rush in to fill the power vacuum left by Egypt's catastrophic demise. The absence of such indications does not mean that the Holy One did not deliver Israel from bondage. It means that "a decision of faith" is needed to come to that conclusion. The belief that the Torah expresses God's will for Israel is in like fashion also a "decision of faith" — there is no way to prove that claim as an empirical fact by means of objective evidence. I am not questioning the reality of the Torah as an expression of the divine will, or the delivery of Israel from bondage, or the raising of Jesus Christ — only their provability.

Within the Christian faith experience, God has established a covenant with the church through a certain son of Israel, Jesus. Christians call him the "Christ" because in their experience of his life, death, and ongoing transcendent glory, they experience relationship with God.

Since Israel has a long communal experience of interacting with God, it might be possible for Jews to engage Christian truth claims by looking for resonances with their own lives of faith. Can lives of holiness be evident among Christians? While over the centuries many Jews would have little reason to answer that question affirmatively, to the extent that holiness is perceived, then it must be the Holy One with whom Christians relate, for where else does holiness originate? Christian claims for covenant with God in Christ might therefore be respected even if Jews do not share in the revelatory religious experiences that for Christians establish their faith identity.

Likewise, for Christians it is possible to understand the work of the rabbis over the centuries as a participation in a process of uncovering God's will for Israel, analogous to the workings of the Holy Spirit in Christian thought.[22] Christians thereby can respect the rabbinic tradition, even though

21. Pontifical Biblical Commission, "The Bible and Christology," 1.2.6.
22. Note these words of the Pontifical Biblical Commission: "Christians can and ought to admit that the Jewish reading of the Bible is a possible one, in continuity with the Jewish Sacred Scriptures from the Second Temple period, a reading analogous to the Christian reading which developed in parallel fashion. Both readings are bound up with the vision of their

the rabbinic project, their living out of their relationship with God, is not their own faith experience.

For a Jewish theology of Christianity to hold that Christians are in covenant with the God of Israel as the result of revelatory experiences in which Jews do not participate, obviously does not mean that Jews must thereby assent to all Christian theological teachings. Christian claims that Jesus was the incarnate Word of a Triune God should certainly be defined as not acceptable for Jews because Jews do not share in the Christian relationship with God that gives rise to such beliefs. However, they might be seen as reasonable within a Christian frame of reference, and their similarities and differences from Jewish notions of the transcendent God's involvement in human history or Jewish mysticism's conceptions of the ten emanations of God could be explored. Understanding Christianity's foundational claim as an instance of God's ineffable self-disclosure might be a useful way to engage Christian truths and yet show why they are not part of the Jewish experience.[23] For Christians, this model can explain why Jews do not share their resurrection faith. For Jews, it might show why such Christian claims lie outside the rabbinic tradition.

This possibility of recognizing defining religious experiences in another religious community without sharing in them because we ourselves have known such moments would logically come more easily for Jews and Christians because of our common rootedness in biblical Israel.

## Conclusion

The perspective I am offering here, that another community's truth claims can be appreciated even if not experienced and embraced, is not an easy one. It requires a deep commitment to solidarity with the other because the Jews and Christians involved believe that this is what God desires of them. It will require years of dedicated perseverance, not only because of the inherited zero-sum binaries of the past, but because we are together finding our way along new and unexplored paths of mutuality.

---

respective faiths, of which the readings are the result and expression. Consequently, both are irreducible." *The Jewish People and Their Sacred Scriptures in the Christian Bible* (2001), II, A, 7.

23. Michael Kogan has made a similar argument from the Jewish side in "Toward a Jewish Theology of Christianity," *Journal of Ecumenical Studies* 32/1 (Winter 1995): 89-106. See also his *Opening the Covenant* (Oxford/New York: Oxford University Press, 2008), 231-246.

# Charting the Unexplored Paths of Mutuality

## Moving toward Mutuality?

Fifty years after its official beginning with the issuance of *Nostra Aetate,* the new Catholic-Jewish relationship might be compared to a newborn human being. Just as a major milestone in child development is learning how to speak, an initial task for interfaith dialogists was to learn how to talk to one another. However, human babies are genetically "hard-wired" toward language acquisition, while pioneering dialogists were challenged by centuries of hostility, suspicion, stereotyping, fear, and oppositional thinking. With this history, could Jews and Catholics (and other Christians) ever really communicate with one another?

Another human developmental challenge is the formation of personal identity that is both in relationship with and in distinction from other human beings. In the first decade of life one's childhood family of origin plays a crucial role, in adolescence one's peers become highly influential, and later one's adult family, friends, co-workers, etc. all play important roles. As mentioned several times in this book, Judaism and Christianity have been interacting historically — and, therefore, also theologically — even as far back as the aftermath of the destruction of the Temple in Jerusalem. This interaction for good or ill inevitably has had consequences for identity formation in each community. Or to put it another way, each tradition's self-understanding has been affected by its experiences of and attitudes toward the Jewish or Christian other.

Although one can only push metaphors so far, if generally speaking Jews and Christians have been interacting for about two thousand years, then the five decades since *Nostra Aetate* amount to only one-fortieth of that entire history. If the human lifespan in the Western world is rounded off to be about 80 years of age, then the new relationship between Catholics and Jews is the equivalent of toddlerhood!

Still, in many parts of the world Jews and Christians have begun to speak to each other beyond surface-level descriptions of their respective customs. They have begun to understand their different perspectives and concerns. They are doing so with few positive precedents from their particular received traditions and with many caricatures and misunderstandings confounding their efforts.

While interreligious dialogue has a primary goal of dispelling ignorance and stereotypes, a profound discovery has also occurred. In the process of opening themselves to each other's religious lives, Jews and Christians have sometimes discerned a deeper spiritual reality. In their interactions, occasionally Jewish and Christian participants found themselves glimpsing the elusive presence of the Holy One in the lives and traditions of their dialogue partners.

Cardinal Walter Kasper has expressed this perception in Catholic theological terms by describing Judaism "as a sacrament of every otherness that as such the Church must learn to discern, recognize and celebrate."[1] His use of the rich theological term "sacrament" is significant. It expresses the Catholic recognition of holiness in their experiences of Jewish covenantal life. And this holiness is mediated precisely through the "otherness" of Judaism — in the distinctiveness of the relationships Jews can have with the Holy One.

This suggests a primary purpose as the Catholic-Jewish relationship matures in the future: We are beginning to chart the unexplored paths of mutuality. By "mutuality" in this context I mean a deepening love for the distinctiveness of the Jewish or Christian other because of their edifying ways of walking with God. The companionship that this presupposes inevitably produces a reconfiguration of the crude oppositional borders that both traditions received from their inimical pasts. To that extent, Christians and Jews will not be the same as they were before profoundly engaging with each other, but if the testimony of many dialogue veterans over the past decades is any indication, they will understand their respective Christianity and Jewishness more deeply than would otherwise have been possible. The mutual enrichment generated by the new relationship between Jews and Christians offers profound hope for a wide variety of long-lasting conflicts around the world.

1. Walter Kasper, "Address on the 37th Anniversary of *Nostra Aetate*," Oct. 28, 2002.

## Emergent Mutuality

Signs of such mutuality can be found emerging in many places. Very prominent, of course, is the long friendship between two religious leaders in Buenos Aires: Cardinal Jorge Mario Bergoglio (the future Pope Francis) and
Rabbi Abraham Skorka. In their joint book, each of them refers to the other
in intimate terms, with Bergoglio writing of the rabbi as "a brother and a
friend" and Skorka describing their conversations as "exposing our souls"
to one another.[2]

Similarly, in a forthcoming book on interreligious friendships, Catholic
theologian Mary C. Boys writes of her long collaboration with Jewish edu-
cator Sara Lee: "Over the years, Sara and I have discussed many demanding
and delicate questions — but the conversations themselves have not been
difficult. To the contrary, our friendship allows us to probe in sensitive areas." Quoting Sara in regard to the most fraught of subjects, she writes, "And
only when Christians and Jews face Auschwitz in one another's presence will
reconciliation be possible."[3]

Likewise, Hanspeter Heinz has written movingly about his more than
twenty-year friendship with the late Michael Signer:

> "Most theologians and bishops operate with a different hermeneutics
> than you do," Michael once wrote to me. "They rely on historical texts of
> the biblical era and the Christian tradition. You, on the other hand, have
> Jewish friends — this is your privilege — and you rely on dialogue with
> living Judaism when you do theology. You thus work on differing levels
> and come to differing results."[4]

The adjective "living" here is crucial: it is the personal encounter with
the vitality and dynamism of another religious tradition that is so transformative. This important insight from Rabbi Signer points to a possible future
direction of the new relationship between Jews and Christians, but Father
Heinz also describes other notable aspects of their mutuality. He writes:

2. Jose Mario Bergoglio and Abraham Skorka, *On Heaven and Earth,* trans. Alejandro
Bermudez and Howard Goodman (New York: Image Books, 2013), xvi and xii, respectively.

3. Mary C. Boys, "Learning in the Presence of the Other: My Friendship with Sara Lee,"
forthcoming in James L. Fredericks and Tracy Sayuki Tiemeier, eds., *Interreligious Friendship
after Nostra Aetate* (New York/London: Palgrave Macmillan, 2015).

4. Hanspeter Heinz, " 'Your Privilege: You Have Jewish Friends,' " in Philip A. Cunningham et al., eds., *Christ Jesus and the Jewish People Today,* (Grand Rapids: Eerdmans, 2011), 5.

The joy we shared as friends was no less important than our [educational] projects together. . . .

Like overgrown boys, we played games that often oscillated between fun and seriousness. . . . Indeed, our free time together and our correspondence brought us much more than relaxation. . . . During our long walks, . . . we regularly lost our way because we were so absorbed in our discussions. At some point we would let someone pick us up in a car and return us to the village. . . .

Without our deep theological discussions, our friendship would have surely lacked seriousness and depth.[5]

Their informal camaraderie likely contributed to developing the trust in each other necessary for deep dialogue. Their experience of leaving the everyday world behind when in the midst of profound conversation recalls the rabbinic practice of *chavruta* study — serious and multidimensional grappling with sacred texts in close relationship with a study partner.

In response to a question about what metaphor might best describe the emerging Christian-Jewish relationship today, Daniel Lehmann has proposed the following:

I would like to suggest a new metaphor, at least something to get us thinking in a different direction. That is the metaphor of what in Aramaic we [ Jews] call a *chavruta,* that is a learning partner. A learning partner is someone with whom you study texts, biblical or other kinds of traditional texts, but you study it in order to have a dialogue — an interlocutor, with whom truth can emerge as you play out your different perspectives on the texts. And it's a kind of relationship which is very intimate, in which there is a sense of shared texts, and even a covenantal relationship, but in which the partners are not just trying to agree, but in fact, trying to see how their different perspectives can enhance the other person's understanding. Again, I would like [Christian-Jewish relations] to shift from dialogue to learning. I think it's really about sharing insights and interpretations in the common texts that we share and some that we don't share.[6]

5. Heinz, " 'Your Privilege,' "4.

6. Daniel Lehmann, quoted at 07:18–8:32 in *Metaphors for a Unique Relationship,* episode 5 of *Walking God's Path: Jews and Christians in Candid Conversation* [video series]. Produced by Philip A. Cunningham, John Michalczyk, and Gilbert Rosenthal (Boston: Center for Christian-Jewish Learning at Boston College, 2004).

If the new relationship between Christians and Jews is giving rise in many places to a *chavruta*-like partnership of learning, this opens up possibilities for a future journey together. Michael Signer made a crucial observation when he noted that having close Jewish friends made Hanspeter Heinz theologize differently than he would have otherwise. He himself found that he had to find new ways of thinking about Christians because of his experiences with them.[7] Mary Boys quoted her friend Sara Lee as saying, "[O]nly when Christians and Jews face Auschwitz in one another's presence will reconciliation be possible." Hanspeter Heinz wrote in a similar vein that Jews and Christians "can — and must — assist each other and search with one another for the way through the depths of history into the future."[8] As adduced earlier in this volume, Pope Benedict XVI has written: "[W]e now see it as our task to bring these two ways of rereading the biblical texts — the Christian way and the Jewish way — into dialogue with one another, if we are to understand God's will and his word aright." Our discussion in chapter 12 about actualizing biblical land promises in today's world concluded with the thought that perhaps it would be best for Jews and Christians to explore the topic together from their rather different perspectives. Personally, my own experiences over the years in collaborating, co-authoring, and team-teaching with several Jewish colleagues have provided precious inspiration.

These examples suggest that the new relationship between Jews and Christians, fifty years after *Nostra Aetate,* may well be developing to the point that it is surfacing profound religious questions that can only be effectively addressed by Christians and Jews working together for extended periods of time as learning partners, in mutuality and friendship. In a way, this is not surprising since Jews and Christians today are discussing topics about their interrelationship before God that literally have not been seriously considered since the era of the New Testament.

To express this conclusion in an extreme form: we may be rapidly approaching the point where Jews and Christians who venture to speak or write about the other community will risk being superficial, unoriginal, or tendentious if they do not engage in creative and rigorous study with friends from the other tradition — with all of the shared commitment, openness, and flexibility that this ideally implies. Those concerned with building *shalom* or right-relationship between Christians and Jews might do well to follow the famous advice of a rabbinic text, *Pirkei Avot:* "Find yourself a

7. Heinz, "'Your Privilege,'" 13.
8. Heinz, "'Your Privilege,'" 9.

teacher, get for yourself a friend" (1:6). In the world of academia, universities committed to interreligious relations ought to deliberately create structures and positions that enable Jewish and Christian scholars to work together on a sustained basis.

## Markers of Mutuality

If it is true that the future maturation of the new relationship — or of theologies of *shalom* — between Christians and Jews demands intensive collaboration, then the experiences of the past fifty years provide some guiding principles.

A. For mutuality to thrive, **the otherness of the Jewish or Christian interlocutor must be cherished.** This was suggested above by Cardinal Kasper's evocative Catholic phraseology, "a sacrament of every otherness." Since cherishing the distinctiveness of the other is not an ideal that today's Jews and Christians have inherited from our adversarial past, it is an attitude that must be consciously cultivated.

   i. It goes without saying that any conversionary motives poison a relationship of interreligious mutuality. However, dialogists must also be alert to the sometimes more subtle influence of inherited constructs that in the past were used to disrespect the other. For instance, technical Catholic theological terms such as "invincible ignorance" — "an ignorance for which [a person is] not morally responsible"[9] — renders the Jewish dialogue partner inferior no matter how benignly employed. The same would be true if a Jewish interlocutor saw the Christian other as engaging at some level in *avodah zarah,* forbidden worship or idolatry. In either case, the Jew or the Christian is closing himself or herself off to learning with and from the other. Both would be "violations of love."[10]

   ii. Cherishing the distinctiveness of the Christian or Jewish other also means that each person must resist the temptation to assess the other only according to their own frames of reference. While the traditions of one's own heritage cannot be abandoned without some loss of identity, it is imperative that the effort be made to appreciate the other's thought-world to the greatest degree possible. Both

---

9. Richard McBrien, *Catholicism* (Minneapolis: Winston Press, 1980), 1001.
10. A phrase used by Hanspeter Heinz, " 'Your Privilege,' " 10-11.

perspectives need to be in play. Developing facility in perceiving the Jewish and Christian relationship from multiple frames of reference is a major contributor to mutuality.[11]

B. Cherishing the distinctiveness of the other means that differences are not to be avoided. However, **the nature of any differences needs to be analyzed carefully**. Several questions could be examined, for example:

   i. *Is the perceived difference premised on an oppositional understanding of the self or the other?* For instance, sometimes people erroneously assume that since Christians believe that Jesus was resurrected, Jews do not believe in the resurrection of the dead or in an afterlife.

   ii. *Do important terms mean something different to Christians and Jews?* An oft-repeated formula is that Christians believe "the Messiah" has come, while Jews insist "the Messiah" has not come. Not always realized is that "the Messiah" may mean something very different to each tradition today, let alone that its meaning may have changed over time. As discussed in previous chapters, Christians today mean something very different when they speak of Jesus as "Christ" (even though the Greek *christos* is equivalent to the Hebrew *mashiach*) than Jews today do when they speak of "the Messiah."

   iii. *Is the perceived difference a question of emphasis?* For instance, it is sometimes said that Christians hold that the world has already been redeemed, while Jews claim that the world is unredeemed. Careful study shows that Jews and Christians both believe (in different ways) that God acts in history for human redemption but also that God's designs for the world have yet to be fully achieved.

---

11. Didier Pollefeyt and I expressed this idea in our "The Triune One, the Incarnate Logos, and Israel's Covenantal Life" as follows: "It is not possible for either Christians or Jews to survey reality, including each other's reality, completely removed from their own religious and historical horizons. There is no 'helicopter perspective' from which we can regard the Jewish or Christian other with majestic neutrality. We are all participants in the interreligious encounter, not simply observers. Since we cannot access some transcendent viewpoint next to or above these living and lived particular Christian and Jewish perspectives, it is necessary that the effort to understand the other in one's own terms be accompanied by a simultaneous, complementary effort to hear and understand the other within the other's frames of reference. This dialectical dynamic mitigates against the imposition of Christian categories on Judaism (or vice-versa).

"During interreligious dialogue, then, there is an exchange of these diverse internal and external points of view, seeking to uncover how, on the negative side, contrasting perspectives can become sources of exclusion and even violence, and on the positive side, how they can enrich each other. Interreligious dialogue is therefore an important touchstone for every theological enterprise that considers religious others" (193-194).

iv. *Are there unstated presuppositions at work?* Jews and Christians have traditionally interpreted certain scriptural passages, such as Isaiah 7:14, quite differently. "Look, the young woman [or "virgin" in Greek] is with child and shall bear a son, and shall name him Immanuel." Prescinding from the translational question over the Hebrew *'almah* and the Greek *parthenos* in reference to the woman, Christians (following Matthew 1:22-23) have typically seen this text as referring to the coming of Jesus in the future. Jews tend to see the son as referring to King Hezekiah or some contemporary of the prophet. But this difference becomes a defining contradiction between Judaism and Christianity only if it is presupposed that a biblical text can have only one correct interpretation. In fact, Jewish tradition has always seen the value of multiple understandings of a text (as in discussions of Psalm 62:11: "One thing God has spoken, two things have I heard"), while the Catholic Church (as seen in the 2001 Pontifical Commission study discussed in chapter 2) teaches that multiple legitimate "retrospective" readings of biblical texts exist. That is why Pope Benedict encouraged dialogue between Jewish and Christian traditions of interpretation. Examining presuppositions is especially necessary because of the oppositional history between Jews and Christians.

v. *Would an apparent difference change if viewed from another philosophical perspective?* In chapter 10 it was proposed that a relational metaphysic is more conducive for Christian and Jewish understanding than one grounded solely in ontological being. The former stresses that identity is grounded in relationship, while the latter emphasizes truth as the foundation of identity. Considering a topic such as the nature of God from the perspective of ontic truth tends to produce antithetical-sounding formulas about Jewish and Christian understandings of God: Jews believe in a God whose essential trait is Oneness, Christians believe in a God who exists in three interrelated ways of being. However, a shift to a relational approach highlights the respective Jewish and Christian experiences of God, and both can then be seen as grappling with how the transcendent Holy One becomes involved in ordinary human history delimited by time and space.

C. Finally, a relationship of mutuality is surely enhanced when both Christians and Jews see the highest purpose of their interactions as **seeking the Holy One together.** For religious people, it is God who is the ultimate source of existence and meaning. Therefore, it is God who gives the mystery of the unique Jewish and Christian relationship its fullest significance.

## Conclusion: Seeking Shalom Together

This book has explored the past fifty years of Christian-Jewish relations, particularly in terms of the new Catholic-Jewish relationship engendered by *Nostra Aetate* in 1965. It traced two interrelated lines of development in ecclesiastical documents: one concerning biblical studies and the other in terms of the church's understanding of Jews and Judaism. In both instances it then put the respective approaches into practice with exercises in scriptural interpretation and constructive theology.

The concluding chapters have brought us to the threshold of a second fifty-year period in the new relationship, with this final chapter suggesting that an unprecedented opportunity for mutual enrichment and growth is upon us.

In the aftermath of the abomination that was the Shoah, Christian theology had to radically reform itself in order to even begin to speak meaningfully with Jews. Traumatized Jews had to struggle with whether to risk speaking with Christians at all. Was a new relationship even possible, let alone desirable?

Decades later, it appears that it is the new relationship itself that is assuming a primary value. It is becoming the very space[12] within which both Jews and Christians can theologize, where they can seek to deepen their understanding of relationship with God.

And in deepening relationship with the Holy One, their own interrelationship will be blessed with wholeness, with divine *shalom*.

---

12. I am indebted to Celia Deutsch for this phraseology.

# Works Cited

## 1. CATHOLIC ECCLESIASTICAL TEXTS

### A. Second Vatican Council

[The following may all be accessed at the Vatican website at: http://www.vatican.va/
archive/hist_councils/ii_vatican_council/index.htm]

*Dei Verbum.* The Dogmatic Constitution on Divine Revelation. (November 18, 1965).
*Lumen Gentium.* The Dogmatic Constitution on the Church. (November 21, 1964).
*Gaudium et Spes.* The Pastoral Constitution on the Church in the Modern World. (December 7, 1965).
*Nostra Aetate.* The Declaration on the Relationship of the Church to Non-Christian Religions. (October 28, 1965).
*Unitatis Redintegratio.* The Decree on Ecumenism. (November 21, 1964).

### B. Popes

Benedict XVI. "Address to Delegates of the International Jewish Committee for Interreligious Consultation." (June 9, 2005). Available at: http://www.ccjr.us/dialogika
-resources/documents-and-statements/roman-catholic/pope-benedict-xvi/355
-b16-05june9

———. "Address at the Great Synagogue of Rome." (January 17, 2010). Available at:
http://www.ccjr.us/dialogika-resources/documents-and-statements/roman
-catholic/pope-benedict-xvi/660-b1610jan17

———. "Address to the Roman Curia." (December 22, 2005). Available at: http://
www.ccjr.us/index.php/dialogika-resources/documents-and-statements/roman
-catholic/pope-benedict-xvi/359-b16-05dec22.html

———. *Ecclesia in Medio Oriente.* (September 14, 2012). Available at: http://www
.ccjr.us/dialogika-resources/documents-and-statements/roman-catholic/pope
-benedict-xvi/1139-b162012sept14

257

————. *Jesus of Nazareth.* Part Two. *Holy Week: From the Entrance into Jerusalem to the Resurrection.* San Francisco: Ignatius Press, 2011.

————. "Letter to Catholic Bishops on the Remission of the Excommunication of SSPX Bishops." (March 10, 2009). Available at: http://www.ccjr.us/dialogika -resources/documents-and-statements/roman-catholic/pope-benedict-xvi/502 -b16-09mar10-1

Francis. "Address to the Chief Rabbis of Israel." (May 26, 2014). Available at: http:// www.ccjr.us/dialogika-resources/documents-and-statements/roman-catholic/ francis/1279-francis-2014may26-rabbis

————. Apostolic Exhortation *Evangelii Gaudium* (January 24, 2014). Available at: http://w2.vatican.va/content/francesco/en/apost_exhortations/documents/ papa-francesco_esortazione-ap_20131124_evangelii-gaudium.html

————. Interview with Eugenio Scalfari. *La Republica.* Oct. 1, 2013. Available at: http://www.ccjr.us/dialogika-resources/documents-and-statements/roman -catholic/francis/1265-francis2013oct1

————. "Letter to a Non-Believer." (Sept. 4, 2013). Available at: http://w2.vatican .va/content/francesco/en/letters/2013/documents/papa-francesco_20130911 _eugenio-scalfari.html

John Paul II. [Unless otherwise indicated, all the items listed below may be accessed in Eugene J. Fisher and Leon Klenicki, eds. *The Saint for Shalom: How Pope John Paul II Transformed Catholic-Jewish Relations.* New York: Crossroad, 2011.]

John Paul II. "Address to the Australian Jewish Community." (November 26, 1986).

————. "Address to Episcopal Conference Delegates and Consultors of the Pontifical Commission for Religious Relations with the Jews." (March 6, 1982).

————. "Address on the Fiftieth Anniversary of the Warsaw Ghetto Uprising." (April 6, 1993).

————. "Address at the Great Synagogue of Rome." (April 13, 1986).

————. "Address to the Jewish Community in Mainz, West Germany." (November 17, 1980).

————. "Address to Jewish Leaders in Miami." (September 11, 1987).

————. "Address to Jewish Leaders in Warsaw." (June 14, 1987).

————. "Address to Representatives of Jewish Organizations." (March 12, 1979).

————. "Address to the New Ambassador of the Federal Republic of Germany to the Holy See." (November 8, 1990).

————. "Address to Participants in the Vatican Symposium on 'The Roots of Anti-Judaism in the Christian Milieu.'" (October 31, 1997).

————. "Address to the Pontifical Biblical Commission." (April 11, 1997).

————. "Address to the Viennese Jewish Community." (June 24, 1988).

————. Apostolic Exhortation *Ecclesia in Europa* (June 28, 2003), II, 56. Available at: http://www.vatican.va/holy_father/john_paul_ii/apost_exhortations/docu-ments/hf_jp-ii_exh_20030628_ecclesia-in-europa_en.html

————. Apostolic Letter *Tertio Millennio Adveniente* on Preparation for the Jubilee of the Year 2000 (November 10, 1994). Available at: http://www.vatican.va/holy

_father/john_paul_ii/apost_letters/documents/hf_jp-ii_apl_10111994_tertio
-millennio-adveniente_en.html

—. *Fides et Ratio. Origins* 28/19. (October 22, 1998).

—. General Audience. (April 28, 1999).

—. "Homily at Mount Sinai." (February 26, 2000).

—. "Jasna Gora Meditation." (September 26, 1990).

—. "Letter concerning Pilgrimage to Places Linked to the History of Salvation."
(June 29, 1999).

—. "Prayer at the Western Wall." (March 26, 2000).

Pius XII. *Divino Afflante Spiritu.* (September 30, 1943). http://www.vatican.va/holy
_father/pius_xii/encyclicals/documents/hf_p-xii_enc_30091943_divino-afflante
-spiritu_en.html


**C. Vatican Offices and Commissions**

Congregation for the Doctrine of the Faith. "*Dominus Iesus.* Declaration on the Unicity
and Salvific Universality of Jesus Christ and the Church." (August 6, 2000).

—. *Mysterium Ecclesiae.* (May 11, 1973).

Pontifical Biblical Commission. "Instruction on the Bible and Christology." (January
6, 1984).

—. "Instruction on the Historical Truth of the Gospels." (April 21, 1964).

—. "The Interpretation of the Bible in the Church." (April 15, 1993). *Origins* 23/29
(Jan. 6, 1994): 497-524.

—. *The Jewish People and Their Sacred Scriptures in the Christian Bible.* Vatican
City: Libreria Editrice Vaticana, 2001.

Pontifical Commission for Religious Relations with the Jews. "Guidelines and Suggestions for Implementing the Conciliar Declaration *Nostra Aetate,* 4." (December
1, 1974).

—. "Notes on the Correct Way to Present the Jews and Judaism in Preaching and
Catechesis in the Roman Catholic Church." (June 24, 1985).


**D. Members and Former Members of the Curia**

Cassidy, Edward Idris Cardinal. "Catholic-Jewish Relations: 1990-2001." Address delivered at the 17th meeting of the International Catholic-Jewish Liaison Committee,
New York. (May 1, 2001).

—. "Reflections: The Vatican Statement on the Shoah." *Origins* 28/2 (May 28,
1998).

Fumagalli, Pier Francesco. "*Nostra Aetate:* A Milestone." Address delivered at the
Vatican Symposium on *The Roots of Anti-Judaism in the Christian Environment.*
(October 31, 1997).

Hofmann, Norbert J. "A Sign of Great Hope: The Beginning of the Dialogue between
the Holy See and the Chief Rabbinate of Israel." In Cunningham, Hofmann, and
Sievers, eds., *The Catholic Church and the Jewish People,* 167-175.

Kasper, Walter Cardinal. "Address on the 37th Anniversary of *Nostra Aetate.*" (October
28, 2002).

————. "The Commission for Religious Relations with the Jews: A Crucial Endeavour of the Catholic Church." Address delivered at Boston College. (November 6, 2002).

————. *Dominus Iesus.* Paper delivered at the 17th meeting of the International Catholic-Jewish Liaison Committee. (May 1, 2001).

————. "The Relationship of the Old and the New Covenant as One of the Central Issues in Jewish-Christian Dialogue." Address delivered at the Centre for the Study of Jewish-Christian Relations, Cambridge, England. (December 6, 2004). §5.

————. "Striving for Mutual Respect in Modes of Prayer." *L'Osservatore Romano* (April 16, 2008): 8-9.

Koch, Kurt Cardinal. "Theological Questions and Perspectives in Jewish-Catholic Dialogue." Paper delivered at the annual meeting of the Council of Centers on Jewish-Christian Relations, Seton Hall University, South Orange, New Jersey. (October 30, 2011).

————. "Unthinkable to Question the Council." *Servizio Informazione Religiosa.* (January 15, 2013). Available at: http://www.agensir.it/pls/sir/v3_s2doc_a.a_autentication?rifi=&rifp=&tema=Quot_english&oggetto=253607

Mejía, Jorge Maria Cardinal. "The Creation and Work of the Commission for Religious Relations with the Jews." In Cunningham, Hofmann, and Sievers, eds., *The Catholic Church and the Jewish People,* 152-158.

Ratzinger, Joseph Cardinal. "The Heritage of Abraham: The Gift of Christmas." *L'Osservatore Romano.* (Dec. 29, 2000).

Willebrands, Johannes Cardinal. *Church and Jewish People: New Considerations.* New York/Mahwah: Paulist Press, 1992.


### E. Vatican Offices and Jewish Representatives

International Catholic-Jewish Liaison Committee. "A Common Declaration on Anti-Semitism." Prague, Czechoslovakia. (September 6, 1990).

Secretariat of the State of the Holy See and the State of Israel Foreign Office. "Fundamental Agreement between the Holy See and the State of Israel." (December 30, 1993).


### F. United States Conference of Catholic Bishops and Committees

Bishops' Committee on Ecumenical and Interreligious Affairs, National Conference of Catholic Bishops. "Criteria for the Evaluation of Dramatizations of the Passion." Washington, D.C.: USCC, 1988.

————. "Guidelines for Catholic-Jewish Relations." Washington, D.C.: USCC, 1985 revision.

Bishops' Committee on the Liturgy, National Conference of Catholic Bishops. *God's Mercy Endures Forever:* "Guidelines on the Presentation of Jews and Judaism in Catholic Preaching." Washington, D.C.: USCC, 1988.

National Conference of Catholic Bishops. "Statement on Catholic-Jewish Relations." Washington, D.C.: USCC, 1975.

**G. Other National Conferences of Catholic Bishops**
[West] German Bishops' Conference. "The Church and the Jews" (1980).


## 2. SECONDARY AND OTHER LITERATURE

Allen, John L., Jr. "Thinking Straight about Israel, the Jews, and the Archbishop." *NCR Online* (October 27, 2010). http://www.ccjr.us/dialogika-resources/themes-in -todays-dialogue/isrpal/896-bustros2010nov1#ncr

Avery-Peck, Alan J., Daniel J. Harrington, and Jacob Neusner, eds. *When Judaism and Christianity Began: Essays in Memory of Anthony J. Saldarini.* Leiden and Boston: E. J. Brill, 2004.

Bacon, Benjamin Wisner. *Studies in Matthew.* New York: H. Holt, 1930.

Becker, Adam H., and Annette Yoshiko Reed, eds. *The Ways that Never Parted: Jews and Christians in Late Antiquity and the Early Middle Ages.* Minneapolis: Fortress Press, 2007.

Berger, David. "On *Dominus Iesus* and the Jews." Paper delivered at the 17th meeting of the International Catholic-Jewish Liaison Committee, New York (May 1, 2001).

Bergoglio, Jorge Mario and Abraham Skorka. *On Heaven and Earth: Pope Francis on Faith, Family, and the Church in the Twenty-First Century.* Trans. Alejandro Bermudez and Howard Goodman. New York: Image Books, 2013.

Berkovits, Eliezer. "Judaism in the Post-Christian Era." In F. E. Talmage, ed., *Disputation and Dialogue: Readings in the Jewish-Christian Encounter.* New York: KTAV, 1975, 284-295.

Boyarin, Daniel. *Border Lines: The Partition of Judaeo-Christianity.* Philadelphia: University of Pennsylvania Press, 2004.

Boys, Mary C. *Jewish-Christian Dialogue: One Woman's Experience — The 1997 Madeleva Lecture in Spirituality.* New York/Mahwah: Paulist Press, 1997.

———. "Learning in the Presence of the Other: My Friendship with Sara Lee." In James L. Fredericks and Tracy Sayuki Tiemeier, eds., *Interreligious Friendship after Nostra Aetate.* New York/London: Palgrave Macmillan, 2015.

———. *Redeeming Our Sacred Story: The Death of Jesus and Relations between Jews and Christians.* New York/Mahwah: Paulist Press/Stimulus Books, 2013.

Brown, Raymond E. *The Community of the Beloved Disciple: The Life, Loves, and Hates of an Individual Church in New Testament Times.* New York/Ramsey/Toronto: Paulist Press, 1979.

———. *A Crucified Christ in Holy Week: Essays on the Four Gospel Passion Narratives.* Collegeville: Liturgical Press, 1986.

———. *The Death of the Messiah: From Gethsemane to the Grave.* New York: Doubleday, 1994.

———. *The Gospel According to John.* Anchor Bible Series. Garden City, NY: Doubleday, 1966.

———. *The Virginal Conception and Bodily Resurrection of Jesus.* New York: Paulist, 1973.

————, Joseph A. Fitzmyer, and Roland E. Murphy, eds. *The New Jerome Biblical Commentary.* Englewood Cliffs: Prentice-Hall, 1990.

————, and John P. Meier. *Antioch and Rome: New Testament Cradles of Catholic Christianity.* New York/Ramsey: Paulist Press, 1983.

Brueggemann, Walter. *Genesis.* Interpretation Bible Commentary. Atlanta: John Knox Press, 1982.

Bruteau, Beatrice, ed. *Merton and Judaism, Holiness in Words: Recognition, Repentance, and Renewal.* Louisville, KY: Fons Vitae, 2003.

Burrell, David B. *Knowing the Unknowable God: Ibn-Sina, Maimonides, Aquinas.* Notre Dame, IN: University of Notre Dame Press, 1986.

Carter, Warren. *Pontius Pilate: Portraits of a Roman Governor.* Collegeville, MN: Liturgical Press, 2003.

Clifford, Richard J., and Roland E. Murphy. "Genesis." In Raymond E. Brown, Joseph A. Fitzmyer, and Roland E. Murphy, eds., *The New Jerome Biblical Commentary.* Englewood Cliffs, NJ: Prentice Hall, 1990, 8-43.

Cohen, Raymond. "The Document that Never Was: People, Land, and State after *Nostra Aetate.*" Paper presented at the 2014 consultation of the "Promise, Land, and Hope" project of the International Council of Christians and Jews, Hochschule für Jüdische Studien Heidelberg, University of Heidelberg ( June 24, 2014).

Connelly, John. *From Enemy to Brother: The Revolution in Catholic Teaching on the Jews, 1933-1965.* Harvard University Press, 2011.

Coote, Robert B., and David Robert Ord. *The Bible's First History.* Philadelphia: Fortress, 1989.

Cunningham, Philip A. "A Catholic Theology of the Land?: The State of the Question." *Studies in Christian-Jewish Relations* 8/1 (2013). http://ejournals.bc.edu/ojs/index .php/scjr/article/view/5182/4666

————. "Celebrating Judaism as a 'Sacrament of Every Otherness.'" In Kristen Colberg and Robert Krieg, eds., *The Theology of Cardinal Walter Kasper: Speaking Truth in Love.* Collegeville, MN: Liturgical Press, 2014, 223-240.

————. "A Challenge to Catholic Teaching." In Philip A. Cunningham, ed., *Pondering the Passion: What's at Stake for Christians and Jews?* Franklin, WI, and Chicago: Sheed & Ward, 2004, 143-156.

————. "A Covenantal Christology." *Studies in Christian-Jewish Relations* 1 (2005-2006): 41-52. Available at http://escholarship.bc.edu/scjr/vol1/iss1/art6

————. *Education for Shalom: Religion Textbooks and the Enhancement of the Catholic and Jewish Relationship.* Collegeville: Liturgical Press, 1995.

————. "How *Nostra Aetate* Transformed the Jewish-Catholic Relationship: 'The Beginning of the Beginning.'" In Eric J. Greenberg, ed., *Transforming the Catholic-Jewish Relationship: Nostra Aetate on Its Fortieth Anniversary.* New York: Anti-Defamation League, 2005, 33-45.

————. "Jews and Christians from the Time of Christ to Constantine's Reign." In Albert S. Lindemann and Richard S. Levy, eds., *Antisemitism: A History.* New York/ Oxford: Oxford University Press, 2010, 47-62.

————. "Official Ecclesial Documents to Implement the Second Vatican Council on

Relations with Jews: Study Them, Become Immersed in Them, and Put Them into Practice." *Studies in Christian-Jewish Relations* (October, 2009) http://escholarship.bc.edu/scjr/vol4/iss1/24

————. "Paul's Letters and the Relationship between the People of Israel and the Church Today." In Reimund Bieringer and Didier Pollefeyt, eds., *Paul and Judaism: Crosscurrents in Pauline Exegesis and the Study of Jewish-Christian Relations.* London/New York: T&T Clark, 2012, 141-162.

————, ed. *Pondering the Passion: What's at Stake for Christians and Jews?* Franklin, WI and Chicago: Sheed & Ward, 2004, 143-156.

————. *Proclaiming Shalom: Lectionary Introductions to Foster the Catholic and Jewish Relationship.* Collegeville, MN: Liturgical Press, 1995.

————. "Reflections from a Roman Catholic on a Reform Theology of Christianity." *CCAR Journal — A Reform Jewish Quarterly* (Spring 2005): 61-73.

————. *A Story of Shalom: The Calling of Christians and Jews by a Covenanting God.* New York/Mahwah: Stimulus Foundation/Paulist Press, 2001.

————, Norbert J. Hofmann, and Joseph Sievers, eds. *The Catholic Church and the Jewish People: Recent Reflections from Rome.* New York: Fordham University Press, 2007.

————, John Michalczyk, and Gilbert Rosenthal, producers. *Walking God's Path: Jews and Christians in Candid Conversation* [video series]. Episode 5. *Metaphors for a Unique Relationship.* Boston: Center for Christian-Jewish Learning at Boston College, 2004. http://www.ccjr.us/dialogika-resources/educational-and-liturgical-materials/curricula/958-wgp

————, and Mark D. Nanos. "Implications of Paul's Hopes for the End of Days for Jews and Christians Today." *Studies in Christian-Jewish Relations* 9/1 (2014): 1-45.

————, and Didier Pollefeyt. "The Triune One, the Incarnate *Logos,* and Israel's Covenantal Life." In Cunningham et al., eds., *Christ Jesus and the Jewish People Today,* 183-201.

————, Joseph Sievers, Mary C. Boys, Hans Hermann Henrix, and Jesper Svartvik, eds. *Christ Jesus and the Jewish People Today: New Explorations of Theological Interrelationships.* Grand Rapids: William B. Eerdmans, 2011.

————, and Arthur Starr, eds. *Sharing Shalom: A Local Interfaith Dialogue Process.* Mahwah/New York: Paulist Press, 1998.

Davies, W. D., and Dale C. Allison. *A Critical and Exegetical Commentary on the Gospel According to Saint Matthew.* Volume 1. Edinburgh: T&T Clark, 1988.

Donahue, John R., and Daniel J. Harrington. *The Gospel of Mark.* Sacra Pagina Series. Collegeville, MN: Liturgical Press, 2002.

Donfried, Karl P., ed. *The Romans Debate.* Rev. exp. ed. Peabody, MA: Hendrickson Press, 1991.

Efroymson, David P. "The Patristic Connection." In Alan T. Davies, ed., *Antisemitism and the Foundations of Christianity.* New York/Ramsey/Toronto: Paulist, 1979, 98-117.

Efroymson, David P., Eugene Fisher, and Leon Klenicki, eds. *Within Context: Essays on Jews & Judaism in the New Testament.* Collegeville, MN: Liturgical Press, 1993.

Eisenbaum, Pamela. *Paul Was Not a Christian: The Original Message of a Misunderstood Apostle.* New York: HarperOne, 2009.

Ellenson, David. "A Jewish Legal Authority Addresses Jewish-Christian Dialogue: Two Responsa of Rabbi Moshe Feinstein." *American Jewish Archives Journal* 52 (2000): 112-128.

Fisher, Eugene J., and Leon Klenicki, eds. *In Our Time: The Flowering of Jewish-Catholic Dialogue.* New York/Mahwah: Paulist Press, 1990.

Fitzmyer, Joseph A. *The Gospel According to Luke, I–IX.* The Anchor Bible. Garden City: Doubleday, 1981.

———. *Luke the Theologian: Aspects of His Teaching.* New York/Mahwah: Paulist, 1989.

———. *Romans.* Anchor Yale Bible Commentary. New Haven: Yale University Press, 1992.

———. "Romans." In Raymond E. Brown, Joseph A. Fitzmyer, and Roland E. Murphy, eds., *The New Jerome Biblical Commentary.* Englewood Cliffs, NJ: Prentice Hall, 1990, 830-868.

Flannery, Edward H. *The Anguish of the Jews: Twenty-Three Centuries of Anti-Semitism.* Rev. and exp. ed. New York/Mahwah: Paulist Press/Stimulus Books, 2004.

Giuliani, Massimo. "The Shoah as a Shadow upon and a Stimulus to Jewish-Christian Dialogue." In Philip A. Cunningham, Norbert J. Hofmann, and Joseph Sievers, eds., *The Catholic Church and the Jewish People: Recent Reflections from Rome.* New York: Fordham University Press, 2007, 54-70.

Grayzel, Solomon. *The Church and the Jews in the XIIIth Century — A Study of Their Relations during the Years 1198-1254.* New York: Hermon Press, 1966.

Greenberg, Irving. "Response to John T. Pawlikowski." *Moment* 15/4 (August 1990): 39.

Gregerman, Adam. "'Have you despised Jerusalem and Zion after you had chosen them?': The Destruction of Jerusalem and the Temple in Jewish and Christian Writings from the Land of Israel in Late Antiquity." Doctoral dissertation, Columbia University, 2007. UMI Publication Number 3266586.

———. "Sacred Past, Secular Present?: Contemporary Church Statements on the State of Israel." Paper presented at the 2014 consultation of the "Promise, Land, and Hope" project of the International Council of Christians and Jews, Hochschule für Jüdische Studien Heidelberg, University of Heidelberg. (June 24, 2014).

Halbertal, Moshe. "'Ones Possessed of Religion': Religious Tolerance in the Teachings of the Me'iri." *Edah Journal* 1 (2000): 1-24. http://www.edah.org/backend/JournalArticle/halbertal.pdf

Harrington, Daniel J. *The Gospel of Matthew.* Sacra Pagina Series. Collegeville, MN: Liturgical Press, 1991.

Harrington, Wilfrid J. *Revelation.* Sacra Pagina Series. Collegeville, MN: Liturgical Press, 1993.

Hartman, David. *A Living Covenant: The Innovative Spirit in Traditional Judaism.* Woodstock, VT: Jewish Lights, 1997.

Heinz, Hanspeter. "Your Privilege: You Have Jewish Friends." In Cunningham et al., eds., *Christ Jesus and the Jewish People Today,* 1-13.

Hoff, Gregor Maria. "A Realm of Differences: The Meaning of Jewish Monotheism for

Christology and Trinitarian Theology." In Cunningham et al., eds., *Christ Jesus and the Jewish People Today*, 202-220.

Horsley Richard A., with John S. Hanson. *Bandits, Prophets, and Messiahs*. San Francisco: Harper & Row, 1985.

Horsley, Richard A. *Jesus and the Spiral of Violence*. San Francisco: Harper & Row, 1987.

International Council of Christians and Jews. "'As Long as You Believe in a Living God, You Must Have Hope': Reflections on the Role of Religious and Interreligious Groups in Promoting Reconciliation about and in the Troubled Middle East." (May 13, 2013).

————. "'Let Us Have Mercy Upon Words': A Plea from the International Council of Christians and Jews to All Who Seek Interreligious Understanding" (July 26, 2010).

Jervell, Jacob. "The Church of Jews and Godfearers." In Joseph B. Tyson, ed., *Luke-Acts and the Jewish People*. Minneapolis: Augsburg, 1988, 11-20.

————. *Luke and the People of God*. Minneapolis: Augsburg, 1972.

————. *The Unknown Paul: Essays on Luke-Acts and Early Christian History*. Minneapolis: Augsburg, 1984.

Johnson, Luke T. "The New Testament's Anti-Jewish Slander and the Conventions of Ancient Polemic." *Journal of Biblical Literature* 108/3 (Fall 1989): 419-441.

Katzew, Jan. "From Other to Brother." *CCAR Journal: A Reform Jewish Quarterly* 52 (Spring 2005): 29-41.

Kertzer, David I. *The Pope and Mussolini: The Secret History of Pius XI and the Rise of Fascism in Europe*. New York: Random House, 2014.

Kessler, Edward, and Neil Wenborn, eds. *A Dictionary of Jewish-Christian Relations*. Cambridge: Cambridge University Press, 2005.

Klassen, William. "Peace." In Edward Kessler and Neil Wenborn, eds., *A Dictionary of Jewish-Christian Relations*. Cambridge: Cambridge University Press, 2005, 338.

Klenicki, Leon. "*Ecclesia et Synagoga*: Judaism and Christianity, A Reflection toward the Future." *CCAR Journal: A Reform Jewish Quarterly* 52 (Spring 2005): 18-28.

Klenicki, Leon, and Eugene J. Fisher, eds. *Root and Branches: Biblical Judaism, Rabbinic Judaism, and Early Christianity*. Winona, MN: Saint Mary's Press, 1987.

Kogan, Michael. *Opening the Covenant: A Jewish Theology of Christianity*. Oxford/New York: Oxford University Press, 2008.

————. "Toward a Jewish Theology of Christianity." *Journal of Ecumen Studies* 32/1 (Winter 1995): 89-106.

Komonchak, Joseph A. "Novelty in Continuity: Pope Benedict's Interpretation of Vatican II." *America* 2003/3 (February 2, 2009): 10-16.

Korn, Eugene. "Covenantal Possibilities in a Post-Polemical Age: A Jewish View." *Studies in Christian-Jewish Relations* 6 (2011): 1-13. http://ejournals.bc.edu/ojs/index.php/scjr/article/download/1911/1717

LaCugna, Catherine Mowry. *God for Us: The Trinity and Christian Life*. New York: HarperCollins, 1991.

Landau, Yehezkel. "An Interview with Krister Stendahl." *Harvard Divinity Bulletin* 35/1 (2007): 29-31.

Langer, Ruth. *Cursing the Christians?: A History of the Birkat HaMinim*. New York/ Oxford: Oxford University Press, 2011.

———. "Jewish Understandings of the Religious Other." *Theological Studies* 64 (2003): 255-77.

———. "Theologies of the Land and State of Israel: The Role of the Secular in Christian and Jewish Understandings." *Studies in Christian-Jewish Relations* 3 (2008). http:// escholarship@bc.edu/scjr/vol3.

Lee, Bernard J. *Conversation on the Road Not Taken*. Vol. 1, *The Galilean Jewishness of Jesus: Retrieving the Jewish Origins of Christianity*. New York/Mahwah: Paulist Press/Stimulus Books, 1988.

———. *Conversation on the Road Not Taken*. Vol. 2, *Jesus and the Metaphors of God: The Christs of the New Testament*. New York/Mahwah: Paulist Press/Stimulus Books, 1993.

Levine, Amy-Jill, and Marc Zvi Brettler, eds. *The Jewish Annotated New Testament*. New York/Oxford: Oxford University Press, 2011.

Linder, Amnon. *The Jews in Roman Imperial Legislation*. Detroit: Wayne State University Press, 1987.

Lux, Richard C. *The Jewish People, the Holy Land, and the State of Israel: A Catholic View*. New York/Mahwah: Paulist Press, 2010.

Martyn, J. Louis. *History & Theology in the Fourth Gospel*. Rev & enlarged ed. Nashville: Abingdon, 1979.

McBrien, Richard. *Catholicism*. Minneapolis: Winston Press, 1980.

Melloni, Alberto. "*Nostra Aetate* and the Discovery of the Sacrament of Otherness." In Philip A. Cunningham, Norbert J. Hofmann, and Joseph Sievers, eds., *The Catholic Church and the Jewish People: Recent Reflections from Rome*. New York: Fordham University Press, 2007, 129-151.

Miccoli, Giovanni. "Two Sensitive Issues: Religious Freedom and the Jews." In Giuseppe Albergio and Joseph A. Komonchak, eds., *History of Vatican II*. Vol. 4, *Church as Communion: Third Period and Intersession, September 1964–September 1965*. Maryknoll, NY, and Leuven, Belgium: Orbis Books and Peeters, 2003, 95-193.

Nanos, Mark D. *The Mystery of Romans: The Jewish Context of Paul's Letter*. Minneapolis: Fortress Press, 1996.

———. "Paul's Relationship to Torah in Light of His Strategy 'To Become Everything to Everyone' (1 Corinthians 9.19-23)." In Reimund Bieringer and Didier Pollefeyt, eds., *Paul and Judaism: Crosscurrents in Pauline Exegesis and the Study of Jewish-Christian Relations*. London and New York: T&T Clark, 2012, 106-140.

Neyrey, Jerome H. *An Ideology of Revolt: John's Christology in Social Science Perspective*. Philadelphia: Fortress Press, 1988.

Novak, David. *Jewish-Christian Dialogue: A Jewish Justification*. New York/Oxford: Oxford University Press, 1989.

O'Brien, Darcy. *The Hidden Pope: The Untold Story of a Lifelong Friendship That Is Changing the Relationship between Catholics and Jews: The Personal Journey of John Paul II and Jerzy Kluger*. New York: Rodale Books, 1998.

Oesterreicher, John M. *The New Encounter between Christians and Jews*. New York: Philosophical Library, 1986.

O'Leary, Joseph Stephen. *Questioning Back: The Overcoming of Metaphysics in Christian Tradition*. Minneapolis/Chicago/New York: Winston Press, 1985.

O'Malley, John W. *What Happened at Vatican II*. Cambridge, MA: Harvard University Press, 2008.

Osten-Sacken, Peter von der. *Christian-Jewish Dialogue: Theological Foundations*. Philadelphia: Fortress Press, 1986.

Passelecq, Georges, and Bernard Suchecky. *The Hidden Encyclical of Pius XI*. New York: Harcourt, Brace, and Co., 1997.

Patai, Raphael. *The Complete Diaries of Theodor Herzl*. Trans. Harry Zohn. New York/London: Herzl Press, Thomas Yoseloff, 1960.

Pawlikowski, John T. *Jesus and the Theology of Israel*. Wilmington, DE.: Michael Glazier, Inc., 1989.

———. "Rethinking Christianity: A Challenge to Jewish Attitudes." *Moment* 15/4 (Aug. 1990): 36-39.

Perkins, Pheme. *Resurrection: New Testament Witness and Contemporary Reflection*. Garden City, NY: Doubleday, 1984.

Phillips, J. B. *The New Testament in Modern English*. Rev. ed. New York: Macmillan, 1972.

Przybylski, Benno. "The Setting of Matthean Anti-Judaism." In Peter Richardson, ed., *Anti-Judaism in Early Christianity*. Vol. 1, *Paul and the Gospels*. Waterloo, Ontario: Wilfrid Laurier University Press, 1986, 181-200.

Reynolds, Joyce, and Robert Tannenbaum. *Jews and Godfearers at Aphrodisias*. Cambridge, England: Cambridge Philological Society, 1987.

Roy, Louis. "Why Is the Death of Jesus Redemptive?" In Cunningham, ed., *Pondering the Passion*, 129-142.

Sabbah, Michel. "Reading the Bible in the Land of the Bible." (November 1, 1993). http://www.lpj.org/newsite2006/patriarch/pastoral-letters/1993/readingthebible_en.html

Saldarini, Anthony J. "Christian Anti-Judaism: The First Century Speaks to the Twenty-first Century." In Thomas A. Baima, ed., *A Legacy of Catholic-Jewish Dialogue: The Joseph Cardinal Bernardin Jerusalem Lectures*. Chicago: Liturgy Training Publications, 2012, 75-90.

———. *Matthew's Christian-Jewish Community*. Chicago/London: University of Chicago Press, 1994.

Sanders, E. P. *Jesus and Judaism*. Philadelphia: Fortress, 1985.

———. *Jewish Law from Jesus to the Mishnah*. Philadelphia: Trinity, 1990.

———. *Paul and Palestinian Judaism: A Comparison of Patterns of Religion*. Philadelphia: Fortress Press, 1977.

Schneiders, Sandra M. *The Revelatory Text: Interpreting the New Testament as Sacred Scripture*. HarperSanFrancisco, 1991.

Schreckenberg, Heinz. *The Jews in Christian Art: An Illustrated History*. New York: Continuum, 1996.

Sherman, Franklin, ed. *Bridges: Documents of the Christian-Jewish Dialogue.* Volume One, *The Road to Reconciliation (1945-1985);* Volume Two, *Building a New Relationship (1986-2013).* New York/Mahwah: Paulist Press/Stimulus Books, 2011 and 2014.

Siegman, Henry. "Ten Years of Catholic-Jewish Relations: A Reassessment." In International Catholic-Jewish Liaison Committee, *Fifteen Years of Catholic-Jewish Dialogue, 1970-1985: Selected Papers.* Libreria Editrice Vaticana, 1988, 26-45.

Sievers, Joseph. "A History of the Interpretation of Romans 11:29." *Annali di Storia dell'esegesi* 14 (1997): 381-442

Soloveitchik, Joseph B. "Confrontation." *Tradition: A Journal of Orthodox Thought* 6/2 (1964): 5-29.

Soulen, R. Kendall. *The God of Israel and Christian Theology.* Minneapolis: Fortress Press, 1996.

———. "Removing Anti-Judaism." Howard Clark Kee and Irvin J. Borowsky, eds. In *Removing Anti-Judaism from the New Testament.* Philadelphia: American Interfaith Institute/World Alliance, 1998, 149-156.

Speiser, E. A. *Genesis.* Anchor Bible Commentary. New York: Doubleday, 1964.

Stendahl, Krister. "The Apostle Paul and the Introspective Conscience of the West." *Harvard Theological Review* 56 (1963): 199-215.

Therrien, Samuel. *The Elusive Presence: Toward a New Biblical Theology.* New York/Hagerstown/San Francisco, London: Harper and Row, 1978.

van Buren, Paul M. *A Theology of the Jewish-Christian Reality.* Part 3, *Christ in Context.* San Francisco: Harper and Row, 1988.

de Vos, Cornelis. "The Book of Joshua on the Land." Paper presented at the Promise, Land, and Hope research project of the International Council of Christians and Jews, Catholic Theological Union, Chicago. (August 14, 2013).

Wilken, Robert L. *The Christians as the Romans Saw Them.* New Haven: Yale University Press, 1984.

———. *John Chrysostom and the Jews: Rhetoric and Reality in the Fourth Century.* Berkeley: University of California Press, 1983.

———. *Judaism and the Early Christian Mind: A Study of Cyril of Alexandria's Exegesis and Theology.* New Haven: Yale University Press, 1971.

Williamson, Clark. "What Does It Mean to Be Saved?" In Philip A. Cunningham, ed., *Pondering the Passion: What's at Stake for Christians and Jews?* Franklin, WI, and Chicago: Sheed & Ward, 2004, 119-128.

World Council of Churches, Executive Committee. "Ecumenical Considerations on Jewish-Christian Dialogue." (1982). In World Council of Churches, *The Theology of the Churches and the Jewish People: Statement by the World Council of Churches and Its Member Churches.* Geneva: WCC Publications, 1988, 34-42.

World Council of Churches, Faith and Order Commission. "The Church and the Jewish People" (1967). In World Council of Churches, *The Theology of the Churches and the Jewish People: Statement by the World Council of Churches and Its Member Churches.* Geneva: WCC Publications, 1988, 13-28.